Remember When...

Adam L'Heureux

Copyright © 2019 Adam L'Heureux.
All rights reserved.
ISBN-13: 9781674970684

You Learned to Tie Your Shoes

Tying your shoes was one of life's first major milestones. You don't remember learning how to sit up, crawl, walk or talk, but learning how to tie your shoes was your first notable triumph, especially since it once seemed impossible.

Remember when you thought you'd never get it because it was just too hard? That's when you made the decision to wear Velcro for the rest of your life. That was the resolution that I made at least, and I can't be alone in that.

There was a problem with Velcro, however, though it had nothing to do with the actual shoes themselves. The problem was that when kids who had already learned to tie their shoes saw you wearing them, they made fun of you. I specifically remember such an incident in my own childhood. It was just after I had told my mom that I would be a Velcro man for the rest of my days when one of the big kids on my street saw my Velcro shoes and made fun of me in front of all the neighbourhood kids. He literally pointed at my shoes and started laughing hysterically, mocking me because he knew I couldn't tie my own laces. His jeering stuck like a harpoon through my little heart, and in one exceptionally embarrassing instant, my plan to wear Velcro for the rest of my life was eradicated. As a result, I had no choice but to do the impossible: I had to learn how to tie my own shoes.

Of course, I would need the help of my parents to do so, because they knew how to do it. Parents are patient teachers. I don't know how many hundreds of times I made my mom take me through the process. It was probably the same for all of us: as she sat on the stairs endlessly demonstrating the proper technique, I watched in awe while she repeated the same words over and over again.

"First, you make the bunny ears. Then the rabbit goes through the hole. Then he runs around in a circle, and then you pull him tight."

I remember sitting on the front steps listening to my mom tell me about the rabbit and the hole, watching her tie my shoes and trying to form the neurological connections that would one day make me a master shoe tier, and it was the first time in my life I remember feeling stressed out. I felt like I would never get it, but I was determined to keep trying until I did. I didn't know it at the time but learning to tie my shoes was teaching me one of the greatest gifts we can possess: the gift of tenacity.

Although tying your shoes first seemed impossible, you kept at it and you got it little parts at a time, first making the rabbit ears, then sending him through the hole. You often hit the wall at that point and had to start again, but your parents were there to guide you through that important rite of passage. They literally held your hands through the entire process, and after so many unsuccessful attempts, you finally tied your own shoes. At that moment, you had done something you once considered impossible, and life would never be the same.

Tying your shoes is a great metaphor for life. If you can learn to tie your shoes, you can learn to do anything. When you first start something unfamiliar, you will try, fail, and think that it's impossible, just like you did back then. But if you keep trying, if you keep making those bunny ears of whatever it is you're trying to do, one day you will master that most difficult of tasks. So if there's something you want to do but feel that you can't, take a lesson from your younger self and just keep trying. You didn't give up back then, and you shouldn't give up now. If you need proof that you're capable of pushing yourself beyond what you thought was possible, just look down at the shoes on your feet and remember that one day, that too was impossible.

Of course, if you're still wearing Velcro, none of this applies.

Your Parents Did The Wiping

There was a short period in your life when you literally lived like a king. Your parents waited on you hand and foot and lovingly responded to your every need. They dressed you, they fed you, they even carried you on walks. Despite all of that extravagant treatment, however, nothing elevated you to the status of royalty quite so much as the fact that you didn't wipe your own butt.

Now, most kids have trainer toilets, or potties, when they're learning how to go to the bathroom on their own. They're usually kept in the bathroom, and the kid must go to where the toilet is when nature calls. In my family, however, it was the other way around, and I was privileged enough that when I felt the need, the toilet came to me. It wasn't your average store-bought plastic trainer toilet that most people used, either. Instead, it had been built by my Opa, with some good old-fashioned German craftsmanship and ingenuity, and it put those other potties to shame. It had a high back that extended all the way above your shoulders, perfectly crafted arm rests, and was painted a beautiful crimson red and yellowish cream colour. Despite the stunning craftsmanship and the fact that the potty came to me, it was its name that made me feel especially regal whenever I had to use it: we called it "the throne."

The throne could be transported to any room in the house so that you could use it anywhere, any time, and in the midst of any activity, whether it was a family dinner or simply watching cartoons. To me, at two or three years of age, that was wonderful. As soon as I felt the need, I called out to one of my servants – also known as my parents or grandparents – and announced that I had to go to the bathroom. Then, someone would hurry to fetch the throne and bring it to me. I did what I had to do, and even if there were other people around, I didn't feel an ounce of shame or self-consciousness, which is impossible to fathom as an adult.

When I was finished, I yelled out, "I'm done!" which was kid code for, "Hey, someone get in here and do the wiping, because I'm not doing it myself."

At that point, one of my minions would come do the job I didn't want or know how to do, as I sat there proud of the fact that not only had I successfully used the potty like I was supposed to, someone else was taking care of the most unpleasant part. I had a good thing going and I knew it, and at the time, the thought of having to do the wiping on my own never crossed my mind.

Maybe you were lucky enough to have a portable toilet too, or maybe you had to actually go into the bathroom to do your business, which in retrospect seems a lot more normal, but regardless of where you went or how you did it, the routine was pretty much the same for all of us. You felt the urge, told your parents you had to go, and when you were done, you called for them to come take care of the cleanup. At the time, it was a perfect arrangement.

That was an idyllic phase of life, and yet, like so many wonderful things, it couldn't last forever. There eventually came a day when your parents told you it was time to start doing your own wiping, and it came as a total shock. You'd thought that the routine you were currently enjoying would last forever, and had never considered the fact that one day you'd have to do it yourself. In fact, you were offended by the very notion. You may have even refused to do it, but your parents, having had their fill of doing your dirty work for you, simply abandoned you on the toilet and refused to give in, leaving you with no choice but to do it yourself or stay on the toilet and die of starvation or boredom, whichever came first.

Yes, that final time your parents did the wiping marked the end of a wonderful era and the beginning of new responsibility. You were now forced to take charge of an unpleasant part of your own life, and you knew that from that moment on things were just going to get tougher. It was a sobering moment, one you likely remember if you think back far enough. It was probably the first time you realized that for some things in life you were completely on your own, and you had to either step up or get shit on - literally.

Here's to stepping up when life gets tough.

You Ran Around Naked And No One Cared

There was a time in your life when you could run out the front door without pants on and no one would call the cops. However, that was a long time ago, and it only lasted until the age of about three or four. After that, you had to wear clothes like everyone else, and that's been the story ever since, except for that crazy camping trip you went on and the time you lost at strip poker.

As an adult, it would take a lot to get you to run out of the house naked: a fire, an earthquake, an alien in your bedroom. Even then, you would grab whatever you could to cover yourself. You might wrap a jacket or a towel around your waist – you'd even grab a sock just to cover your shame. When you were a kid, however, you didn't think twice about leaving the house naked, and if someone tried to force you to put clothes on, you ran away from them.

Now, you may not have any memories of running out of the house naked, but you probably did it at least once or twice. Even if you don't remember doing it yourself, you can probably remember a time when you were outside minding your own business, and all of a sudden some kid ran out of their house buck naked with their parents chasing them and yelling for them to put some clothes on.

Growing up on my street, which was filled with kids of all ages, that happened on a regular basis. When it did, the other neighbourhood kids and I could tell that the naked child's parents were mortified, but it wasn't a big deal to us. It was just a regular part of childhood, something we all accepted as normal because we had done it ourselves not long ago. In fact, I clearly remember hanging out on the cul-de-sac with the other kids one day when a newly arrived neighbour named Scott, who was about three years old, burst out the front door of his house, ran up to us stark naked and started showing us some new toy he had got for his birthday. The only person who seemed the least bit unsettled was his mom, who came flying down the front steps after him, shrieking for him to put some clothes on. In our minds, it was Scott's mom who was out of line for making such a big deal about something so little, no pun intended.

Of course, once Scott got a little older, it would be hard for him to imagine himself doing something like that, because like the rest of us, he would have developed shame. Once that happened, no one ever voluntarily left the house naked again. Developing shame was literally like someone flipping a switch in our brains, and in one life changing moment, we became self-aware. If we happened to be naked at that moment, which I'm sure many of us were, it was the most horrifically uncomfortable feeling we had ever experienced.

The day that I became self-conscious and aware of my own shame was a beautiful summer day. The sky was blue, the sun was a golden yellow, and there wasn't a hint of a cloud in the sky. I was at my Oma and Opa's house, swimming in a small, vinyl kiddie pool with my brother and my cousins, while several adults relaxed in lawn chairs and enjoyed that perfect afternoon. I had just turned four, and as was often the case at that age, I was running around naked and having the time of my life, without a care in the world. The other kids and I were taking turns doing cannon balls into the pool, and as I lined up for another leap into that cool refreshing water, it suddenly dawned on me that I was the only person there who wasn't wearing any clothes. In that dreadful moment, one that changed my life forever, I realized I was naked, and that it wasn't ok.

It was the most vulnerable feeling I had ever experienced, and the worst part was that once I realized it, there was nothing I could do to cover myself, since I had left all my clothes inside and hadn't brought a towel with me. I was left with two terrible choices:

jump back in the pool and remain there until night fall, or run soaking wet through the house and risk a spanking for getting the carpets drenched. I chanced the spanking, which thankfully never manifested, especially since it would've resulted in me not wearing pants again and have defeated the purpose of running inside in the first place.

Regardless of what made you feel self-conscious and aware of your own shame for the first time, that moment marked the end of a carefree and innocent era when you could do anything you wanted and not feel weird about it. From that point on, there would be no more naked pool parties, no more exploring the backyard in the nude, and definitely no more running out of the house naked.

Unless, of course, strip poker had gone seriously wrong.

You Worried You Would Fall Through the Cracks on the Playground

It's funny to think about now, but there was a time in your life when you were certain that you would meet your unfortunate end by falling through the cracks on the playground. In fact, you were so worried about it that when you set foot on a new playground, you didn't even walk on it - you crawled. Despite the fact that it was physically impossible for your body, let alone your toe, to fit through one of those cracks, you were certain that if you took even the slightest misstep, you would meet your demise and forever be remembered as the kid who fell through the cracks and died. You would become the cautionary tale for children around the world, and they would make a safety video about you that elementary school kids would have to watch at assemblies to learn about playground dangers, the way they do with firecracker videos at Halloween.

Come to think of it, why weren't you watching videos like that already? Every kid had heard stories about some poor sap who had fallen through the cracks and died, yet the adults were silent on the issue. Talk about a conspiracy! Sure, they showed you videos on traffic safety and how to avoid strangers, but where were the videos about playground mortality? Kids knew that it could happen, yet the adults refused to acknowledge it. And so, not wanting to miss out on the fun, but wanting to stay alive, you did what you had to, which was to crawl around on your hands and knees and get laughed at by the older kids, who had been doing the same thing only a couple years earlier.

So today when you see kids crawling around on playgrounds, it's not because they're playing a game or pretending they're some type of animal, it's because they're scared for their lives, and crawling is the only way they can have fun while staying alive. You have to admire that kind of courage. They're like old people who refuse to give up their drivers' licenses in order to maintain their independence, but a lot less dangerous to others.

Parents, if you want to put your child's mind at ease, maybe you should give them a science lesson about the impossibility of them actually slipping between those wooden slats and falling to their death. Not only will it help them feel more confident on the playground, it will also spare them from being ridiculed by the bigger kids, which as every kid knows, is the second worst thing that can happen on a playground.

You Had to Get to Your Parent's Room After a Nightmare

Frodo's expedition to Mordor. The Apollo astronauts' mission to the moon. Perseus' quest through the Underworld. None of the heroes on those perilous journeys felt even a fraction of the fear you did when you had to get to your parents' room after having a nightmare.

When you awoke from a bad dream and needed to get to the safety of your parents' room, it felt like the longest and most dangerous trip imaginable. It wasn't a simple matter of get up and go, either. First, you had to decide whether or not to even risk the trip in the first place. If you stayed where you were, you would spend the night sleepless and terrified, but if you ran to your parents' room you risked being eaten by a monster on the way. Of course, if you stayed in your room, there was a good chance that monster would get you anyway, so it was better to take your chances in the hallway in order to reach the safety of your parents' bed, where nothing could ever get you.

After you made up your mind to reach your parents, who hadn't had a full nights sleep since they let you stay up and watch *Ghostbusters* the night it was on TV, the next terrifying part of the ordeal was actually getting out of your bed. You knew that as soon as you did, the monster who could be lurking under your bed might yank you under and eat you alive, so it was with extreme trepidation that you slowly lowered one toe to the floor, ready to pull it up at the first sign of danger. You felt exactly the same as the Apollo 11 astronauts did when they opened the door of the lunar lander and stepped onto the moon for the first time. They knew it might be the death of them, but they had to risk it, and so did you.

With your feet safely on the ground and not yet having been pulled into the abyss by any monsters under your bed, you were ready for the next phase of your journey, which was by far the most terrifying: opening your bedroom door and actually entering the hallway, where all kinds of dangers could be lurking. There were two ways to traverse the hallway to your parents' room. One was a full speed sprint where you crashed through their door like an escaped prison bus ramming down the gates of the penitentiary, and the other was a silent tip toe, which was even scarier because of the terrifying creatures your imagination conjured up that might be lurking behind you as you slowly made your way down the hall.

Even if you started with a silent tip toe, however, every trip to your parents' room ended in a full sprint with you screaming like a banshee as you crashed through their door at 3 am, waking them from their peaceful slumber and nearly giving them heart attacks in the process. You threw yourself into their bed, buried yourself between them, and fell peacefully asleep in a matter of moments, knowing that you were in the safest place in the world, and no monster could ever get you there.

It had been perilous, and it could have been the end of you, but you had made it. Once more you had braved the dangers of the midnight hallway and lived to tell the tale. In the sanctuary of your parents' bed, you quickly fell sound asleep, embraced by the warmth of their bodies and the protection that was beyond anything imaginable, and for you, that was Heaven.

For your parents, it was confirmation of two things: they needed to schedule that vasectomy they had been talking about, and they would never let you watch another scary movie until you turned 21.

You Thought You Would Marry Your First Love

Remember when you were young and thought you would marry your first love? It's almost a shame that doesn't happen more often. If you only ever loved one person you would never experience the pain of a broken heart, or the hassle of trying to find a new love. Your idea of a perfect partner would no doubt change over time, especially if you fell in love when you were in elementary school, because back then all you wanted was someone who could tie their shoes and go to the bathroom on their own. Of course, when you're a senior those traits are still important, so it would only be in your middle years that you might wish you had been more selective with your criteria, but other than that things might have worked out just fine.

We all remember our first love. For me, it was a girl named Robyn. I was only five, but I was sure I'd found the girl I wanted to spend the rest of my life with. Sure, she was the first girl I'd ever socialized with, but still, I was certain she was the one. There were a lot of things that made me believe we were going to get married. For starters, she was the most beautiful girl in kindergarten, and that was counting both the morning and afternoon classes. We also got along like old friends from the beginning, so I knew we were compatible. And the main reason I thought we would get married, the thing that made me believe it more than anything else, was because she told me we were going to and I didn't have a choice.

You know what's funny about that? My reasons for deciding to get married in kindergarten weren't that different from the reasons many people decide to get married as adults. In fact, they were almost identical. The world is full of guys who marry their first girlfriends because they find them attractive, have gotten comfortable in their relationship, and are told that they have to.

Really, the only difference between those types of marriages and the one you were planning on when you were in kindergarten is that as an adult you can actually go through with the marriage, whereas in kindergarten it was just a tantalizing idea. Also, when you were a kid no one took your wedding plans seriously, so no one tried to talk you out of it.

Looking back, it's almost a shame I didn't marry Robyn. She was a babe back then, and still is today. I would have wound up with a beautiful, smart, sexy wife, and maybe all those times we played house and she pretended to cook for me would have become reality and manifested into a wonderful life for the both of us, but it's too late to think about that now. She probably already forced some other guy to marry her even though he didn't really want to, but did it anyway because she told him he had to. Oh well, that's life. You can't change the past; all you can do is hope for a better future, but sometimes it's hard not to think about what could have been if you had only made different choices.

I'm sure you can also look back on your first love and wonder, "What if...?" Even if it's unrealistic, it's fun to think about, and if you had followed through on the innocently immature plans you made when you were a kid, your life would have turned out completely different. Maybe you would be happier than you are now, maybe not. Who's to say? Of course, if people followed through on all the plans they made when they were kids, the only jobs that would exist in society would be policemen, firemen, race car drivers and astronauts, so maybe it's a good thing that most of the plans we made back then didn't pan out.

At least we have the memories to look back on, and if we actually think that getting in touch with our first love and asking them to marry us is still a good idea, there's always Facebook.

You Went To Sleep Before The Sun Set

As a kid, you were unhappy about having an early bedtime because it meant your playtime was cut short. There was nothing more frustrating than lying in bed watching the sun's evening rays poking through the blinds and still being able to hear your friends playing outside while you were tucked under the covers with the fan on, wondering if there was a hotline you could call to report your parents for such an unspeakable act of cruelty.

You would have done anything to trade positions with your parents and stay up late. Little did you know, they would have done anything to trade positions with you and go to bed early. You always thought they did fun adult things after you went to bed, and you were partly right. They did do adult things, but there was nothing fun about them. While you were fuming about having to go to bed so early, they were washing dishes, doing laundry, paying bills, and were sometimes still at work! They were doing the million things parents have do to keep their children alive, and they would have given anything to be able to go to bed early for once in their adult lives, but they couldn't, because you had come along and ruined that for them. But hey, you didn't ask to be born.

That's the difference between kids and adults when it comes to bedtime. Kids think they have to go to bed too early, and adults know they have to stay up too late. Neither group is happy, and they would love to trade places, but that's not how the system works. Eventually, however, those kids who were furious about being forced to go to bed before the sun set will grow up and have kids of their own, and their childhood wish of getting to stay up late will come true, although by then they'll wish it hadn't. While they're up late trying to keep their families afloat, their parents, who will be in their golden years, will be tucked under their covers relishing the fact that they can finally go to bed as early as their children used to.

You Had to Wear a Life Jacket

When you were little, and I mean really little, swimming with a life jacket wasn't a big deal. All the little kids had lifejackets, and they were kind of fun to wear. You could splash around, bob up and down, and not worry about drowning. When it did become a big deal, however, was when a paranoid adult made you wear one, even though you were way too old for it.

Usually, it was your grandparents who made you wear a lifejacket, or one of your friend's overprotective parents. They refused to let you go in the water without one, and it was downright humiliating, especially in front of the other kids who frequented the same swimming hole you did. That's because those other kids had all seen you swimming perfectly well on your own countless times before, so to suddenly see you in a life jacket gave them something to make fun of you for, and they did just that, because kids can be downright mean.

At that point, a life jacket wasn't so much a life saving device as it was a bright orange badge of shame. It was worse than being the chubby kid, and even worse than the kid who had to wear a T-shirt in the water because his parents didn't want him to get burned. If you wanted to go swimming though, you knew you had to wear one, even though that damn life jacket nearly ruined the whole experience for you. Not only did it make swimming difficult, it handicapped you socially because none of the kids you usually hung out with wanted to be seen with you. At that point, you wondered if it would have been better to drown, because at least that way you would have been remembered as the valiant child who gave their life for a cause they believed in, rather than the wiener kid who had to wear a life jacket well beyond the time they should have.

Yes, being forced to wear a life jacket when you didn't need one was a terrible injustice and could ruin what would have otherwise been a perfect day at the beach. You couldn't swim properly, you couldn't hang out with your friends, and you couldn't even enjoy yourself because some adult thought they knew your limits better than you did. The irony was that it was always the adults who couldn't swim who made you wear a life jacket, and they were simply projecting their own insecurities onto you. Maybe if they had sucked it up and gone to swimming lessons like you'd had to, they would have been less paranoid, but unfortunately that wasn't the case, and you had no choice but to obey their tyrannous rule or sit on the beach and completely miss out on all the fun.

I guess you could have built a sand castle, but those were for babies. At least you would've fit in with them though, since they had to wear their life jackets too.

You Wore a Speedo

When I was little, I only knew of one type of bathing suit, and that was a Speedo. But I didn't call it a Speedo; I called it a bathing suit, and so did everyone else, because that's what it was. I never felt weird in my Speedo, either. I always thought it was awesome, and completely normal, because at one point in time, it was.

You likely felt the same way about your bathing suit back then, too. You loved your Speedo, with its bright colours and flashy designs, and the way it hugged your body and propelled you through the water like a human dolphin. You proudly wore it to all types of swimming lessons and pool parties, and never once felt self-conscious about it, since it seemed that all the other kids at the pool were wearing the same thing as you. But one day, that all changed.

You can probably remember the exact moment in your life when you were at some swimming related event, wearing your Speedo, and all of a sudden, it dawned on you that the bathing suit you were wearing left absolutely nothing to the imagination, and you were completely exposed to the world around you. You felt like Adam in Eden, suddenly aware of your own shame and near nakedness, and it was an awful experience to go through.

Mine was especially bad, because it happened in front of my entire swim class. It was the day we were supposed to jump off the dive tower, a day I'd been dreading for weeks. I was always the runt back in those days, and being the smallest kid in swim class, the dive tower seemed even more intimidating to me than to the other kids, who literally stood head and shoulders above me.

As I stood on the slippery, wet pool deck, fearfully waiting my turn to climb the ladder to my imminent demise, the sound of shrieking children filled the air around me. I watched my classmates each take their turn climbing the cold metallic ladder to the top of the dive tower, walking to the edge of the diving board, and jumping off. I don't know if they were as scared as I was, but if they were, they weren't showing it. I figured I must have been the only one who was petrified to take that terrifying leap of faith, and as I stood on the pool deck shaking and shivering in my bright red, star spangled Speedo, my turn was getting ever closer.

Finally, the last kid in front of me climbed the ladder, walked to the edge of the board, and jumped in. That meant that I was the only one left to go, and my entire swim class, all dozen or so kids, was waiting at the edge of the pool deck below, watching and waiting for me to take my turn. I'd never been so terrified of something in my entire life. It was the first "damned if you do, damned if you don't" situation" I'd ever faced, and I knew there was no way out. If I climbed to the top of the tower and walked out onto the diving board, the surface of the water and my peers terrifyingly far below, I knew I might die of fright. If I chickened out, I would be teased into oblivion and remembered forever as the sissy who didn't have the guts to jump. I was screwed either way, and I knew it.

I don't know how, but I managed to summon the courage that all little children are able to muster on a routine basis when doing anything for the first time, and I put my foot on the first rung of the ladder. I grabbed the railings and hoisted myself up, and put one foot in front of the other, making sure not to look down, until at last, I was at the top of the tower, a whole three meters above the pool deck. To me, it was the equivalent of scaling Everest, and that was only the beginning. Now came the hard part: actually walking to the edge and jumping off.

With my entire class below me, watching and waiting for me to chicken out, I took my first cautious steps out onto the fiberglass death trap that lay before me. Slowly, one little step at a time, I made my way to the edge of the board, my whole body trembling with fear as I went. Ever so cautiously, I approached the edge of the board and looked down into the abyss below, and I was immediately flooded with panic.

The diving board felt ten times higher than it had looked from the pool deck, because now I could see straight to its bottom. This hammered me with a sense of vertigo I'd never experienced before, and I literally felt my head spin, creating the sensation that I was about to be catapulted off the edge and into the oblivion below.

I bent down and grabbed the sides of the board to steady myself, then slowly stood back up. I stood frozen in terror, and the muscles in my body refused to budge. I couldn't jump for fear of death, and I couldn't turn back for fear of the shame that awaited me. I would die there, and the paramedics would have to climb the ladder and inch their way out to the edge of the board themselves if they wanted to remove the corpse of the little kid who had died of fright, frozen in place at the edge of the high dive.

As I stood there contemplating my fate and wondering if the girl I liked would come to my funeral, I had the most unexpected awakening of my life. Right in the middle of that most terrifying experience of my life, I looked down, and for the first time, I suddenly saw what I was wearing. I'm not sure if it was a moment of realization brought on by extreme terror, or the fact that I was literally on display for every pair of eyes in the pool that day, but all of a sudden I noticed that what I was wearing left absolutely nothing to the imagination, and for the first time, I realized that I wasn't wearing a bathing suit; I was wearing a star-spangled Speedo. And in that exact same moment, I jumped.

The next thing I knew, my head was breaking the surface of the water and I was coming up for air. I had jumped, and lived to tell the tale. My entire class was cheering for me and waiting at the edge of the pool to give me high-fives and congratulations, but those kudos would never be received. That's because in one life changing moment, I had come to know the indignity that only a Speedo can inflict, and there was no way I was getting out of that pool and exposing myself to the other kids wearing something so revealing that even a male stripper would feel vulnerable in.

With that in mind, I swam the length of the pool as my instructor called out for me to come back, leaped out of the shallow end and ran into the change room before anyone could stop me. In a dizzying flash, I threw my clothes on over my bathing suit and ran out the front door of the rec center to find my mom waiting for me in the car and told her swimming lessons had ended early that day, which was the absolute truth.

They hadn't ended early for everyone, just me, but that was a semantic I wasn't about to get into.

Later that day, I took a pair of scissors to my Speedo and cut a giant hole in the crotch so that even my mom, the most talented seamstress I knew, wouldn't be able to repair it. Shortly after that, it was off to Sears to explore the wonderful world of bathing suit options. This time, I walked right past the Speedo section my parents had never seen the need to look beyond and found myself the coolest pair of board shorts I could. From that moment on, I would never again be the weirdo in the Speedo, and it would be up to people's imaginations if they wanted to know what I looked like naked, rather than a tiny piece of spandex Lycra.

Although your moment of epiphany may have been different than mine, chances are that for a significant part of your youth, you too were stuck wearing a Speedo, until the day you realized that you might as well have been naked. Actually, being naked may have been a better option, because Speedos have a tendency to compact the male form into small, oblong, unrecognizable shapes, and the same is true for one's self-esteem while wearing one.

The day you decided to stop wearing a Speedo marked one of the first independent decisions you ever made, and it would be the first of many to come. As life would have it, however, while a Speedo may have been the first embarrassing fashion trend you ever experienced, it wouldn't be the last, though nothing that came after could ever induce as much indignity… hopefully.

You Fried Ants With a Magnifying Glass

Kids are cruel. If you want proof, they're the only members of society who burn people alive for fun. Well, they don't burn people, they burn ants. And they don't actually burn them, but they sure give it the old college try. It's a very social thing for kids to do, and it always starts the same way. Some kid hears a rumour that you can light ants on fire with a magnifying glass, and before you know it all the kids in the neighbourhood are gathered on the sidewalk putting the theory to the test.

In my own experience, frying an ant with a magnifying glass never worked, but it didn't stop us from repeatedly trying to do it. We never actually lit an ant on fire, although I'm pretty sure we killed a couple in the attempt. Much to our disappointment, however, no ants ever spontaneously burst into flames in front of us. I think we all had visions of one fiery ant making its way back to the nest, climbing inside and lighting all the other ants on fire, and then watching in amazement as a river of flaming ants burst forth while we ran away screaming, knowing we had a story that no kid could ever top.

Even though we never managed to light an ant on fire, it didn't dispel the belief that it was possible. We just figured we weren't doing it right. We must have been holding the magnifying glass at the wrong angle, or the one we were using wasn't powerful enough to do the job. Although we repeatedly failed in our cruel science experiment, we were sure that somewhere in the world some kid had lit an ant on fire with a magnifying glass, and we lived forever in awe of that urban legend that we knew just had to be true, even if we hadn't been able to do it ourselves.

I don't know why, but the fascination with lighting ants on fire with a magnifying glass continues to this day. Wherever there are children and ants gathered together in one place, you can be sure that those kids are trying to light the ants on fire, though maybe today they're using a magnifying app on their smartphones. Either way, they'll probably have the same results and ensuing disappointment we did. At least today's kids can make a Snap Chat story or iMovie about it, and with some fancy editing, maybe even convince their friends that they proved the old urban legend was true.

That's one video I'd like to see, if only for old time's sake.

Your Stuffed Animals Were Real

To adults, stuffed animals are dust collectors and future items for the Salvation Army. To kids, they're real.

When you were young, your stuffed animals were as real as any animal you ever had. That's why you had a name for each of them, and the names you gave them were always so clever. For example, if you had a monkey, his name was probably "Monkey." If you had a mouse, it was likely "Mousey", or "Mouse," and if you had a bear, well, you guessed it, his name was probably "Teddy," or "Bear."

Remember when you went to bed with your stuffed animals and you always made sure they had their faces above the covers so that they could breathe? The same rules applied for making your bed. You were always careful to keep their snouts and mouths just above the covers so that they would still be alive when you came home from school. If your parents made your bed for you, sometimes they made the mistake of putting your animals under the sheets, and that always caused you to freak out because you knew that was a potentially fatal mistake. When you came home and saw little tiny lumps buried beneath the covers, you always reacted the same way.

"What are you doing?!" you screamed as you came upon the potential murder scene.

You frantically pulled back the covers, hoping your animals were still alive, while reaming out your parents for being so careless. To your relief, your animals hadn't suffocated, even after being smothered for the whole day. They sure were resilient, as this wasn't the first time they had survived an attempted murder by your parents, who just never seemed to learn.

Remember when you took your stuffed animals with you when you went places? If you were having a sleepover somewhere, at least one stuffed animal normally came along, and it was usually your favourite one. You loved all your animals, but there was always one that you liked better than the rest, the way some parents love one child more than the others, though they can't admit it. That's why you tried to be a bit stealthy when you smuggled your favourite out of the room, as you didn't want the others to get jealous.

Did you ever do something scary, like lose your stuffed animal or drop it out the window of a moving car? I did, despite repeated warnings from my parents that I was going to do just that. I was holding Alvin, my stuffed mouse, who by prior logic should have been called Mousey, out the window of the car, bouncing him up and down by a string that was attached to his head as my parents drove along the highway at 100 km/h, all the while telling me not to do that because I was going to drop him. But did I listen? Of course not, because I knew Alvin liked being held out the window and bounced up and down by his head.

Seconds later, I accidentally dropped Alvin onto the highway, just like my mom and dad said I would. I had never been so terrified in my life, and my parents probably felt the same way as they pulled over on the shoulder and ran into traffic to get him, again proving that parents are the true super heroes of this world.

My parents risked their lives that day to get my stuffed animal back, because they knew that I thought he was real. Deep down, I think that's because they remembered how they felt about their stuffed animals when they were kids, and they understood how traumatic it would have been for me to lose Alvin. Actually, who are we kidding? The real reason they dodged traffic on the highway to get him back was because it was easier than listening to me scream my lungs out for the rest of the ride home. The former reason is more endearing though, so let's stick with that one.

You Ran Away From Home

If you were like most kids, there likely came a time in your life when you just couldn't take the strain of living by your parents' rules anymore, and you decided to run away from home. This bold decision was probably reached in early childhood, when you decided that rather than live at home, eat your vegetables, and go to school, you'd instead live a life of freedom and set out on your own. Of course, this whole affair only lasted about an hour or so, but when you first came up with the idea you were certain it would be forever.

There were several things that could trigger your decision to leave home. It could have been a fight with your parents about having to do your homework, or finishing your broccoli, or having to clean up your room one too many times. Whatever it was, you knew that if you were out there on your own, you'd never have to do any of those things again. You'd never do homework, eat another vegetable, or clean up your room for as long as you lived, mainly because you wouldn't have one.

For my own part, when I finally decided I'd had enough of my parents' tyranny and had made up my mind to strike out on my own, I did what the characters in my favourite books and TV shows did when they ran away: I tied a hanky to a long stick and put all my stuff in it. Even back then, I knew that method was flawed, but since it seemed to have worked for the characters in my books and cartoons, I figured it would work for me too. Well, it didn't, and here's why.

The first problem was that I didn't know how to tie knots very well. The second was that once you fold up a hanky so you can actually try to tie a knot with it, there's not much room left to put anything inside. That meant that if I was going to be facing the world on my own terms, I wasn't going to be able to take a lot of things with me, and even back then, I knew that trying to survive with only candy, gum, a few pennies and my stuffed mouse was going to be really difficult, but since I'd already made up my mind, and more importantly, announced to my parents that I was leaving forever, there was no turning back.

So there I was, my mind firmly fixed on a parent-free future, and my flimsy stick and hanky combination precariously holding all the things I could take with me, none of which would be of any use to me in the real world. Well, I could buy some more candy with the few pennies that I had, and that would keep me going for a while, but everything else was useless. Forget warm clothing, food and water. As a kid, I didn't think about stuff like that, because back then all I cared about was candy and toys, since my parents had always taken care of everything else. I had yet to experience the real world, and as a result, I was totally unprepared for it. Running away would give me my first reality check, and it was extremely unwelcomed, as reality checks usually are.

With little thought to what the future would bring, I set out the front door, boldly stepping out into my new life. I thought of all the places I could live: in the woods, in a cave on a mountain, or in a log fort by the ocean. There were a million incredible places I could spend the rest of my days, so I was surprised and somewhat disappointed with myself for settling on the ditch beside the park that was just up the street from my house.

Oh well, it would do as a starter home. The important thing was that I had taken that initial step of actually running away. I could figure out the rest as I went. Besides, the playground was close by, and it would give me something to do while I planned out the next phase of my adventure.

It was while I was sitting in that ditch, however, that the reality of my situation began to set in. There were three major problems I hadn't considered when I'd decided to leave home. First, I had no food besides the candy I'd brought with me. I figured if I was careful and rationed it though, it could last for at least 10 minutes. After that, I'd have to go to 7-11 to buy more, but it was a long walk for my little legs, and I was afraid to go there on my own. That's because the parking lot was always full of teenagers, and they posed a serious threat to my safety, and I was afraid of what they might do to me if they found me alone. Second, I realized that if I stayed in that ditch long enough, eventually it was going to get dark, and since I was afraid of the dark, that was going to be a serious problem. Third, and most importantly, sitting in that ditch without any of my toys, I was overwhelmingly bored.

As the difficulties of my new circumstances slowly came to light, it also dawned on me that I didn't have any of the necessary skills or effects to survive on my own. I couldn't cook, I barely had any money, and I didn't know how to build a shelter. And then, much to my surprise, something totally unexpected happened, something I never would have thought possible when I first decided to run away: I found myself missing my family.

Despite the overwhelming sense of dread that was washing over me, I didn't want to give up. I didn't want to let my parents win. I wanted to show them that I could make it on my own, and make them think twice before they ever tried to make me do homework or clean my room again. I'd show them, and they'd be sorry.

But in reality, I was the one who was shown, and I was the one who would have to apologize for being a brat and running away. Living in a ditch for a whole 20 minutes was my first real wake-up call, the first time my perception of the world had been challenged. I wasn't the Uberman I thought I was, and living in the real world was a lot harder than I had imagined. It was in that moment of unpleasant epiphany that I realized that maybe I should have appreciated my parents more for all that they did for me, and having to clean my room once in a while or doing some math problems wasn't such a big deal if it meant having a roof over my head, food to eat, toys to play with, a night light to keep the darkness away, and a family that loved me. With newfound understanding, I picked myself up out of the ditch, packed up my belongings and headed for home, feeling an overwhelming sense of humbleness for the first time in my life.

The funny thing about going back home was that I thought it was going to be this emotional celebration between my parents and I, where I would apologize for running away, beg them to take me back, and they would wrap their arms around me, tears streaming down their faces, and welcome me back into the fold. But that's not how it went. Instead, it was as if nothing had happened. That's because my parents hadn't changed at all – only I had. But they didn't know that. They didn't know that suddenly I had a new appreciation for them, and that maybe I loved them just a little more than I had before I ran away. To them, my running away was barely a blip on the radar because they already knew how it would end, but for me it was the first time I had seriously examined my life and the choices I had made that had led me to that point, and it was my first, but not my last, transformative experience. The person who ran away that day was not the same person who came back home, and never would be again.

Settling back into my room, I unpacked my stuff, took a look around, and for the first time, was filled with gratitude for the beautiful life I had and the magnificent people who were my family, things that only an hour earlier I had taken completely for granted. In that moment, I vowed never to take anyone or anything for granted ever again, and to never even think about running away for as long as I lived.

And I kept that promise and that sense of gratitude for a long time, right up until the next time my parents asked me to take the garbage out.

You Caught Butterflies

Catching butterflies was a wonderful part of childhood. As much fun as it was to catch one though, there was always something sad about it, and that's because no matter what, the butterfly always died. However, that didn't stop you from catching another one, treating it exactly the same as all the others, and somehow hoping for a better outcome. I believe that's the definition of insanity, but back then, you didn't know the meaning of the word.

Every time you caught a butterfly, the routine was the same. You went out with your butterfly net and caught a beautiful, healthy butterfly, then brought it inside to its new home, which was an old yogurt container with holes poked in the lid, or some kind of butterfly dome you bought from the kid's science store. You put your butterfly in its new home, which the butterfly would have called a death trap, and watched it frantically flap its wings and flutter around the jar in a desperate bid to escape its impending doom. Once the butterfly had exhausted itself and damaged its wings in a futile attempt to escape, it lay on its side on the bottom of the container, pitifully moving one wing up and down as if somehow still hoping to escape its plastic tomb. At that point, you realized that you were once again about to kill one of nature's most beautiful creatures, but you clung to the faint hope that somehow, this butterfly would make a miraculous recovery and be different from all the others who had died under the exact same circumstances.

That night, you went to sleep and asked God to save your butterfly, and in the morning, you woke up and found it lying dead at the bottom of its container. You felt an overwhelming sense of sadness, maybe cried for a few minutes, and then buried it in the backyard. Right after that, you were back on the street trying to catch a new one, hoping against hope that this time would be different, but it never was.

Eventually, you stopped catching butterflies because you realized that there are some things that just aren't supposed to live in tiny little plastic prisons, and butterflies were one of them. Or, you stopped catching them because a big kid saw you running around with your butterfly net and made fun of you. Either experience was enough to make you give up your obsession, but in the end, allowing the butterflies to live and be free was the right thing to do, whether your reason for stopping was altruistic, or born from shame.

Knowing that you had grown tired of accidentally murdering God's innocent creations, you vowed never again to catch a butterfly, and instead you asked your parents for a more robust pet, like a hamster, fish, or bird, because you knew they would live long and healthy lives under your studious care. If only you had known how much God's little creatures would suffer at your murderous but well-intentioned little hands, you may never have asked for a pet again. But you didn't know, and that's what life is all about: learning from our mistakes and correcting ourselves along the way. Of course, with insects and small animals, it took us a long time to learn from those mistakes, and many unfortunate animals were harmed in the process. At least we could take solace in the fact that we believed all those animals were going to Heaven, and by the time we got there, they would probably be ready to forgive us… we hoped.

You Thought His Name Was "Dark Vader"

As a young boy, I loved watching *Star Wars*. It had everything I wanted: action, adventure, spaceships, laser swords, heroes, bad guys, you name it. I loved that movie, though I didn't always understand what was going on. Speaking of not knowing what was going on, am I the only person who thought Darth Vader's name was Dark Vader? It just made sense, didn't it? His suit was dark, his heart was dark, he was the epitome of evil – of course his name was Dark Vader. That made perfect sense to me back then.

You can imagine my confusion when my uncle, who introduced me to the movies, tried to tell me that his name was "Darth Vader", not "Dark Vader." It was the first time I remember thinking that an adult was wrong about something, and I couldn't fathom how anyone could be that mistaken about such an obvious subject. Darth Vader? What the heck was a Darth? No one had ever heard of that, and it didn't make any sense. Dark Vader, on the other hand, was totally reasonable, so there was no way some misinformed adult was going to change my mind, even if I'd previously believed that adults knew everything. Clearly, they didn't know everything about *Star Wars*.

As time went on and I began to develop a deeper understanding of the movie, however, I was eventually humbled by the realization that his name actually was Darth Vader, despite the fact that it was a stupid name for a character who dressed all in black and was the personification of evil. My epiphany came at the end of Return of the Jedi, when Luke pulled off his mask and Vader was white. That blew my mind. I was whole-heartedly expecting a black guy, or at least someone with a darker skin tone, and I know I'm not the only one. It was at that moment that I realized I'd been wrong all along, as the man behind the mask was actually the whitest person I'd ever seen, and therefore, could not have truly been called Dark Vader.

It was a paradigm shattering experience, and my concept of reality exploded like the second Death Star when I saw a frail old white man behind the black mask that had epitomized so much evil. It was the first time in my life I had been truly shocked by something on screen, and also the first time I had been wrong about something despite my utter conviction that I was right. I'm confident that kids today who see the original trilogy will make the same mistake I did, and discovering the truth about Vader's name will be their first humbling experience as well. We thought we knew it all back then, but as we would learn over and over again, sometimes we were just plain wrong. Of course, once we became teenagers, we really did know everything, and would never have to worry about being humbled like that again…or so we thought.

You Had To Finish Your Vegetables

For hungry people all over the world, having to finish a plate full of vegetables would be a dream come true. When you were a kid, it was your worst nightmare. If your childhood was anything like mine, you spent countless nights at the dinner table, long after everyone else had finished and your parents were cleaning up, staring at a plate picked clean of all but the veggies, and you couldn't leave until you finished them all. That was your parents' way of trying to get you to eat healthy, but for you, it was cruel and unusual punishment.

Being stuck at the table with a plate full of disgusting vegetables while everyone else was off playing with their toys or watching TV was the worst punishment you could endure. That's why if someone wanted to interrogate kids they wouldn't need a rack, a whip, or a water board, they would just need a plate full of vegetables and they'd have them squealing in seconds.

For some reason, your parents always thought they could shame you into eating your vegetables by making you feel bad. That's why they told you the same tired line every time, which was, "Children in Africa would give anything to eat those."

To which your response was always, "Good, let's send them over!"

If there had been a way for you to pack your vegetables into an envelope and mail them to Africa, you would have, because it was a win-win situation. You wouldn't have had to eat your disgusting corn, or broccoli, or carrots, and those hungry kids could've had a nutritious meal. Why wasn't that an option?

Everyone had a vegetable they hated above all others. For me, it was corn. I hated everything about it: the taste, the smell, the texture. Maybe for you it was broccoli, or peas, or cauliflower. Whatever it was, it was awful, which is why you always saved your vegetables for last, when it became like a showdown between you and your parents. They were determined to make you finish your veggies, while you were resolute in finding a way out of doing so, even if it meant sitting at the table all night, which of course, your parents threatened you with.

Although your parents thought they had you cornered and you would eventually cave, you always had a couple tricks up your sleeve to save you from actually having to eat your vegetables. The first trick was to mash them up and swirl them around on your plate, mixing them in with other little food scraps and trying to disguise them in one giant multi-colored mess. In your mind, that was a pretty good scheme. Instead of one big pile of vegetables, there was now an evenly dispersed mound of hard to recognize food spread around your plate. Of course, that never fooled your parents, and they let you know.

"You didn't eat your vegetables, you just mashed them up and swirled them around," they'd say. "Finish those veggies, or you'll sit there all night."

Rats. Your parents weren't going to be as easy to fool as you first thought - time for plan B – or plan D, actually. Plan D stood for "Plan Dog," which involved feeding your unwanted greens and whatnots to your trusty companion, who was patiently waiting beside the table for their turn to chow down. Unfortunately for you, however, even your dog, who would eat gum off the sidewalk and other people's dirty underwear, often spat out your vegetables after they'd had a taste. If someone who ate garbage and underwear couldn't stand the taste of vegetables, how the heck were you supposed to eat them? It was madness, but your parents, being the way they were, refused to relent, so you were forced to resort to an even more elaborate deception – the milk trick.

This third, and usually final trick, was to ask for a glass of milk. Your parents knew you loved milk, so there was nothing suspicious about you asking for a cup of the white stuff to help drown out the taste of those awful vegetables. Ideally, the milk would come in a coloured plastic cup. The reason for this, of course, was to help you in your deceptive endeavour, which was to spit your vegetables into your cup without your parents noticing, at which point they'd sink to the bottom and be concealed by the milk.

With your parents busy washing dishes, you proceeded with your plan, which at the time seemed like pure genius. You'd take a heaping spoonful of vegetables, suppress your gag reflex, and put them in your mouth, being ever so careful not to accidentally swallow any. Right after that, you'd pretend to take a sip of milk. To the outside observer, it looked like you were just washing your vegetables down, but what you were really doing was spitting them back into your cup. It was disgusting, but it worked. Once you had repeated this process three or four times and had cleared your plate of all remaining evidence, it was time for inspection.

When you announced to your parents that you had finished and they came over to make sure that you actually had, you felt like a prisoner who had dug an escape tunnel in their jail cell and only had to pass the nightly check-in before making his escape. Of course, while the prisoner would hope that the guard wouldn't look under the bed to find the tunnel they had dug, you were hoping your parents wouldn't look in your cup and see all the broccoli and cauliflower floating in it, and would only see your empty plate instead.

If you were lucky, your parents took one look at your plate, saw that your vegetables were gone, and gave you the all clear to leave the table. Once they'd done that, you put your cup of milk in the fridge and told them you'd finish it later. Your parents, knowing you'd never waste a glass of milk, were satisfied with the final bit of your charade and gave you permission to do so. Later, when the coast was clear, you'd sneak back into the kitchen, steal the cup and dump the evidence down the toilet or the garburator, reveling in the fact that you had just outsmarted your parents once again.

Getting away with not eating your vegetables wasn't making you any healthier, but it was certainly making you craftier. In fact, it was probably some of the first real life problem solving you ever did. It took a tremendous amount of trial and error, creativity, careful planning, good acting, and perfect execution, but eventually, you became adept at the art of deception. You didn't know it at the time, but getting away with not eating your vegetables would be the first of many routine deceptions you'd start to put over on your parents, including sneaking out at night, telling them it was a pro-D day at school when it wasn't, and keeping your girlfriend or boyfriend a secret for as long as you could. And to think, it all started with some mushy corn.

25 Cents Was a Lot of Money

What is 25 cents today? One-quarter of a can of pop? 10 minutes of parking? Something to give a homeless person when they ask for change? Today, it's nothing. When you were a kid, 25 cents a fortune.

If you had 25 cents back then, you were rich. You could buy any assortment of candy and have more than enough to share, since it only cost a penny a piece. You could get anything you wanted: double-bubble, sour keys, licorice, gummy candies, whatever you wanted. It was all so cheap, and one quarter went a long way.

When you were young, you could buy 25 candies with a quarter. Now, you can buy two and a half, because even the cheapest candy is 10 cents, and then there's tax on top of that too. If you gave a kid in today's world a quarter and told him to enjoy himself, he would probably assume you were joking and wait for the other $4.50, because nowadays, you need at least five bucks to buy anything good. No one in our generation ever got five bucks at the candy store. That's because we would have been able to buy 500 candies with that, and no parent in their right mind would have ever let that happen – not even a grandparent, the same people who used to let us put sugar on Frosted Flakes.

One quarter was once a small fortune, and bought us more candy than we should have been allowed to eat. I guess in some ways then, inflation is actually a good thing because it means kids today can't afford to buy as much candy as we could, which means fewer cavities and a lower risk of diabetes nationwide. Just don't expect a kid to agree with you on that one, because they would gladly trade cheap candy for a few cavities. Speaking of which, do you remember when…

You Put Sugar on Frosted Flakes

Today, most of us don't eat Frosted Flakes. Even if we did, there is no way we would ever do what we did as kids, which was to put spoonfuls of sugar on them. As adults, we'd call that asking for diabetes. As kids, we just called it delicious.

I have to admit that putting sugar on Frosted Flakes wasn't my idea, though it was so genius that I wished it had been. It was my grandpa who came up with the concept, and the first time he asked if I wanted sugar on my Frosted Flakes, I thought I'd died and gone to Heaven. That's something that no sane parent would ever do, but grandparents? They spoiled you in a million ways, and putting sugar on your Frosted Flakes was one of them.

Unfortunately, that perk didn't carry over when I went back home. The next time my mom poured me a bowl of Frosted Flakes, which in itself was a rarity, and I asked her to scoop some sugar on them, she looked at me like I was crazy.

"You can't put sugar on Frosted Flakes!" she exclaimed. "They're pure white already!"

"Grandpa let me do it," I replied.

"He did?!"

And then Grandpa got a talking to, where he was told there was absolutely no way he could ever do that again. But, being the awesome grandpa that he was, he just pretended he forgot about that the next time I went for a sleepover. Aren't grandparents the best?

Eating Frosted Flakes with extra sugar on them is something you could only do when you were a kid, much like how partying hard was something you could only do in college. If you tried to indulge in either of those things now, you'd pay a heavy price and wind up passed out on the couch with a killer headache, wondering why you ever thought you could abuse your body like that and get away with it.

There are so many nostalgic parts of childhood we can look back on and think, "I wish I could experience that again," but putting sugar on Frosted Flakes isn't one of them. It's a part of our childhood that was unique and exciting at the time, but that we're better off without, kind of like the clothes we wore in the '80's. Come to think of it, do you remember when…

Everything You Wore Was Based On A Cartoon Or Movie

For you and countless others, there was a brief period in your life when everything you wore was based on a cartoon or movie. Whether your outfits were festooned with Ninja Turtles, GI Joe, Superman, Batman, Super Mario Brothers, or any other lovable characters from you childhood, your favourite clothes were the ones that had your favourite characters on them, and you wore them every day, except for laundry day, when your parents finally forced you to put them in the wash.

As a child in the late 80s, my favourite cartoon was *Teenage Mutant Ninja Turtles*, so naturally, my favourite clothes bore the Ninja Turtles. On my best days, I was covered from head to toe in Turtles apparel, and wore so much lime green that I was certain people would mistake me for one of the gang. And why not? According to my clothes, I belonged in the group. I had a Ninja Turtles hat, a Ninja Turtles t-shirt, Ninja Turtles shorts, a Ninja Turtles fanny pack, a plastic Ninja Turtles ring that I got from a box of Shreddies, and a Ninja Turtles fanny pack that I filled with all the essential things a kid needed: gum, pennies, and some rocks that I thought were neat. And that was only my daytime outfit. At night, I had a full Ninja Turtles pajama set. At every sleepover I went to, I proudly donned those pajamas, which to me felt more like an official uniform than a pair of jammies.

Wearing clothes with your favourite superheroes and cartoon characters on them was awesome. It was a way to separate yourself from the herd, and it also helped you identity potential friends who shared mutual interests, since they would often be wearing similar apparel. The best part about wearing those clothes was that you felt like the super heroes you were representing, and it took your imagination to a whole other level.

That's why there's nothing I love more than seeing a kid at the playground dressed up as Spiderman or Batman, because when they dress the part, they act the part. If you pay attention, you'll notice that the kid dressed up as the super hero doesn't act like the other kids. They don't play on the swings, and they don't go down the slide. Instead, they stand on the periphery with their arms crossed or on their hips, keeping an eye on things and watching for any signs of trouble, ready to spring into action should the need arise. That, or they're running around the playground with their arms stretched out, making flying noises and pretending to shoot lasers from their eyes.

Whether you dressed up in clothes with your favourite characters on them or actually dressed up as your favourite character, wearing clothes with super heroes on them made you feel like a super hero: you could run faster, jump higher, fight better, and you were invulnerable to any enemy. Any enemy except your parents, actually, who once they had decided you'd had enough running around for one day, scooped you up and put you into the car to take you home. That was ok by you though, because in your mind you were riding in the Turtle Van or the Batmobile, and you had no problem with that, especially if you were going to stop for ice cream on the way home.

Hey, even super heroes deserve a treat once in a while.

You Had To Be The One To Press the Elevator Button

As a child, you had very few responsibilities. The one thing you always stepped up to the plate for, however, was pushing the elevator button. You had to be the one to press that button. It was too important a matter to leave up to some amateur, and no one could push that button like you could. If someone beat you to it, it was the ultimate upset.

There was no greater feeling than actually being the one to push the button, especially if you were in an elevator with other kids. If you were the one to push it, you felt totally superior to them. You were better than them, and you knew it. They knew it too. In fact, everyone knew it. To kids, pushing the elevator button was akin to being the one to pull the legendary Sword from the Stone. It gave you ultimate power, and it was up to you to decide the fate of all who rode in that elevator car with you.

Who got to push the button was always a great way to start a fight in a family. That's because your brothers and sisters wanted to push the button just as much as you did, and it was always an argument to see who got to do it. I can only imagine how ridiculous this seemed to your parents, but for kids, it was more important than anything. Your family probably wasn't much different than mine, and therefore, the conversations you had every single time your family got in an elevator probably weren't much different either. Each time my family took a ride in an elevator, the dialogue was exactly the same:

> Older brother: "I get to push the button!"
> Me: "No! You pushed it last time! It's my turn!"
> Younger brother: "No! It's my turn! I never push the button!"
> Older brother: "You always push the button! I haven't pushed it in forever!"
> Me: "Yes you did! You pushed it yesterday!"
> Younger brother: "It's my turn! I'm pushing the button!"

And then my parents let my younger brother push the button, because that's the way it goes. If you were an only child or your brothers and sisters weren't around, pushing the button was a lot easier. There was no one to fight with about whose turn it was, and your parents always let you do it, even though they still had to tell you what button to push, and sometimes had to lift you up so you could reach it, but they still let you push it, and that's what mattered.

Wasn't it awful when someone else pushed the button before you did? It was especially upsetting when it was some poorly mannered adult who should have waited for you to do it, and worse yet, who obviously didn't derive any satisfaction from doing it. You could tell they got no joy out of doing it, so why did they push the button? Didn't they know how much it meant to you? The only thing you could conclude was that if they were willing to rob you of that simple joy without even batting an eye, they must never have been a kid themselves. Either that, or they'd been a kid who really loved pushing the button and just never grew out of it, though time and habit had numbed they joy they'd once derived from it.

As an adult, I don't think there is any equivalent to being the one to push the elevator button. The only thing that even comes close is finding a good spot in a mall parking lot during Christmas season or being at the front of a big lineup waiting to get into a movie, but they still fall short of how you felt when you mashed that elevator button in your youth. Yes, that kind of satisfaction is something you lose with childhood, but it's probably better that way. After all, it's stressful enough competing with each other for parking spaces and grocery store lineups; we don't need one more thing to fight over.

We can leave that to the kids.

A Stick Was Whatever You Wanted It To Be

A sword; a laser gun; a sword that doubled as a laser gun. When you were a kid, a stick could be all of these things and more. You were only limited by your imagination, which at the time, was limitless.

As an adult, I love seeing kids running around with sticks because I know that in their minds they're not carrying sticks. They're carrying a blaster rifle from *Star Wars*, or a magic wand from *Harry Potter*, or the Master Sword from *Legend of Zelda*. They're carrying something special, magical even. That's why they want to bring those sticks home with them. To kids, sticks are something wonderful; to parents, they're just dirty pieces of wood that have bugs on them and will scratch the car seats.

When you were a kid your imagination gave you so much freedom, and so much pleasure. There was nothing more fun than going to the beach or the woods and running around with a stick because that stick became whatever you wanted it to be and intensified whatever fantastical experience you were already having. Instead of a kid in gumboots, you were a soldier on the front lines, or fighting aliens on a distant planet, or undertaking a heroic quest to slay a dragon. As long as you had a stick, you could be and do anything, because that stick was a wonderful extension of your infinite imagination, but to the adults around you, it was just a stick.

Now, that's not to say that adults didn't have any imagination at all when it came to sticks – they did. When they went camping, a stick could be a hot dog roasting stick, or a marshmallow stick, or a kindling stick, but that was about it. There was nothing magical or wondrous about them, and whatever they were using them for, they were still just sticks. They weren't for slaying dragons or fighting off aliens; they were just for roasting, toasting, or getting a fire going, and that was about it. Of course, if one of the adults around you happened to roast you a perfectly golden marshmallow with one of those sticks, you easily forgave them for their lack of creativity.

I'm not sure what age it happened at, but eventually, you started to become like one of those adults who couldn't imagine more than a few good uses for a stick, and you grew out of playing with them. I guess it's a good thing that happens though, because if people saw adults running around the beach with sticks pretending to shoot people or swinging them around like swords, the police would be called, the sticks would be confiscated, and the adults would be taken to the loony bin or the drunk tank. That's kind of sad actually, because it drives home the point that as adults we're not allowed to have fun anymore and can never be as carefree and imaginative as we used to.

While we may not be allowed to enjoy ourselves as much as we once did, at least we can live vicariously through our children. We can take heart in knowing that when they're running around with sticks in their hands, swinging them in wide circles casting spells and making machine gun noises, their imaginations are wonderfully alive, and so are they. And even though we may be able to recognize the brilliance of their minds and understand that they're creating entire worlds with those sticks they're wielding, there's no way they're bringing them home.

They have bugs on them, and they'll scratch the car seats.

You Sat in Toy Cars For Haircuts

Without a doubt, there is nothing fun about getting a haircut now, but when you were a kid it was awesome. There was usually at least one place in town that totally catered to kids, and it was the best place to get your haircut. In my hometown, we had just such a place. It was called "Tickety Doos", and every kid who was in the know got their hair cut there. Not only did the waiting room have Super Nintendos with all the latest games for you to play while you waited, it also had a slushee machine. On top of that, there were no barber chairs. Instead, there were kid-sized cars and trucks you could sit in while you got your hair cut; there was even a motorcycle! Of course, the vehicles were stationary (let's face it, they had to be), but still, sitting in an army jeep instead of a boring old barber chair made getting your hair cut so exciting. As if that wasn't enough, when you were finished your haircut, you got a giant lollipop and could even hang around and play video games for a while.

When you're an adult, you don't get anything even close to that. All you can do is read a boring magazine called *Golf* or *Tennis*, or stare at magazines filled with beautiful people whose hairlines and hairstyles are far superior to yours and make you long for the days when you didn't have to choose a haircut based on the one that covers your bald spot or receding hairline the best. And there's no lollipop when you're done, either.

That's why I hate being an adult sometimes, because nothing's fun anymore. Everything's a problem, and all we do is worry about stuff. When you were 10, coming off your latest Super Mario high, sitting in a miniature jeep and talking to your stylist about all the different haircuts you were considering, since you had more hair than you knew what to do with, life was so much better. What I wouldn't give to be able to have an experience like that again. Heck, I'd even settle for just having a perfect hairline. You can keep your Super Nintendo and your jeep. Actually, on second thought, it would still be fun to sit in the jeep.

You Only Walked On The Coloured Tiles At The Mall

Kids have been doing this since the dawn of time, and no one knows why. Well, the dawn of time since shopping malls were invented, at least, and they continue to do it to this day. If you go to any mall anywhere in the world, you will see kids walking, hopping, or crawling along only certain coloured tiles. No one tells them to do it, and no one has ever asked them why they do it either. It's never been explained. It's just something they do, and when you were a kid, you did it too.

Along with begging to go to the toy store and lying about not wanting to buy anything, only walking on certain coloured tiles is something every little kid does when they go to the mall. Though it was too long ago for you to remember exactly why you were doing it, I'm sure it had something to do with pretending that most of the floor was covered in lava, and tiles of a certain colour were rocks that you could safely traverse, though the design of the tiles often made it impossible for you to go in a straight line. You'd walk sideways, diagonally, and even backwards, but never straight, and it drove your parents crazy.

"Let's go," they'd holler at you.

"Just a minute," you'd plead back.

And then you'd line yourself up, get up to maximum speed as quickly as possible, and hurl yourself over an abyss of white tiles to safely land on the brown ones three feet in front of you while your parents watched in exasperation and considered what would happen if they just decided to leave you there and drive home without you. I guess that's the irony of that whole game. The only real danger you were in was tempting your parents to abandon you at the mall, but back then that never crossed your mind. You were more concerned with imaginary lava.

This eccentric game that kids play must be something instinctual, something left over from our ancestors who had to traverse semi-frozen bodies of water or treacherous lava fields by only stepping on certain areas in order to make it safely to the other side, being careful to avoid thin spots in the ice or slippery rocks leading across a river, where one misstep could send them into the frigid waters to be carried off to their doom. Whatever it is and wherever it comes from, it's alive and well in children today, just like it was when you were a kid. And of course, the same is true for the frustration parents feel while waiting for their dawdling children to hurry up and walk ten feet without making a life or death decision, but they're not having nearly as much fun as their kids are.

You Had Pez Dispensers

Pez was once a staple of your childhood. It was cheap and delicious, but you didn't love it for its economic or gustatory merits; you loved it because of the dispensers it came with.

Back in the day, you could get all kinds of Pez dispensers: super hero Pez dispensers, Disney Pez dispensers, cartoon character Pez dispensers, you name it. If it existed in the world and was marketed to kids, you could get a Pez dispenser created in its image, and every kid's dispenser was different.

You could do a lot with a Pez dispenser. You could make new friends. You could let someone know you liked them. You could even trade the Pez inside of it for other things, like small toys and hockey cards. Pez was so much more than just candy; it was currency of every kind.

Your Pez dispenser was your pride and joy, one of the first status symbols you ever owned. The kind of Pez dispenser you had said a lot about you, the way your car does as an adult. For example, I had a Mickey Mouse dispenser that I bought from Disneyland, and it was my claim to fame. It was my way of letting other kids know that not only had I been to the Magic Kingdom, I'd actually met Mickey himself, and in the kid world that was akin to someone in Biblical times being healed by Jesus.

You used to love showing off your dispenser to other kids. It was like a classic car show, only with Pez dispensers instead of cars, but you and your friends acted the same way those old guys do at those shows. You marvelled at other kids' dispensers and asked them all kinds of questions about where they got it, how much they paid for it, and if they'd ever consider selling it.

In a way, Pez was kind of like cigarettes for kids. That's because when a group of kids were hanging out talking about video games or cartoons, they'd all have their Pez dispensers out, lazily sucking back on their candies the way adults do with cigarettes. Pez was also kind of like drugs, not just because it was addicting, but because every time you went to a kid's birthday party or some other event, there was always one kid who would come up to you and go, "Hey man, got any Pez?"

The only weird thing about those dispensers was that the candy inside of them came out of your character's throat. I'm sure the original idea was for the candy to come out of their mouth, but for some reason that didn't manifest in the final design, and there was always something unsettling about that.

I remember thinking that eating candy out of someone's throat was gross, but I guess eating it out of someone's mouth would've been pretty disgusting too. Come to think of it, that was one of the major reasons I stopped eating Pez. I just couldn't come to terms with that aspect of it, and eventually it grossed me out enough to stop eating it altogether.

Of course, the other reason I stopped eating Pez was because I got too old for it. Like so many other wonderful parts of childhood, age and time had their way of ruining things for you, and being in love with Pez dispensers was one of them. It's probably a good thing you outgrew them though because you didn't want to get to high school and still be walking around with a Pez dispenser. It would have ruined the cool image you were trying to create for yourself with your baggy jeans, oversized T-shirts, and styling mushroom cut. A Pez dispenser would've just made you look stupid.

You Only Drank Milk

Nowadays, you probably can't remember the last time you had a glass of milk. As an adult, it's a drink that's just not on the menu anymore. On the rare occasions you do drink milk, something about it seems gross. Today, your palate prefers drinks like coffee, tea, beer and wine, and the most hated of all kid drinks, water. When you were a kid though, milk was only one drink that could satisfy you.

Remember when you'd come in from playing with your friends on a hot summer day, and you were dying for a glass of the white stuff? You were sweaty, overheated, and parched, and any normal person would have reached for a cold glass of water, but not you. Instead, you wanted a huge glass of milk, and you downed it the way people down beer at frat parties. You drained the entire glass in one go, and as soon as you did, you immediately went for a second, and maybe even a third. To you, milk was the nectar of the gods, and you were guzzling the whole reserve.

Back then, you used to brag to other kids about how much milk you could drink, the way adults brag about how much liquor they can imbibe. For example, everyone knows someone (who hasn't realized they're an alcoholic yet) who loves to brag about how much they drank on the weekend. On Monday morning, they'll tell you the details of their binge drinking as if it's something to be proud of.

They'll say something like, "I drank two bottles of wine, polished off a six pack, did four shots of Jaeger, and then I puked all night."

When you were a kid, you did that with milk, minus the puking part.

You'd tell your friends things like, "Yesterday, I had a whole carton to myself, and then drank a 250ml just for fun!"

At that point, your friends would tell you about how much milk they drank, and try to one up you. Drinking milk may have been the only time when you didn't exaggerate your stories, because you really did consume it like crazy. You could drink unbelievable amounts of the white stuff, and you were proud of it.

Of course, all kids knew that the only drink better than regular milk was chocolate milk. It was the ambrosia of childhood, and if your parents had allowed it, chocolate milk would have been the only thing you ever drank.

Any kid who got chocolate milk in their lunch was the envy of all the other kids in class. Whenever someone got chocolate milk, they never drank it right away. Instead, they'd leave it on their desk for a while, making sure everyone saw it, and then they'd slowly sip it back, savouring every last drop and making big "Aaah" sounds after each delicious gulp. This was not only a way of showing off, but also a way of making their peers jealous by saying, "Look what I got," the same way adults use Facebook and Instagram to make people think their life is better than everyone else's.

Milk wasn't always the drink of choice though. Sometimes, it was just plain gross, like when your parents packed it in your lunch for you to take to school. By noon, it was room temperature, stinky, and disgusting. That was the only time you were turned off by it, and it was mainly because of the smell. You'd open your thermos and immediately be hit by that horrible odour, and you couldn't bring yourself to consume that wretched, disgusting liquid. I remember being so turned off by milk in a thermos that I begged my parents to give me juice boxes like the cool kids had, but my mom said that they were bad for the environment, so I had no choice but to keep drinking my foul-smelling warm milk, which was awful for both my taste buds and my social status.

Although you loved milk more than anything when you were a kid, somewhere along the way, things changed. You've moved on and evolved since then, to the point where you either don't drink it at all, or only have it once in a while. Now, you prefer the kinds of drinks that kids find disgusting, like coffee, beer, and water, and in turn you're revolted by children's insatiable lust for milk. Once again, there's a huge disconnect between kids and adults, and you're on the opposite end of the spectrum from where you used to be. Kids will never understand adults, but at least you can understand kids, since you used to be one and had the same weird habits they do. Old people, however, continue to remain a mystery to you, and they forever will until you become old yourself, and then it will all make sense. By that time, you'll probably be drinking milk again...just hopefully not out of a thermos at lunchtime.

You Had Bathtub Toys

As an adult, you don't take toys in the bathtub, because it sounds wrong on many levels. As a kid though, toys in the tub were par for the course. In fact, sometimes they were the only way your parents could coax you into the tub in the first place, as they were the decisive, heck, the only element of the negotiation process.

"It's time for your bath," your parents would say.

"No! I hate baths!" you fired back.

"If you go in the tub, you can play with your bathtub toys."

"Deal!"

How could you resist an entire collection of toys specifically dedicated to the bathtub? The simple answer was, you couldn't. Your parents had an array of toys explicitly designed for the purpose of coaxing you into the tub and keeping you there for more than 30 seconds, including rubber ducks, floating boats, submarines, little plastic scuba divers, and so on. Those toys took the experience to a whole new level, and they were the adult equivalent of lighting candles, having a glass of wine, and reading a book, though much more exciting.

The truly great thing about bathtub toys was that they were entirely different from your regular toys. For that reason, they maintained a type of novelty your other toys didn't. There was still a spark of excitement with your bathtub toys, and you didn't take them for granted because you knew your time with them was short. For that reason, you appreciated them more than your regular toys, which were like a stable partner that you trusted would always be there for you, while your tub toys were more like a sexy fling that you knew wasn't going to last forever, so you appreciated the hell out of them while you had them.

In addition to your toys, sometimes your parents even put other people in the tub with you to make it that much more exciting: your brother or sister, your best friend, your cousin who you had a crush on and were young and naïve enough not to feel weird about it, whoever. Some people even took their pets in the bath. Whatever it took to get you to have a bath, your parents were willing to do it, and because of that, bath time was always awesome - except when you got soap in your eyes – but other than that, it was a wonderful experience that always started with a big fuss but wound up being something that made you feel good afterward, kind of like exercise today.

As an adult, baths aren't nearly as pleasurable as they used to be. Most of us only have baths when we're feeling sick, tired, or stressed out, and there's nothing fun about them. It may be different for women, but most men only have baths when the outside world has become too much and the walls are closing in around us. We never take toys in the tub anymore either, although maybe we should. Of course, our imaginations have become so stagnant that we wouldn't even know what to do with them. We'd probably just step on them and hurt our feet, or slip on them and kill ourselves, so maybe it's a good thing we don't include them as part of our bathing ritual anymore.

Also, the bathtub used to seem huge to us, almost like our own personal swimming pool, but nowadays they always seem tiny. You can barely move in them, and even though the idea of having a bath with another person sounds like a great idea, it's always terrible in reality because both people wind up cramped and uncomfortable.

Now, I already said that adults don't take toys in the tub, but we try to do other things to make baths more enjoyable. For example, maybe you'll try to read a book, which always seems like a great idea until you try it. That's because no matter what, your hands always get wet, and inevitably, the book you're reading gets wet too. The condensation damages the pages, and it's a lot of work holding a book in front of your face the entire time, especially if it's a hard cover, so you give up on reading pretty quick.

If you don't want to read, maybe you'll take your iPad in the tub with you, resting it on the ledge or a TV tray, but this is worrisome for two reasons. First, you're concerned that water is going to get in your iPad, shorting it out and putting you out a few hundred dollars, and second, you're worried that it may fall into the tub and electrocute you, putting an end to your bath and your life in one fell swoop.

If the book and the iPad don't work out, maybe you'll light some candles, but still, you can't relax because of the danger involved. Every time I light a candle in the bath, I'm worried that the shower curtain is going to catch fire, and I'm going to wind up standing buck naked in the street while my house burns down in front of me. As a kid, something like that would never have crossed my mind, and even if I did find myself standing naked outside my house I wouldn't have cared, because remember, back then that was acceptable.

Clearly, taking a bath when you were a kid was so much better than it is as an adult. Ruining literature, electrocuting yourself, and burning down your house were things you never worried about back then. Instead, you just played with your toys and had a great time, then ran around the house naked to dry off, which is just one more fun thing on the long list of stuff you're not allowed to do anymore.

You Built Coffee Creamer Pyramids

For adults, coffee creamers are for coffee. For kids, they're for building pyramids. That's why you built stuff out of creamers every time you went to a restaurant. The reason those creamers were on the table in the first place was for adults to use in their coffee, but for you, they were a means of entertainment. That's why when the adults started using the creamers for what they were intended for, it made you mad.

"Hey! What are you doing putting those in your coffee? I'm trying to build something here!"

So your parents would have to call the waitress over and ask her to bring more creamers, not because they wanted more coffee, but because you hadn't finished your pyramid yet, and you'd run out of building materials.

"Excuse me, could we get a couple more creamers please? My son is trying to build the Sphinx."

Eventually, your parents decided to stop bothering the waitress for more creamers, and you were forced to finish your masterpiece with the materials at hand, like a construction company that runs out of funding before a project is complete. To add to your disappointment, your parents had also decided that they were more interested in enjoying a nice meal and some fresh coffee than encouraging your budding architectural career, and soon enough, they started picking your creation apart because they'd run out of creamers. The more coffee they drank, the smaller your pyramid became, until eventually, it was just one lonely creamer. Your great pyramid had been reduced to a mud hut, and it wasn't impressing anyone.

Fortunately, it was usually around that time that your dessert came, so you tossed your lone creamer aside and enthusiastically dug into whatever treat lay in front of you.

Although your architectural aspirations had been put on hold, at least you could contemplate future projects over some delicious ice cream.

You Played Hide and Seek

There is no game more cherished by children around the world than hide and seek. It involves everything kids love: excitement, running around, crawling into small spaces, fooling adults, and yelling. That's why when you were a kid, it was one of your favourite games.

The great thing about hide and seek was that it could be played almost anywhere, and whether it was inside or outside, it was always exhilarating. Of course, everyone remembers the quintessential catch phrase of hide and seek, which was, "Ready or not, here I come!"

Wasn't it the worst when the person who was coming to find you yelled that out, and you hadn't found a hiding spot yet? The adrenaline at that moment was incredible. It was life and death, and you had only seconds to get to the bottom of that laundry basket or buried under some leaves before they came looking for you. Fortunately, if you were like most kids, you had a few tried and true spots that you could always go to in a pinch.

Most of us had one perfect hiding spot, our go to spot, that we used all the time. To us, it was the greatest spot in the world. The funny thing about that spot though was that once you were caught there the first time, it was no longer the world's best spot, because now other people knew about it too. Even though everyone else knew about it, however, you kept going back there all the time, still thinking it was perfect. It was the childhood equivalent of a bad relationship that you keep leaving and crawling back to. You know it's flawed, but you don't think you can do any better, so you just keep returning to it...until you find a better one, that is.

The only thing that made hide and seek better than playing with your friends was playing with adults, because they were terrible at it. That's the impression they gave off, at least. They always did a good job of pandering to your ego by pretending they couldn't find you, even though they knew all your hiding places by heart. Even if they didn't know where you were, all they had to do was follow the giggling or the heavy breathing that came with the adrenaline rush you got when you were hiding, and they could find you in an instant. But they didn't, because they wanted to let you have a little fun. That's why every adult always did the same thing when they were looking for you. For example, I remember my grandma walking around the laundry room, knowing full well that I was in the laundry basket, and checking everywhere but there.

The whole time she was there, she kept saying things like, "Where did he go? I can't imagine where he went. It's like he disappeared!"

To a kid, that was the ultimate compliment. Wasn't that wonderful to hear? It was as if you had super powers, and you were finally getting recognized for them. As far as you were concerned, it was about darn time, too.

No matter where you were hiding, there was no better feeling than hearing the seeker's voice call out those magic words that let you know you'd won the game: "Come out, come out, wherever you are!"

Victorious, you materialized from beneath that pile of laundry, or out of that cupboard, or from inside of that dryer, even though you knew you weren't supposed to be in there, and you re-emerged back into the world knowing that whoever had been looking for you would be astounded that you hadn't actually disappeared into the void.

When you won hide and seek, your ego got a massive boost, and that feeling was magnified tenfold if you'd been playing with adults. Of course, what you didn't realize at the time was that hide and seek was the only bit of peace and quiet your parents or grandparents got when they were looking after you, so pretending they couldn't find you just meant more down time for them. It was a win-win situation. You got to feel great about yourself and your abilities to seemingly vanish into thin air, and the adults around you got some well-deserved respite, until you emerged from hiding, announced your victory, and then forced them to play another round. If they were smart though, they went along with it, since they knew it would guarantee them at least ten more minutes of serenity.

Hide and seek was one of the most fun and exhilarating games you could play, and there is no adult equivalent of it. No matter what you do now, you will never quite be able to recapture the same kinds of thrills and excitement that you felt when you played it as a kid. You had to out think your opponents, master the art of stealth, and be able to hide in the bottom of a clothes hamper without overheating or giggling when someone came in the room. Without a doubt, it was, and still is, the world's best game, and no one is better at it than kids...except the adults who are looking for them, but we won't tell the kids that.

"Are We There Yet?" Was The Only Question You Asked

I don't have kids. It's a conscious decision: the conscious decision to enjoy my life and remain stress free. But my friends have kids, and I get to hear what it's like to have them, which is a big reason why I don't have any of my own. For example, my friend just got back from a camping trip with his wife and his kids. When I asked him how it was, he only used three words to describe it: "Hell on wheels."

Of course, he eventually went into more detail, but that was the initial description, and it only got worse from there. He told me he had booked a spot at a campsite about a three-hour drive from his home, and he had explained to his kids numerous times before packing them into the car and leaving that it would be a very long drive. Despite all his efforts to prepare them for the extensive journey and telling them not to expect to arrive at the campsite for several hours, within ten minutes of leaving the house his four year old daughter asked the question we've all asked so many times: "Are we there yet?"

And in that moment, my friend realized that his life had just come full circle, and he was now on the receiving end of the world's most annoying question.

It's the question that never needs to be asked, because everyone already knows the answer.

But my friend, trying to be a good dad, remained calm, and gave his daughter the best answer he could. "No sweetie, we're not there yet. It's going to be about three hours, so you're just going to have to wait patiently, ok?"

His daughter considered that for a moment, and then, happy with that answer, sat back and said, "Ok, daddy."

And two minutes later, she asked the exact same question. "Are we there yet?"

To which my friend calmly replied, "No sweetie. It's going to be a few hours, so just wait patiently."

"Ok."

And two minutes after that, she asked it again. And again, and again, and again. In fact, she asked every few minutes for the rest of the trip, while my friend repeatedly asked himself why he thought taking two young kids on a road trip was a good idea, and whether he should just cut his losses, head back home, and stop for a vasectomy on the way. But of course, being the good parent that he is, he didn't do that – he just kept driving the car, while his daughter kept driving him insane, and finally, after hours of endless torment, when his daughter asked, "Are we there yet," he could say yes, and no one was more relieved than him. At that moment, he stepped out of the car, looked up at the beautiful blue sky, took a breath of fresh mountain air, and vowed never to take his family on vacation again.

That story is familiar to all of us, because at one point in our lives we all did the same thing my friend's daughter did. I don't know why we asked, "Are we there yet," because it was obvious that we weren't. We knew it as well as anybody. If we had been there, we wouldn't have been sitting in the car anymore, so what was the point in asking? I think that asking that question was actually our way of telling our parents to step on it a little, despite the fact that they were already going as fast as they could. In fact, if there were two people who wanted that car trip to be over sooner than you did, it was your parents.

Your parents really suffered on vacation. Not only were they responsible for planning, packing, and paying for everything, they never actually got to relax, and "Are we there yet" was only the first in a series of trials they'd have to endure throughout their "holiday", which as they quickly came to realize, was a lot more stressful than staying home. After the first family road trip, no matter how long or how short it was, it's amazing that any family ever went on vacation again, which leads me to my next point. Remember when…

Your Parents Vowed Every Vacation Was Your Last

If your family was anything like mine, it's probably a safe bet that every time you went on vacation, your parents vowed it would be your last. That's what always happened on my family vacations, without fail. Yet year after year, we found ourselves on holiday again, repeating the exact same patterns and bad behaviours from the previous ones, and my parents making the same empty threats they always did. They had to make those threats though, because they had no alternatives. They slaved and struggled all year doing the unappreciated, endless, and exhausting jobs that parents do, and all they wanted was a few days away from it all to rest and recharge. Your parents were probably no different, so even though going on a holiday always wound up being just as stressful as staying home, they took you anyways, even if every time they did they said they'd never do it again.

Now, there is a chance that your parents may have never threatened you with this kind of thing, but that probably means the makeup of your family was different from mine. For example, if you were an only child, I imagine vacations were relatively stress free and enjoyable for your parents, and the idea of threatening to never take one again didn't enter their minds, because there was no need for it. Or, maybe you came from one of those exceptional families where the siblings didn't fight. My friend Steve came from such a family. He had an older sister who was relatively close in age, and for some reason, they never fought. But then there were the rest of the families I knew, usually made up of two or more boys, and maybe a sister thrown in for good measure, and those families fought like crazy. My own family, made up of three boys, was no exception, and my brothers and I could've been the poster children for contraception, though we wouldn't have understood what we were advertising.

Now, it was no one's fault that families fought on vacation and parents had to make empty promises they knew they'd never keep. We were all victims of false advertising and brainwashing by the media, because we'd seen TV shows and movies of families on vacation where everyone was happy and getting along, and each year companies put out ads for their hotels and resorts that showed loving, happy families having the time of their lives. If those companies had wanted to advertise authentically, however, they wouldn't have shown families enjoying themselves and everyone getting along. Instead, they would've featured dads with veins popping out of their foreheads, mothers screaming at their children, and the kids in the background fighting, crying, and ruining the vacation for everyone.

It didn't matter where you were or what you were doing, you could always find something to fight about on a trip. You fought in tents, cars, restaurants, bathrooms, on ski lifts, airplanes, even in swimming pools and on diving boards. It drove your parents crazy and ruined every vacation they ever took you on. When you and your siblings had pushed them too far and nothing else had worked, they finally said the thing they didn't want to say, but felt they had to, and in my family it was always my dad who said it first.

"That's it! You've ruined our trip! We are never going on vacation again!"

As kids who didn't appreciate anything as much as we should have, especially our parents, my brothers and I didn't take that moment to reflect on our poor behaviour and how we were spoiling everything for our parents. Instead, we responded with the most smart aleck answer we could think of, albeit an honest one.

"That's what you said last time!"

This was always met with stunned silence by my dad, because he knew it was true. You could see his initial shock as he realized we were right, and you could also see the wheels begin to turn as he tried to come up with a rebuttal that would make his threat more meaningful.

"Well, this time I mean it!"

"You said that last time too!"

I can't imagine how my dad must have felt at that moment, because he knew we were right about that too. But, he also knew that we didn't deserve another vacation as long as we lived, and we knew he was right about that. It was a real "touché" moment in my family.

Despite the fact that we were pretty sure the threat was empty, we always feared that maybe we'd pushed our parents too far, and this time they may keep their promise. Once that threat had been made, we knew they'd reached their limit, and we didn't want to give them any more incentive for leaving us at home the next time they took a holiday. The moment my dad vowed never to take us on vacation again always marked the climax of our fighting, and slowly but surely the hostilities began to subside. Screaming matches didn't last as long, name-calling wasn't as frequent, and hitting and pinching ceased to exist. From that moment on, we had to be on our best behaviour and hope that our parents could still salvage a little enjoyment out of the last few days of vacation, and that come next year, they'd forget about our current holiday from hell and the promise they'd made to never take us on another one.

Inevitably, they always did, except for the year they made good on their threat and went to Kauai without us. I'll never forget how upset we were when they told us we weren't coming. At the time, my brothers and I hated them for it, and we thought they were the worst parents in the world. We threatened to disband from the family, but my parents went anyways, and I hope they had the time of their lives, because they deserved it. Do you know what happened as a result of them going on vacation without us? That's right – the next vacation we got to go on, we were perfect angels. Well, that may be pushing it a little, but we were better behaved than we'd ever been, because now we knew the threat was real. As a result, family vacations were a whole lot more enjoyable from then on, and all it took was for my parents to keep their promise and show us they meant business.

Parents, I think you should take your kids on vacation if you can. But I also think you should leave them at home sometimes, because if your kids are anything like my brothers and I were, it'll serve them right. They'll learn a powerful lesson, and I guarantee you that the next vacation you take them on they'll behave a whole lot better because they'll never want to be left behind again.

Take it from someone who knows.

The Ice Cream Man Came

When you were a kid, there was nothing more stressful than knowing that the ice cream man was coming and not being able to find your money. It was distressing for two reasons. First, you had a perilously short amount of time to get inside, find your money, and get back out before he was gone, and second, when you were a kid, you almost never had your own money. If you did, you didn't keep it in a wallet, but in a piggy bank, which was nearly impossible to open, especially when you were panicking, which you always were in those situations. That's because you could hear him getting closer and closer, and if you didn't get your money in time the absolute worst thing would happen: you'd miss him and be left with nothing while all the other kids savoured their ice cream and ate it in front of you. It was the same feeling people have in the movies when they're trying to diffuse a bomb and they're watching the timer tick closer to zero.

Sometimes, you managed to scoop up enough of your own money to pay for your ice cream, and you dashed outside as quickly as you could. It didn't matter if you couldn't find your shoes, your pants, your anything, you'd run out naked if you had to. In fact, it wasn't uncommon to see a kid with no pants on waiting in line for the ice cream man. He didn't care, and everyone else understood, because they would have done the same thing. Heck, they probably had at one point. When the naked kid finally bought his ice cream, he wouldn't even go inside right away. He'd stand around with all the other kids eating his ice cream until his mom came out and shooed him into the house. You had to respect that kind of commitment to a cause.

A lot of the time, you didn't have enough of your own money to pay for your ice cream when you heard that far off siren, so you had to find your parents and shake them down. That was even more stressful than trying to get money out of your piggy bank, because much like a cop, there was never a parent around when you needed one. You had to race through every room in the house, frantically screaming for your mom or dad, just to get a quarter. The worst thing was if your parents were in the bathroom, because you had to wait until they were done before they'd give you anything. Unlike you, running around with no pants on so someone could get ice cream wasn't something they were going to do, and you never understood why.

I've never been a parent, but I imagine that being in the bathroom when the ice cream man was coming must have been a stressful situation. They were trying to get a moment's peace in the one place they should have been able to, but even then, their child was practically breaking down the door in a frenzied panic, just because they wanted some ice cream out of a truck rather than from the store. It was at those moments that I think many parents probably reconsidered whether having children was a good idea or not, but by then it was too late to do anything about it.

No matter where they were when the ice cream man came, every conversation between you and your parents went the same way. Out of nowhere, you burst into the house in a panic and started screaming at the top of your lungs, scaring them half to death.

"MOM! DAD! COME QUICK"!

Your parents, thinking someone must've been injured, responded immediately.

"What is it!? What happened?!"

"Come quick!"

"Did someone get hit by a car?"

"No, worse!"

"What!?"

"THE ICE CREAM MAN IS COMING!!!!!!"

I can't imagine what that must have been like for parents. One minute, they were fearing for their child's life, and the next, they were thinking about taking it themselves because their crazy kid had nearly given them a heart attack over something as trivial as ice cream. Despite the initial shock, however, they were usually pretty good about fronting you a little change, probably because they knew how much drama they'd have to deal with if you didn't get out there in time.

However, there were those rare times when your parents just didn't feel like giving you the money for free, and that was torture. Instead, they'd lay into you with a line of questions you just didn't have time for.

"Have you done your chores for the week?"

"No."

"Then why should I give you money?"

"Why should you give me money? Because the ice cream man is here, is that a real question?!"

"Do your chores first, then you can have the money."

"Are you crazy? There's no time for that, can't you hear the siren!? The clock's ticking lady, cough up the dough!"

After promising to do your chores right after you ate your ice cream, a promise you both knew you weren't going to keep, your parents gave you some money. Sometimes, just to torture you a little, they thought they'd give you a math lesson also, which to you was insane.

"How much does the ice cream cost?"

"I don't know, I just give him what he asks for!"

"Ok here, take fifty cents. Do you know what a quarter looks like? It's the one with the moose head. That's 25 cents. So you need two of these. But if it's 30 cents, you have to give him a quarter and a nickel, which is five cents, and if it's 40 cents, give him two quarters, but you need to ask for a dime back."

"This isn't time for a math lesson, just give me the damn money!"

Of course, you never said damn to your parents, but you may have been thinking it, or at the very least, darn. Once you'd finally gotten your money, you ran outside, usually barefoot, as fast as your little legs could carry you, running as if a pack of wild dogs was chasing you, when in reality you were running to join a pack of wild kids who were chasing the ice cream man.

On my street, the ice cream truck's siren heralded the arrival of every kid on the block, and as we stood there in the hot summer sun, each of us feeling the same sense of elation that we'd made it in time, we eagerly awaited our delicious reward from one of the most revered people in the world: the ice cream man.

One by one, kids lined up next to the truck, making the most important decision of the week, and each of us got our 30 seconds with the ice cream man. Once you got your ice cream, you stood around with the other kids, relishing every delicious lick of that tastiest of treats, in a perpetual race with the summer heat to eat your ice cream before it melted onto your hands, or worse, off the stick and onto the street.

Once more, you'd beaten the odds, and the world's most delicious treat was your reward. If the ice cream man was a god, then Heaven was eating that ice cream beneath a clear blue sky, surrounded by your friends on a perfect summer day as that colourfully swathed white van leisurely drove off to spread joy to the rest of the world, its siren slowly diminishing in the distance.

In that moment, life was perfect, and it only cost a quarter.

You Had Pet Caterpillars

Who needs pet stores when you've got the sidewalk? Forget dogs and cats, many kid's first pet was a caterpillar, and you loved them to death even if everyone else thought they were disgusting.

If you were like most kids, I'm sure you have fond memories of spending summer days searching for caterpillars, finding the perfect one, and then getting it to cling to a stick so you could introduce it to its new home, which was a washed out yogurt container or an empty plastic butter jar.

Once you'd placed your pet into its new home, which ironically would also be its final resting place, it was time to give it a name. You always gave them names based on what they looked like, so a lot of caterpillars wound up with names like Furry, Fuzzy, Stripey, or George. Giving your caterpillar a name created an instant bond between the two of you. You immediately fell in love with your new friend, and you were sure the feeling was mutual.

Remember when you used to take your caterpillar everywhere you went? You brought them with you in the car, to your friend's house, you even tried to bring them into restaurants. There was no way you were going to leave your little friend behind; you were so attached to them and you were certain they would miss you if you did. For that reason, you took them everywhere you went.

As much as you loved your pet caterpillars, unfortunately, you weren't very good at keeping them alive. No matter how hard you tried, they always died. Maybe it was because you forgot to feed them and give them water, or maybe it was the fact that they never survived the baths you thought they might enjoy from time to time. Truly, there was nothing more disgusting than finding a wet, dead caterpillar lying on the bottom of its butter jar, and even you, with your empathetic little heart and natural love for all things great and small, felt more repulsion than remorse at the sight of the soggy black mess that had once been your friend.

Losing your caterpillar was always heartbreaking, and much like the ending of an intimate relationship in adulthood, the only way to truly get over your loss was to move on and find someone else, or in this case, something else – that thing being a brand new caterpillar, which looked exactly like your old one, and unfortunately, was doomed to the same fate.

Yes, when you were a kid, you were crazy for caterpillars. You cherished them, you loved them, but in the end, you always accidentally killed them, either by drowning them, starving them, poisoning them, or accidentally crushing them in your pocket when you took them outside to play. But such is life - you always hurt the ones you love, and your caterpillars were no exception. Fortunately, as time passed and you got older, you started to take a shining to more durable pets, like cats and dogs, which were a lot more robust and usually lived longer.

At the end of the day though, all the animals you ever owned still loved you...except for your caterpillars. They were the first one-sided relationship you ever experienced, but they wouldn't be your last.

Losing A Tooth Was A Life Goal

There are many rites of passage in life, but one of the earliest and most important, the one that proved you weren't a little kid anymore, was losing your first tooth.

Losing your first tooth was a lot like losing your virginity: it was something that no one could truly describe, and the experience was different for everyone. For some, it would be a celebrated event. For others, it would be painful. And for many, the tale of how it happened would be grossly exaggerated.

When you were a kid, you had a weird obsession with losing your first tooth. It wasn't something you necessarily looked forward to, but at the same time, you wanted it to happen because it would elevate your social status, since kids who had lost a tooth commanded a high level of respect from their peers. You spent countless hours poring over what it might feel like, how much it would hurt, and whether or not you might bleed to death as a result. You also spent countless hours thinking about how much money you'd get for that first tooth, and let's not lie, that was half the motivation for wanting it gone.

Without a doubt, the best part about losing your first tooth was the attention and praise that was lavished upon you when it finally happened. Your whole class knew about it, and the teacher always made a big deal about it too. If you were lucky, your teacher even gave you a prize. The most cherished prize in my grade three class, the year I lost my first tooth, was a plastic tooth on a necklace. The tooth opened up, and you could put your real tooth inside of it. Every kid desperately wanted to lose a tooth that year because those necklaces were the coolest things going, and anyone who got one proudly wore it around their neck for the whole day and was the envy of the entire class.

On the other hand, the worst part about losing your first tooth was when it was so close to falling out that you could wiggle it around and it was just hanging on by a piece of connective tissue. You were morbidly fascinated with that. You'd stand in front of the mirror, wiggling it around, pushing it with your tongue and watching it sway back and forth, wondering what it was going to take for it to fall out. It grossed you out, yet intrigued you at the same time. It was perhaps the first paradox you'd ever experienced. Oh, and let's not forget that it also grossed out everyone around you who you insisted on showing it to, though that was all part of the fun.

Remember how much mental trauma you experienced when your tooth was close to falling out and you decided to make that final push? There was always a little bit of blood, but in your eyes you were like a wounded soldier on the battlefield gushing blood from a critical wound. Despite the gore, you wanted that tooth out, so you stood in front of the mirror wiggling it with your tongue. You were so afraid to make that final push, but knew that on the other side of that thrust the admiration of your peers awaited you, as well as one of those plastic tooth necklaces and some money from the Tooth Fairy, so there was no shortage of motivation for you to finish what you started. Summoning all your courage, you closed your eyes and gave it one last push, and the next thing you knew your tooth was in your hand.

Once that happened, you found that all the fear and apprehension you'd built up was for nothing, because the other kids had been right – it didn't hurt at all. You'd now joined the ranks of gap-toothed wonders who proudly showed off their gaping smiles, and you'd crossed a bloody threshold into another world where respect, admiration, and a visit from the Tooth Fairy would be yours. At that point in time, it was the proudest moment of your life.

While losing a tooth was a major accomplishment when you were a kid, there's nothing glorious about it as an adult. If it happened now, you wouldn't be proud of it the way you used to be, and you certainly wouldn't show it off like you used to either. In fact, if it happened today, you'd take the day off work to get it fixed and pray to God that no one would see you as a toothless wonder. That's just one more difference between who you are today and who you used to be. Losing a tooth used to be your top priority, and now it's your worst nightmare. Of course, unless you're a dentist, you don't get money for teeth anymore either, so that may be the greatest reason for the difference in perspective.

I guess money really does change people.

You Believed In The Tooth Fairy For The Money

Every kid believed in Santa. Some kids believed in the Easter Bunny. No one really believed in the Tooth Fairy, and here's why.

Santa was the best of all make believe holiday characters. He was a kind hearted, magical old man who brought you presents for free, and you loved him for that. You could even arrange to meet with him before hand to discuss exactly what he should bring you in case there was a special size, colour, or specific criteria that had to be met, and he always promised to deliver. You met with him early enough in the season that he would have plenty of time to fill your order and deliver it to your house in time for Christmas, and he didn't ask for a penny in return. All he wanted was for you to be good, and if you were, you'd be showered with gifts. Sure, there were a couple questionable things about him, like how he was able to fly around the world in one night and how he was able to get down chimneys without being burned alive or getting stuck, but your parents had a logical explanation for all that: Santa was magic. You chose to believe that, because everyone knew that if you didn't, you may not get presents, and that wasn't worth the risk. Blind faith was better than being disappointed on Christmas morning, so we all chose to believe, if only for material gain.

Now, to a lesser extent, you also believed in the Easter Bunny, at least for a few years. Granted, it made no sense that a giant bipedal bunny was going to break into your house on a holiday that was meant to pay tribute to Jesus Christ, the Christian Savior of mankind, and leave you chocolate eggs and jelly beans (why a rabbit is laying eggs is another question entirely), but as a kid, that wasn't important. What was important was that despite the fact that a bunny had no real connection to the original purpose of Easter, the Easter Bunny was still going to come to your house and give you candy, chocolates, and possibly other presents as well. As a kid, that was all that mattered. So, as an act of good faith, you chose to believe that the Easter Bunny was real, even though when you met him at the mall you knew he was just a guy in a fuzzy rabbit costume who was desperate for a better job. As with Santa though, if believing in the bunny meant candy and chocolates on Easter morning, you'd do it.

Then there was the Tooth Fairy. No one really believed in the Tooth Fairy, but you were open to the idea that maybe, just maybe, she could be real, although it seemed doubtful, even in your most impressionable years. Besides the fact that you couldn't meet with the Tooth Fairy in person like you could with Santa and the Easter Bunny, and that there was no physical evidence of her existence, the Tooth Fairy was hard to believe in for one other reason as well, and that's because she was inconsistent with her paydays and everyone knew it. For example, when some kids in my class lost a tooth, they got a quarter. Other kids got 50 cents. Some kids, however, got a whole dollar. To a kid back then, that was a fortune! You know what I got when I lost my first tooth? A nickel, and I was outraged.

Do you know who I blamed for only giving me a nickel? It wasn't the Tooth Fairy, because after that happened I knew she wasn't real. Instead, I blamed my parents, because I knew that they were real, and I also knew that they could afford to pay me a lot more than a nickel for my first tooth! At that price point, if I had lost my entire set of teeth, I would've only made one dollar. One dollar for an entire mouthful of teeth seemed like a terrible deal, and I wasn't about to let my frustration go unnoticed. When I came home and found that one measly nickel under my pillow in place of the tooth I'd left there that morning, I was furious. I marched straight into the kitchen where my mom was making dinner and demanded a raise from the only people who could do anything about it, and do you know what my mom said to me?

"Well, it wasn't me; it was the Tooth Fairy."

I didn't know the word bullshit at the time, but I would've blurted it out if I had. After that, I never again entertained the idea that the Tooth Fairy might be real. In fact, that whole episode made me start questioning the existence of other holiday entities as well, like the Easter Bunny. I never doubted the existence of Santa though, not even for a second; it just wasn't worth the risk.

Your Favourite Restaurant Was Chucky Cheese

If little kids went on dates, they'd be completely different from the kinds of dates adults go on. For one thing, they'd probably be a lot more fun, and for another, little kids would never go to a fancy restaurant to eat. Instead, they'd go to Chucky Cheese, and they'd both have an awesome time.

As a kid, Chucky Cheese was one of the best restaurants in the world. It had everything you wanted: pizza, arcade games, and a ball pit. What more could a kid ask for? For your parents, it was their worst nightmare because it was the opposite of everything they wanted in a restaurant. It was loud, dirty, greasy, and full of screaming kids. It was the last place in the world they wanted to be, and yet there they were, time after time and birthday after birthday, desperately hoping you'd grow old before your time so they'd never have to go there again.

The way your parents felt about Chucky Cheese was the way you felt about the kinds of restaurants they wanted to go to. You hated those kinds of places because they were the opposite of what you considered a good time. You had to be well behaved, quiet, and everything was neat and orderly, or in your opinion, boring. Your parents loved it, because deep down, all they wanted was a little peace and quiet. That's why Chucky Cheese was such hell for them.

That's also why parents are heroes. Despite the suffering they endured each time you wanted to go somewhere like Chucky Cheese, they still went because they wanted to make you happy, but you never did the same for them. Sacrifice and compromise were a one-way street when you were a kid, and it only went the way you were going.

That way was straight to Chucky Cheese.

You Had to Have Time Outs

To an adult, two minutes is nothing. It'll fly by without you even noticing. To a kid who has no choice but to stand in the corner and face the wall, it's an eternity.

When you were little, there was no time period longer than the two minutes you had to spend having a time out. This punishment seemed so long, in fact, that part way through you actually had to ask your parents how long you'd been standing in the corner. Your parents, who probably weren't really timing you anyways, relished those moments because they held all the power and they knew it.

"How long has it been?" you'd ask.

"30 seconds," they'd say.

"30 seconds?! It's been longer than that!"

"Be quiet, or it'll start at two minutes again."

They had you. You couldn't handle your two-minute time out as it was, forget starting over. There was nothing you could do, so you just stood there fuming. When those two minutes were finally over, you left the corner angrier than ever, and the only reason you didn't throw a tantrum was because you didn't want to get sent back.

Wasn't it the worst when that happened? There was nothing more unbearable than finally being released from a time out and getting another one right away. I remember that happening a lot, and it was infuriating. It was almost as bad as a two-minute time out being escalated to a five-minute time out, which back then seemed like a violation of your human rights. God forbid you ever got the dreaded ten-minute time out. That was pretty much the end of the world; death would have seemed more merciful.

Getting a time out back then was kind of like getting solitary confinement in prison, only worse. That's because you could still see and hear what everyone else was doing, but you couldn't be a part of it. Remember when your siblings would pretend they were having extra fun doing whatever they were doing just to rub salt in your wounds, or to try to make you leave your corner and have your punishment escalated? I used to do that to my older brother. It was the only time that I knew it was safe for me to have a go at him, and I did whatever I could to make him suffer. If I couldn't best him physically, I could do it psychologically. He had no choice but to stand in the corner and agonize while I put on Oscar winning performances about how much fun I was having, even if I wasn't doing anything special. I laughed louder, pressed the controls more emphatically on the

Nintendo, and celebrated ten times louder when I beat a level or got some kind of power up on a video game. It was torture for him, and I cherished every second of it.

Although it's absurd now, short time outs used to seem like a terrible form of punishment, but if someone tells us to "take five" nowadays, we welcome the opportunity for it. It's just a shame those five-minute breaks don't seem nearly as long as they did when we were kids. What we wouldn't give to trade our perspective on time with our younger selves. Talk about a win-win situation!

You Had A Kiddie Pool

What would you do if someone told you that you could have a pool in your backyard that would give you room to swim around in, had a slide, and only cost $20? If you were a kid, you'd tell them to bring on the kiddie pool.

Kiddie pools were an absolute highlight of summer. There was nothing better than sitting in the backyard on a hot summer day, splashing around with a couple friends or a sibling by your side and enjoying the kiddie pool. Of course when you were a kid, you didn't call it a kiddie pool. You just called it a pool, because back then there was nothing "kiddie" about them. To you, it was a regular pool. It's not that your pool was that big, but more that you were that small. So small in fact, that at one point in your life you could actually swim in your kiddie pool. Sure, you could only swim in circles around the perimeter, much like a goldfish in a bowl, but it was still a perfect way to spend a hot summer day.

You did all kinds of stuff in your kiddie pool: you made tidal waves; floated boats; pretended you were a shark or a sea monster; someone usually took their bathing suit off and ran around naked. It was crazy, but it was awesome, and you loved every minute of it.

Unfortunately, the era of kiddie pools was a short one. That's because kids grow so quickly, and the manufacturers who produced those pools never saw fit to keep increasing the size of the pools for higher age brackets, despite the fact that you would've continued to buy them. They really missed the boat on that one, because you would've been a lifetime customer if you could have been. They should have had the Kiddie Plus Pool, and the Teenie Pool, followed by the Young Adult Pool, all the way up to the Geriatric Pool, and still made them affordable. If they had done that, they would've had you in their pocket for life.

Sadly, however, that wasn't the case, and being able to lounge in the luxury of a kiddie pool was something you had to leave behind much sooner than you would've liked. While they lasted though, kiddie pools were an amazing and most memorable part of your childhood. Sure, some adults still try to use kiddie pools nowadays, but there's something unsettling about seeing an overweight, full-grown man having a few beers on a hot summer's day in a kiddie pool...though it doesn't stop people from doing it.

You Had a Crush On Your Babysitter

At one point in their lives, everyone had a babysitter they had a crush on. In fact, your babysitter was likely your first crush. They were also probably the first person who ever turned you down, but given the age difference, that was a good thing, though still disappointing at the time.

I still remember the babysitter I had a crush on. I can't recall her name or the finer details about her, but I do remember that she was attractive, female, and had been forced into close proximity with me for $1.50 an hour, and that was good enough for me. You'd think that a child's life would be worth more than that, but apparently kids weren't worth much in the 80s. Besides, I didn't care what my parents were paying her. All I cared about was that she was coming over to my house and wasn't legally allowed to leave until they came home, and you better believe I took every opportunity to turn on the charm while I could.

I'm sure you found yourself doing the same thing when the babysitter you liked came over to your house. The funny thing was, you knew there was an insurmountable age gap between the two of you and that there was no chance of actually being together, but it didn't matter. You just liked them, and you weren't afraid to let them know it. To do that, you pulled out every trick you could think of, like pretending you'd fallen asleep on the couch so they'd carry you into bed, asking them to read you a story and telling them your parents always lay under the covers with you, feigning you were afraid of monsters so they'd stay in your room with you, or even going so far as to tell them that you might be able to fall asleep, if only they'd give you a kiss on the cheek. You did whatever you could do to get some extra time or affection from your babysitter, and you knew you had two bulletproof fail safes if they thought you were pushing your luck: innocence and cuteness, and you took full advantage of both.

Deep down, you knew you didn't have a realistic shot, and at the end of the night they'd go home and be out of your life forever, or at least until the next time your parents needed a night out, but that wasn't important. What mattered was making that connection with them in the moment. You weren't thinking about the last babysitter you'd blown your chances with, or where the relationship was going in the future. You also weren't afraid to let them know how you felt. Despite the odds of them reciprocating your feelings being almost zero, you put it out there anyways. You were honest and unafraid with your emotions, and it was a wonderful way to be.

At the end of the night, you'd laid it all on the line, gotten nowhere, and felt great about it anyways, because at least you'd given it your all. You hadn't tried to hide your feelings, or let the fear of rejection get in the way of letting someone know that you liked them. How come when we were kids we could be so bold with our hearts, but we're so bad at it as adults? Maybe it's because as kids, we'd never been rejected before, so we didn't know the pain that came with it. Or maybe we had more faith in love, and we believed that on some level, our feelings for our babysitter had to be mutual. Or maybe, just maybe, we knew that we didn't have a shot in hell, but we didn't give a damn. All we wanted was for someone to know that we liked them, and that was all that mattered. Such selfless affection was a beautiful thing, and it's something we don't give enough of anymore.

Your babysitter was your first crush, and your first rejection. They were also probably the first person who ever sent you mixed signals. That's because they were nice to you, spent their Friday or Saturday nights with you, and even told you that you were cute, yet when you tried to get them into bed with you it was a total shut down. That was confusing, but no matter how many times you struck out you never stopped trying. After all, they thought you were cute, so in your mind all you had to do was wait until you were a little older and then you'd have a shot. Of course, what you hadn't considered was that by the time you were old enough to actually date your baby sitter, you wouldn't need them anymore, so there'd be no way to get them over to your house for that final charm offensive, but that wasn't the kind of thing you thought about back then.

No wonder you were so much happier.

You Pretended to Fall Asleep in the Car

One of the best parts about being a kid was pretending to fall asleep in the car so your parents would carry you inside. For you, it was the ultimate comfort. For your parents, it was the ultimate pain in the ass. That's because 99 percent of the time you were faking it, and your parents knew. They also had to carry other things inside which weren't capable of walking in on their own, like groceries, or your younger siblings, who unlike you, were actually asleep.

Despite how inconvenient it was for your parents to carry you in, it was actually their own fault that you tried to trick them into doing it. That's because they made the mistake of carrying you in once when you were actually asleep, and you went from sitting in the back of the car to waking up nestled in your bed wearing your pajamas, snuggled up with your teddy bear and being as comfortable as a human can possibly be. And you thought, "Hey, this is awesome." From that moment on, you started pretending to fall asleep so you'd get that royal treatment every time.

Being as sharp as they were, however, your parents soon caught on to your scheme. Just like how they knew when you were faking sick to stay home from school, they also knew when you were faking being asleep, and after one too many times of carrying you inside, they'd had enough. From that point on, there was no more Mr. and Mrs. Nice Guys. Instead of gently unbuckling you and softly lifting you from the back seat, ever so careful not to bump your head on the way out, they'd just open your door, stand there and go, "We're home. Wake up!" And then there was silence. The game was on, and you intended to win, which meant you intended to wind up in your own bed without having to move a muscle.

But your parents weren't having it, so they tried again.

"Hey, wake up. We're home. I can't carry you, I have to bring in the groceries."

And you were thinking, "That's fine, you can make two trips."

It was a stalemate, and neither side was willing to concede. It was at this moment that your parents pulled the trump card, the one thing they knew would get you up and out of the car on your own steam.

"Ok, well, if you don't want to walk on your own, you can stay in the car all night."

That was a terrifying notion. Your parents knew your Achilles heel, and you had no greater weakness than your fear of the dark. At that point, your mind started racing.

"They won't do that, will they? They can't; it's got to be illegal. I don't want to stay here all night...there are probably monsters in the bushes. Maybe I should just give in."

But you weren't willing to give up quite yet, so you tested them. You sat there, still as a statue, while your parents stared you down, laser beams shooting from their eyes, searching for a hint of consciousness on your face...but if you were really good, there was none.

It was the ultimate standoff, and more often than not, it was your parents who cracked first. They were going to carry you in - but they weren't going to be nice about it. Laden with grocery bags and exhausted after another impossible day of parenting, they somehow managed to summon the strength to lean inside the car, scoop you up, this time not being careful to avoid hitting your head on the door jam in the hopes that you'd never do this again, and carry you into the house, groceries and all.

Despite the potential bump to the noggin and the frustration you could feel radiating from your parents, you were ecstatic. You'd won the battle and were being carried into the house. However, once you were inside, the free ride was over. Instead of being lovingly tucked into bed with your pajamas on, you either got dumped on the stairs, or unceremoniously tossed into your bed, clothes on and everything. You'd gone way over the line, and your parents wanted you to know it. From there on in, there would be no more special treatment. Once those initial perks disappeared, being carried inside wasn't nearly as rewarding as it used to be, but you were willing to sacrifice a few frivolities for the luxury of not having to use your own two legs to walk inside the house. Besides, there was an added bonus to this whole charade: you didn't have to brush your teeth.

Being carried in from the car was something you knew couldn't last forever, but you wanted to keep doing for as long as possible. Like a chopper pilot flying dangerous missions in Vietnam, you knew that every time could be your last, and one day, your final carry-in came. From that moment on, your parents decided to make good on their promise of leaving you in the car. You had finally pushed them over the edge, and at that point, the thought that you might get kidnapped while you were out there seemed like more of a blessing than a curse to them.

Although you'd managed to manipulate your parents so many times in the past, one night they finally decided they'd had enough, and rather than giving in to your selfish charade, they instead left you sitting alone in the dark. And it was terrifying. Fortunately, that only lasted for about five seconds before you bolted from the car and followed them towards the front door, where they were not at all surprised to see you sprinting up the walkway, scanning the bushes for monsters as you ran to catch up with them.

That first night you were abandoned in the car marked a turning point in your life. You realized that you weren't going to be treated like a baby anymore, and that your parents had a limit of what they were willing to do for you. In that moment, you looked at them with new eyes and you understood that they were people too, and it wasn't fair to keep taking advantage of them the way you'd been doing. In that same moment, your parents were looking at you, feeling absolutely guilt ridden that they'd left you alone in the car for that five seconds, and they vowed never to abandon you to the elements again. It was a turning point for everyone, one that resulted in greater maturity for you, and the first of many times your mom or dad would unwarrantedly think that they were the worst parents in the world, even though they were doing the best they could.

You Knew Exactly How Old You Were

While writing this, I'm not sure if I'm 32 or 33. I'm pretty sure I'm 33…not 100 percent sure, but 85 percent sure. That's good enough for me. Once you pass a certain age, and I'm not sure what age that is, you start to lose track of your years, and it doesn't matter to you or anyone else exactly how old you are. When you were a kid though, that was not the case. You always knew exactly how old you were, and you wanted the world to know it too.

When you were young, you talked about your age all the time. It was almost a daily conversation at school, and everyone knew exactly how old everyone else was. That's because everybody got invited to each other's birthday parties, even if they didn't like each other, because it was the polite thing to do.

Everyone in your class wanted to be the oldest back then. That's why no one was ever just five, or six, or seven. They were all five and a half, six and nine months, seven and three-quarters, and so on. You added any measure of time to your age, even to make yourself a day older than someone else.

You lied about your age the way adults do, only in reverse. As an adult, it's an enviable position to be the youngest in the group, even if that group is made up entirely of senior citizens. The 70 year old is a young pup to the 80 year old, and they're both babies to the guy who is 90, who would do anything to trade places with them. Alternatively, if you were the youngest in a group of kids, you were looked at as the runt and the pipsqueak, the one everyone else had to watch out for. You would have done anything to make yourself older, and that included lying about your age.

It's funny how our obsession with age changes over time, from wanting to be older when we're young to wanting to be younger when we're old, and not being exactly sure how old we are for some time in the middle. It seems like the ultimate paradox, another classic example of always wanting the opposite of what we have. It's part of the human condition, I guess. We're weird like that, and that behaviour doesn't just apply to our age, but to other aspects of our lives too. When we're single, we want to be in a relationship. When we're in a relationship, we want to be single. When we're bored at work, we long for freedom, and when we get that freedom we yearn for structure and purpose.

We're peculiar creatures who routinely express contrasting desires. It's a strange behaviour that started when we were very young, probably only about five years old...no wait...five and three-quarters.

You Didn't Know The Meaning of Important Words

Remember when you thought you knew what certain words meant, but you were way off? That led to a lot of confusion at times. For example, when I was a kid, I thought arson was a person.

I'd be watching the news with my parents and the reporter would come on and say, "There was another fire in the warehouse district last night. Police believe it was started by arson."

And I'd be sitting there going, "Well, why don't they just arrest him already? They know who's doing it; he's doing it all the time. Last time it was Arson. This time it was Arson. I'm pretty sure that next time it's going to be Arson. I'm six years old and I can figure this out, why can't they?"

I also didn't know what a virgin was, but apparently it was a big deal to be one. I remember watching shows like *Beverly Hills 90210*, and the characters were always shocked when they found out someone was a virgin. I remember thinking that if it was such a big deal to be a virgin, I didn't want to be one. Of course, I had no idea what a virgin actually was, so like all kids do when they have a question that needs to be answered, I asked my mom. Apparently, that wasn't a question she was ready for.

I can still picture it clearly. It was about 4 o'clock in the afternoon on a beautiful spring day, and my mom was in the kitchen cutting up carrots for dinner.

I figured it was the perfect time, so I walked up to her and innocently asked, "Mom, what's a virgin?"

There was a long pause, and I could tell I'd hit her with something she hadn't been anticipating, though I wasn't sure what the big deal was. She put down the knife she was using and just stood there for a few silent moments, looking vacantly out the kitchen window and thinking about how to answer that most delicate question.

After what seemed an eternity, she looked at me and calmly but seriously said, "A virgin is someone who's never slept with anyone before."

What a relief! The next day, I was at school telling people I wasn't a virgin because I had slept with both my parents, at the same time. Despite my enthusiasm, that announcement didn't go over so well when my teacher heard me telling my classmates about it, but I couldn't help it. I was so excited that I wasn't the social outcast that everyone on *90210* looked upon with such scorn that I just had to share it with the world.

While my claim that I wasn't a virgin caused confusion for my teacher and resulted in an awkward call home from the principal, it also symbolized my absolute innocence and naiveté, two hallmarks of childhood. Being young was all about not understanding the world, and not being afraid to question it. It was taking things literally when they should have been taken figuratively, and believing anything an adult told you because they were supposed to know everything. Back then it made for a lot of misunderstandings, but in retrospect it makes for great comedy.

Being able to laugh at ourselves is a great gift. If we can do that, there's humour all around us. And let's be honest – there's a lot to laugh about.

You Got a Jockstrap and Made People Kick You

This is one of those things that only little kids do, because it's crazy, and so are they. They have minimal life experience, and most of them don't know how much it hurts to get hit in the groin. That's why they're the only people on the planet who will put on a jock strap and actually encourage people to kick them there, just to make sure it works.

There's nothing funny to adults about getting hit in the groin, but kids love it. That's why when you were a kid (providing you're a male who played tee-ball or baseball), you wouldn't just get one of your friends to kick you in the groin, you'd get the whole team to line up so they could each take a turn. Every kid in that line up had a huge smile on their face, including the person who was on the receiving end of those kicks. It was the craziest thing you could imagine, but it happened on every single tee-ball and little league baseball team you ever played on. The really crazy part was that after the whole team had tested your jock strap by kicking you in the groin as hard as they could, another kid took your place so he could get kicked in the groin too, and the process repeated itself until the entire team had their chance to get booted, or until the coach put a stop to it. It was absolutely insane, but we loved doing it, and being on both the giving and the receiving ends was equally enjoyable.

This is one of those rituals that only little kids partake in, because no adult male would ever voluntarily let himself get kicked there. It is the most painful thing a man can experience, and we avoid it at all costs. I think that's the reason most adults stop playing sports as they get older. They just can't handle the thought of another stomach churning shot to the crotch, and they'd rather get fat and lazy than hit down there. Even if men continue playing sports that require a cup, they will never test that cup out the way they did when they were younger; they'll simply hope that it works.

For example, when I was in my early 20s my brother and I took up kickboxing, a sport that required athletic protection. The difference between needing a jock in my 20s compared to when I was a kid though was that I didn't put it on right away and tell my brother to kick me as hard as he could. In fact, it was the exact opposite. If he even got close to my groin when we were sparring, I freaked out.

"Hey, watch the groin! This isn't tee ball, here!"

Hot Water Came Out of the Hose

Remember when you had to hose your feet off after coming home from the beach and hot water came out of the hose? It felt so good and always caught you off guard, and every time was like the first time. Your parents or your grandparents would uncoil the hose, you'd brace for the cold, and when that hot water hit you, it blew your mind.

Getting sprayed with warm hose water was especially enjoyable if you'd just been swimming somewhere cold. It was like a hot shower you weren't expecting, right in your front yard. If your friends or your siblings were around, they wanted their share of hot hose water too. There was little time for everyone to get their fix, so whoever was in charge of the hose had to be quick and fair, and they took charge like a drill sergeant in basic training.

"Get in there! Give me those feet! One, two! Now, you! Let's go, get those sandals off! Next kid, move it, move it, move it!"

That whole experience was magnificent, right up until the moment the water suddenly turned cold, and now instead of begging for the person with the hose to spray you more, you were yelling for them to stop because it was freezing. If they didn't stop right away, what had been a delightful surprise became a torturous ordeal.

Yes, hot hose water on a summer day was amazing, but like so many wonderful things in life, it never lasted as long as you wanted it to. I guess warm hose water is a lot like love. When it's there, it's the most incredible feeling in the world, but when it's gone, often in what seems like a heartbeat, you're left feeling cold and miserable, and you'd give anything to get it back. But you can't, so you just have to move on and know that another summer day will come, and when you least expect it, love will find you…or hot water will come out of the hose. Hopefully both.

You Hated Coffee

I've heard that in the future, coffee will be extinct; it will no longer be available on planet Earth. You know what? When coffee goes, I want to go with it, because I don't want to live in a world without coffee. When I was a kid though, I would have thought that was great news because I thought coffee was the most disgusting drink in the world, and I'm sure you did too.

To kids, coffee was just plain gross, and you could never understand why adults liked it so much. It was a toxic black sludge that all the adults you knew couldn't live without. They needed it in the morning to get themselves going; they wanted it in the afternoon to perk themselves up, and every time you got a donut or something to eat with your parents, they had to have a coffee then too. What was the deal with adults and coffee? Why didn't they drink milk, pop, or juice like you did? It was something you couldn't understand, and you vowed you would never drink a coffee in your life.

To make things even stranger, my grandpa used to drink coffee on hot summer days. Before we went swimming at the lake, he'd make himself a piping hot coffee and take it with him. He couldn't go to the beach without one, and my brothers and I thought he was crazy.

"When you're older, you'll understand," he told us.

The way he was talking, you would think he was telling us about the birds and the bees. Frankly, that would have made more sense to me. Back then, I thought he was nuts for drinking coffee on a hot summer day, but now I do the exact same thing.

When someone asks me, "Do you want to go sit at the beach for a while?" I say, "Sure. Mind if we grab a coffee first?" To which they reply, "I wouldn't go without one."

I have several vices, and coffee is my strongest. When I go to bed, I'm already thinking about having coffee the next morning, and when I wake up it's the first thing on my mind. I need coffee, and I have to have it at the start of any workday. In fact, even if I'm going to be late for work, I'll still stop and grab a coffee, and you know what? My boss would understand.

"Sorry I was late," I'd say. "I was running behind, but I just had to stop and grab a coffee."

"Well," my boss would reply, "I can't say I'm happy about it, but I understand. I wouldn't want you coming to work without having had a coffee first. Say, all this talk about coffee is making me thirsty. You want a coffee?

"Sure, I'll have another coffee."

That's life now. Coffee is literally the kick-start to your day, and the "pick me up" when you need it, but it didn't used to be. When I was a kid, a huge glass of milk or some bright red, sugary Kool-Aid always hit the spot, and I vowed that I would never drink coffee as long as I lived. Of course, I swore I would never do a lot of the things I now do on a regular basis, and drinking coffee is just one of them. That includes the promise I made to never have a girlfriend.

Oh well, at least I have someone to go for coffee with now.

Your Imagination Was Awesome

Compared to the imagination you had when you were a child, the one you have now just plain sucks. In fact, if you're like most adults, the only time you even use your imagination is when you get caught doing something you're not supposed to be doing and you need to think of how to lie your way out of it. Despite how hard you try, however, your excuses are always pathetic, and it's because your imagination is nothing compared to what it used to be.

When you were a kid, your imagination was awesome. It was a powerful, creative tool that you exercised constantly, and so did all the other kids around you. That's why life was so much more fun when you were younger. You were rarely present in the real world; instead, you constantly lived in the fantastic realities that you created in your mind. It didn't matter where you were or what you were doing, you could always use your imagination to make life magical. That's why I love seeing kids running around playgrounds screaming their heads off and acting like maniacs. They're so intense, and you know they're acting out some incredible fantasy they're creating in their minds, and they're doing it in perfect synchronicity with the other kids around them. Their imaginations can collectively form alternate realities, and it's the reason they can have fun wherever they go.

Long ago, you could do the same thing. There was no stopping your imagination, and there were no limits as to what it could conjure up. On top of that, you didn't have an ounce of self-consciousness, so you didn't care what anyone else thought of you or how you might look to others when you were running around with a stick making machine gun noises and throwing yourself into the sand like a soldier storming the beaches at Normandy.

When adults watch kids playing out their fantasies, it looks like they're just running around making noises, but kids are operating on a whole other level that grownups can barely comprehend. Maybe those kids are fighting off a swarm of zombies, or blasting away an army of outer space aliens, or getting ready to board a pirate ship. Whatever they're doing, they're doing it with absolute commitment. They're yelling out orders to other kids and sprinting around the playground like their lives depend on it. They've got sticks in their hands and they're firing away at enemies that remain unseen to the adults around them, who simply sit and watch, barely able to remember that at one time, their imaginations were just as powerful as those of the children they're now struggling to understand.

It's hard for them to relate, because although they used to do the exact same things, slowly, almost imperceptibly over time, they stopped using their imaginations. It's sad, but it's something that happens to all of us. We quietly become self-conscious, and all too quickly, we stop having fun the way we used to. In fact, if it wasn't for being able to watch children exercise their imaginations while we sit on the sidelines and worry about how we're going to pay our next bill or what we're going to have for dinner, we might completely forget that at one time, we too were powerful creators of our own worlds that existed entirely within our minds.

I guess if humans never grew up and started living in the real world though, humanity would never have gotten as far as it has because we'd all still be pretending to be sailors charting new lands, or space explorers traversing distant planets instead of doing it in real life. Shedding our imaginations must be part of human evolution, something we do in order to ensure the survival of our species, but I think it's important that we don't lose them completely. We should remember the wonderful creative minds we possessed when we were children, and how much fun we had simply by thinking about how things could have been instead of just looking at them as they were.

It's always important to imagine, whether you're visualizing a better future for yourself, who your perfect partner may be, or what it would be like if you were really going after the things you wanted and living the life of your dreams. I think that if we stop imagining, some wonderous part of us ceases to exist, and a life without imagination is no life at all. After all, it's in our imaginations that we can escape to new realities and get some much-needed reprieve from the dulling monotony of everyday life. If it's been a long time since you have allowed yourself to exercise your mind, there is no shortage of screaming kids running around with their imaginations operating at full blast, who I'm sure would be happy to give you a few pointers, and maybe even let you join in on the fun. After all, I'm sure they could always use one more pirate for their adventure.

Just check with their parents first.

You Watched The Same Movie Everyday

Every kid had at least one movie they watched every single day. For my little brother, it was *Pinocchio*. Others watched *Homeward Bound*, or some other feel good film. *Mortal Kombat* was also a popular choice among kids in my generation. If you ask me though, there was no movie as re-watchable as the original *Teenage Mutant Ninja Turtles*. It had everything a kid wanted: action, comedy, and no sappy love story, because we hated that kind of thing back then.

When I was a kid, I watched that movie every day and never got bored of it. There was something so addictive about the music, the karate, the pizza, the high threes - it was amazing. When I watched it, I always felt like the fifth ninja turtle, the way Lou Pearlman, the guy who founded "Backstreet Boys", claims he was the sixth member of the band, despite the fact that he was twice their age, grossly overweight, and couldn't sing. That's how I felt with the Turtles, although in that case I was half their age, didn't know karate, and wasn't a turtle, but I still felt like one of the gang.

No matter what movie you loved back then, you never just watched that movie - you were the movie. You understood the characters as intimately as your own friends and family. You could recite every line from start to finish. You knew exactly how the movie ended, but you still felt suspense every time you watched it. Maybe somewhere in your imagination, you thought that somehow, this time would be different, and the bad guy might win. You were pretty sure it wouldn't happen, but you hadn't ruled it out entirely. After all, your imagination was as fertile as a spring forest, and life was full of possibilities.

It was also full of free time. That's why you could come home from school and watch that same movie every day and never get bored, or think for even a second that you were wasting your time. As an adult, you can't do that. First, you don't have time to watch a movie every day. You have to go to work, drive your kids around, cook meals, clean the house, help with homework, pay bills, grocery shop, and so on. Second, even if you had that much free time, you wouldn't want to watch the same movie day in and day out. You want some variety. Sure, *Gran Torino* is a great film, but you don't want to watch it every day, and you especially don't want your kids around while you're watching it because that's the last movie you need them quoting lines from at school.

When you were a kid though, you knew what you loved and you loved what you knew, and that meant watching the same movie every day until you actually wore out the VHS tape and were forced to get a new one. It was probably a tremendous relief for your parents when that happened, because inadvertently they too had been forced to watch or listen to that same movie day after day until they probably felt like going insane. That's why when it was finally time to pick out a new movie, your parents always tried to coax you into getting something they might enjoy too, like *The Sound of Music*, but being the selfish little brat you were, you shut them down every time. After all, if your parents didn't want to hear *The Goonies* or Disney's *Robinhood* constantly playing in the background, they shouldn't have had kids.

You Got a Toy When You Went To The Dentist

As an adult, there is nothing satisfying about going to the dentist. All you get are lectures about how you're not brushing properly, not flossing enough, and are generally doing a poor job with your oral hygiene. Then, at the end of the appointment, you get a huge bill. What did you get as a kid? A job well done, a high-five, and a toy, and it was a heck of a lot more enjoyable than it is today.

Going to the dentist was great as a kid. They didn't hassle you much about your brushing, they went easy on the scraping, and at the end, you got to pick a new toy from the treat basket. Sure, the toys weren't great, but it was still something to look forward to. Even if you didn't deserve one, you still got a treat of some kind because it was part and parcel of the experience.

Take my younger brother, for example. He literally had the worst brushing habits of anyone I knew when we were kids. In fact, he prided himself on how little he brushed his teeth. Combine this with the fact that he had an unparalleled sweet tooth and the absence of any self-control and you had the makings of someone who came to be known as the Cavity King. He had to get a cavity filled almost every time he went to the dentist, yet he always got something from the treat basket. I'm not sure what the dentist was rewarding him for, because it certainly wasn't his brushing habits. Maybe it was more of a thank you for always racking up a huge bill and helping the dentist to put his kids through college, but that's how it was. Even if you were the worst patient the dentist had, you could still come out smiling because you knew you had something to look forward to.

As an adult, you have nothing to look forward to at the dentist. They go hard on the scraping, force cancer-causing x-rays upon you, and charge you an astronomical amount of money for some basic dental hygiene that everyone needs to stay healthy. Not only that, but things get worse as you get older because eventually you may need things like root canals, crowns, or even dentures, and not only are those procedures more painful than a simple check-up, they're also more expensive. You don't even get to pick fun flavours of fluoride anymore; you just get plain or mint. Whoop dee doo.

Like so many things in life, going to the dentist was better when you were young. You were treated like a star, and even the worst habits were rewarded. Today, it's painful, expensive, and you're always made to feel guilty about your oral hygiene efforts, no matter how hard you try. Maybe there's a way to get your dentist to go easier on you, like when you were a kid, but there's probably an extra fee for that service.

It might be worth it though...especially if you get a little toy at the end.

You Loved Lucky Charms

When you were a kid, there was one breakfast cereal that was superior to all others. It was the most magically delicious thing you'd ever tasted, and for kids, it was the childhood equivalent to ecstasy. That cereal, of course, was Lucky Charms.

Everything about that cereal was amazing. Even the box was enticing. It was a beautiful candy red, accented by an array of colourful magic marshmallows: red, orange, yellow, green, blue, purple; all the colours of the rainbow! When even the box made your taste buds start to water, you knew you were in for a treat.

Lucky Charms were said to be magical. Maybe that's because it took so much effort for you to convince your parents to buy them that it seemed like a miracle when they finally caved. Despite the leg work required to get them, when you got home and poured yourself your first heaping bowl and all those colours came to life before your eyes, it was worth the effort. It was nature's most mesmerizing sight, displayed in high definition marshmallow form and floating around your cereal bowl. In fact, Lucky Charms were so vibrant that they even turned the milk a different colour, a type of greyish purple, if I remember correctly. Despite how much I loved Lucky Charms, I do remember trying to eat them before the milk changed colour, because as delicious as they were, something about grey milk always turned me off. Up until that point though, the experience was enchanting.

Of course, there was no way you could settle for eating just one bowl of Lucky Charms. That's why as soon as you were done your first helping, you immediately poured yourself another. And another, and another, until your parents finally saw what you were doing and put a stop to it.

In my house, my brothers and I loved that cereal so much that my parents had to take it out of the cupboards and hide it from us, because they knew that if they didn't, it would be gone by morning, and the fights that would ensue over who ate more than their fair share would be a hell storm to endure. For that reason, they not only had to hide the cereal from us, but also carefully ration it out, because they knew we couldn't control ourselves. Although my brothers and I desperately wished we could gorge ourselves to our hearts' content and not be under the stingy thumb of our parents rationing, deep down, we were grateful for it. That's because Lucky Charms were such a rarity that we were willing to suffer a little if it meant being able to prolong the experience, since we knew it would be a long time before it happened again.

Yes, Lucky Charms were an incredible part of being a kid, and if we had been forced to choose one cereal to eat for the rest of our lives, most of us would have picked Lucky Charms. Sure, Frosted Flakes, Fruit Loops, and Cocoa Puffs were delicious too, but they lacked that certain allure. Speaking of which, in an attempt to recapture some of the wonder of my childhood, I recently bought a box of Lucky Charms because I thought they might help me relive some of my youthful nostalgia. Not so.

For starters, I couldn't eat it fast enough to keep the milk from turning grey, which grossed me out and made me struggle to finish even a single bowl. Next, it gave me diarrhea. After that, I experienced a massive sugar high, followed by an immediate crash, and then I got a terrible headache. The combination of all of those side effects made for a terrible day at work, and as a result, I vowed never to eat Lucky Charms again, something my childhood self would have been unable to believe if he could have seen into the future.

Despite the fact that Lucky Charms and I don't get along anymore and I'll probably never eat them again, whenever I see that candy red box with those colourful magic marshmallows, there's still a small part of me that wants to buy it. That's the kid part of me, the part that didn't get sugar highs or know about diabetes. The adult part of me looks on that box the same way a patient looks at a former stimulant after undergoing electro shock therapy and recoils in horror. Like so many things in life we can't go back to, Lucky Charms were good while they lasted. I'd say they were great, but I don't want to step on any toes here.

You Had a Lunchbox

Transformers. GI Joe. Barbie. If they were your favourite cartoon, there was a good chance they were also on your lunchbox.

When you were a kid, your lunchbox was your unique representation of yourself to the world around you. It would shape your identity not only for your first day of school, but for the entire year, and depending on your family's socio-economic status, possibly for years to come. For that reason, picking the right lunchbox was one of the most important decisions you had to make back then.

You couldn't just go into a store and buy the first one you saw. Instead, you had to think carefully about what was going to best represent you when you walked into class for that first day of school, and what would still be cool in six months to a year. Selecting a lunchbox was your first experience with brand marketing, and in this case you were marketing yourself to the most judgmental group of people on the planet: your peers. Choosing the right lunchbox was a major decision, and it wasn't something that could be rushed into, unlike when you promised to marry your Kindergarten crush.

When choosing a lunch box, you had to think long term. Sure, the Smurfs might have been great when you were in Kindergarten, but would it still be cool a year or two later, or would you be mocked by your peers for a short-sighted decision you made when you were young and foolish? What would happen if your lunchbox's cartoon was cancelled the following year? Would it have any retro value, or would you just be seen as the loser who fell behind the times and suffer the loss of your social standing as a result? It was a monumental decision, one you spent countless minutes in the K-mart or Zellers aisle contemplating, but one we all had to eventually make.

There were so many options, and in an ever-changing world, trying to choose the right one was always a gamble. I guess in a way, it was good practice for choosing a marriage partner later in life. You had to be selective and think about whether or not your choice would be feasible in the long run. Sometimes, you also had to be realistic about what you could actually get. Even though you wanted the one with all the bells and whistles, you knew you just couldn't afford it, and therefore, had to settle for a scaled down version of what you really wanted. Of course, unlike a marriage partner, if you picked the wrong lunchbox, you could easily return it to the store, no hard feelings would be had, and it wouldn't be entitled to half your assets if you felt you'd made a mistake.

Lunchboxes were one of the first ways you expressed yourself to the world, and they also taught you the importance of long-term planning, a skill you would need to master to navigate the ever increasing demands of life. Who knew a plastic box with a picture of He-man or The Care Bears on it could teach you so much?

You Roasted Marshmallows

To a child, there is no culinary treat more appealing than the roasted marshmallow. It is the piece-de-resistance of all dishes, and they were only available a few times a year when you were somewhere that called for such a delicacy, and when there was no fire ban preventing you from enjoying them.

Roasting marshmallows usually happened in summer when you were camping with your family, up at the cabin, or anywhere else that was special enough to encourage that kind of activity, provided there was no fire-ban. Back then, half the fun of roasting marshmallows was doing all the preparatory work that was first required. Before you could even think about roasting, you had to find yourself the perfect stick. You couldn't just pick up any twig off the ground and head off to the bonfire, either. Instead, you had to look for a stick with the right amount of thickness that wouldn't just burn up in the fire, and one that didn't have any sharp bits along the shaft and would be strong enough to hold one or two marshmallows at a time.

You always tried to get your stick to be absolutely perfect. You'd find a long twig, pull out your Swiss Army knife, and immediately set to work shaving and shaping its end, stripping away layers of bark to make a perfect spear point on which to skewer your mallow. You literally could have poked someone's eye out, and that was always your parents' fear. I remember trying to get that stick so sharp that I could kill a bear with it if I needed to. It's not that I was actually worried about a bear showing up and stealing my marshmallows, but that was the level of sharpness I was going for.

If you were lucky, you found a stick with a forked end, because you thought it would be a good idea to roast two marshmallows at once. Unfortunately, you always wound up burning one or dropping it into the fire, and it never worked out as well as you thought it would. In fact, the two-pronged stick may have been your first experience where the idea of something was better than the reality. As an adult, you have lots of opportunities to learn that: relationships, consumer goods, cheap vacation packages and so on, but as a kid, your first life lesson in theory versus reality was the two-pronged marshmallow stick. You quickly discovered that it was better to focus on one good thing than to try to juggle two at a time, because otherwise you got burned. Well, you didn't, but your marshmallows certainly did.

Once your stick was prepared and the fire had been lit, you set about trying to roast the perfect marshmallow, but that wasn't something you could nail the first time. It took years of practice, persistence, and knowing where the best spots in the fire were to get that golden brown masterpiece you were after, yet most of the time, too impatient to achieve. There was an art to it, much like there was an art to how the Samurai made their swords in Ancient Japan. You took the same serious approach to perfecting your marshmallows as they did to crafting their blades, though with far less patience and a severely compromised end product.

Although you started off telling yourself you would be patient and let the coals do their job to give you that cinnamon coloured perfection, you usually got fed up after about 30 seconds and just shoved your marshmallow into the hottest part of the fire and let it catch flame, quickly blowing it out to reveal a charred and blackened outer shell, which you still ate it anyways, even if it wasn't quite what you had wanted.

Despite your desire to be a master roaster, it was a position you couldn't rush into, but that was ok, because there was at least one person in your family who already held that title. In my family, it was my grandpa. He was, and probably still is, the world's greatest marshmallow roaster. My mom and dad were my go-to for many things, but for the perfect marshmallow, it was always my grandpa. He had been roasting all his life, and possessed two traits I didn't: experience, and more importantly, patience. He had the knowledge of a man who had lived many years and done many things, and he knew that like so many of the finest things in life, roasting a marshmallow required time, commitment, and a little bit of love.

And so, while the rest of my family and I burned through many mallows, scorching them to a crisp, dropping them into the fire, and eating ones that had barely been singed, my grandpa patiently worked his marshmallows to perfection. He was like a master blacksmith at his forge, knowing just when and where to dip it into the fire, when to turn it, and when to pull back. He was a master craftsman, and if you were lucky, he'd give you his prize: the world's most perfectly toasted, golden brown marshmallow.

My grandpa is a man of many talents, but even as an adult, whenever I think of him, one of the first things that comes to mind is his ability to roast the perfect marshmallow. Life is funny like that. You never know that in your most ordinary of moments, you may be making a lifelong impression on someone, and you do it with the simplest acts of kindness and love. To my grandpa, it was just roasting a marshmallow, but to me it was a creating a memory I'll cherish forever.

You Drank From The Hose

Remember when your favourite way to drink was straight from the hose? Hose water always tasted better than tap water, and I don't know why. Maybe it was the way the rubber mixed with the water, or the dirt around the edges that gave it that extra tang. Or maybe it was because it was a perfect summer day and you were having fun with your friends, and drinking from the hose meant you didn't have to interrupt the moment and go inside just to get a drink.

However, I'll never forget the day my friend Steve and I were playing tag in his yard with a bunch of the neighbourhood kids. We had stopped to take a break, and Steve decided he needed to quench his thirst, so he turned on the hose and started drinking from it. When I lined up behind him and asked if I could take a sip, he lowered the hose from his lips, looked me in the eyes and said, "You've got your own hose."

Steve and I are still friends, and to this day we still can't figure out what the hell his problem was that day. Oh well, that's water under the bridge now. Hose water, I guess.

People's Insults Were Terrible

Kids have the worst insults. Much like their jokes, they often make little or no sense, but being on the receiving end of another child's barb was always upsetting. Even something as ridiculous as being called "a stupid" was heart breaking, but having someone make a rhyme out of your name was even worse, despite how terrible that rhyme might have been. For example, I remember some kids used to call me "Adam Bobadam." As an adult, it's hard to even register that as an insult, but it enraged me as a child and forced me to come up with a retort related to the offending kid's name, something like "Greg the Peg" or "Jenny the Penny," which was equally ridiculous but served the purpose nonetheless.

To further illustrate this point, when we were about 11 or 12 my best friend came up with a chant that would turn my little brother into a miniature version of the Hulk, yet there was no genius to the rhyme. It was simply this: "Baby, baby, stick your head in gravy!"

When he heard that, he would get this look of sheer ferocity on his face and his entire body contorted with rage. He would stare straight into the soul of the person singing the song, then scream at the top of his lungs and attack them like a wild animal, little arms and legs flailing as he kicked, scratched, bit, and shrieked at the top of his lungs to get them to stop singing. The problem was, my brother's reaction was so entertaining that we would sing even louder just to see how crazy he would get. It was literally like watching him develop super powers in front of us. We were still strong enough to handle him, but I'm not going to lie, it wasn't as easy as it normally was.

That was 25 years ago, when I was bigger and stronger than my brother. Today, he is about 6'1, 220 pounds, and works out with a personal trainer several times a week. He's a lot bigger and stronger than I am, so it probably wouldn't be a good idea to tease him like I used to.

But sometimes, I still wonder what he would do if I sang that song to him now...

You Had Glow In The Dark Stars

I just got home from visiting my brother. When I was at his place, I noticed something remarkable in his room: glow in the dark stars on the walls and ceilings. Seeing those stars and planets light up as I fell asleep took me back to being a kid, when decorating your room with the cosmos was the most awe inspiring thing you could do.

Wasn't it awesome when your parents let you get a pack of glow in the dark stars from the toy store? They were happy because they got away with buying you a toy that only cost two dollars, and you were happy because you knew that come nighttime, you were going to have the coolest room on the planet.

It was so much fun going through that package and seeing all the different planets and stars you could put on your ceiling. There were big planets, small planets, planets with rings, the moon, and countless little stars as well. We took such pride in carefully choosing our favourite stickers and placing them in areas where they would garner the most attention. We spent hours putting those stars up, making sure they were just right, and then we turned on all the lights in our bedroom to super charge them so that they'd be at their brightest come night fall.

What an unforgettable experience it was when we first lay under our star-filled ceilings and stared up at the beautiful universe we had created. There was something about the soft glow of those stars that brought us so much joy and created such a sense of wonder. We knew they were just stickers, but they seemed like so much more. To us, it was as if the whole universe was contained in our tiny little bedrooms. We felt like we had created something beautiful, and in a sense, we had. We had created a picturesque star scape to fall asleep under, and although we didn't know it at the time, we had also created a beautiful memory, one that we would look back on years down the road and think about how much happiness a few stickers could bring us, back when we were young and full of wonder for the world.

Those stars were more than just stickers. They were the manifestation of everything beautiful about our imaginations, a symbol of our youth and innocence. We didn't care about money, or power, or status – we just cared about staring up at something wondrous we'd created, and that brought us more happiness than those other things ever could. We were so simple back then. I think that's why to this day, I love seeing glow in the dark stars on someone's ceiling. It's a good indication that that person is very much in tune with their inner child and with the simplicity of life. Back then, those stars were beautiful, and so were we. I think I'll put some up again, for old time's sake. Actually, wait a minute. They'll be a pain in the ass to take off when I need to paint. Forget it, I'll just go visit my brother again if I need some magic in my life.

You Played Guns

It's a sad reality that kids can't safely play guns anymore, or "Cops and Robbers," as we used to call it. They can get expelled from school for even making a gun with their fingers, and if a cop sees a kid with a toy gun, the consequences can be even worse. The world has gone crazy, and as a result, today's kids are missing out on one of the best, albeit one of the most frustrating games you could play when you were young.

I'm not sure why playing guns was so much fun when you were a kid. Maybe humans are inherently violent, or maybe you were just mimicking what you saw on TV. Whatever the reason, "guns" was one of the best games you could play. You had the most epic battles imaginable and adrenaline pumped through your veins as if you were fighting in a real war. You dove over rocks, under cars, sprinted like lightning, and cut up your knees sliding for cover across freshly mowed lawns, every grass stain a badge of honour for your mom to wash out at the end of the day.

There were barely any rules to the game, and no one followed them anyways. The general idea was that you and your friends would shoot at each other and every so often someone would have to pretend to get shot and die, or at least get mortally wounded before miraculously coming back to life 10 seconds later, just like in your video games.

Of course, everyone had one friend who pretended that they never got hit, even when they were dangerously out in the open. For me, that was my friend Steve. He obviously thought that I had the worst aim in the world, because in all our years of playing guns he never once allowed himself to be shot. Even when he was out in the open, five feet away, and I was behind cover with a clear shot, he never got hit. It was unbelievably irritating, but I played with him anyways because I loved the game. He was also the only other kid on the street with a cap gun, so my options were limited.

Steve's rampant cheating and refusal to be shot was exasperating, because it defeated the whole purpose of the game. Like so many things in life, you had to take your turn. Sometimes you had to let yourself get shot so that your friend could feel good about himself, and when the favour was returned, it made for an exciting, rewarding game. Playing with a person who refused to do that was infuriating, and sometimes made me wish I could shoot Steve for real. Well, not really, but at least it would have settled the argument of whether or not I was as bad a shot as he said I was.

I'm sure the neighbours hated our gun battles because of the noise we made, not to mention the fact that we ran all over their lawns, but fortunately for them, our skirmishes never lasted that long, because one of two things always happened. We would either run out of caps and have to wait a few days until we got our allowance and could buy more, or Steve would cheat, I would quit in protest, and we vowed never to play guns again. Of course, that only lasted a day or so and then we'd be right back out there for as long as we could tolerate each other, or until our ammunition ran out.

You never see kids playing guns anymore. It's too bad, because they're missing out on what was an absolute staple of childhood for so many of us. Of course, kids are still playing guns nowadays, but not outside like we did. Instead, they're inside on their Xboxes and PlayStations, blowing kids away who are on the other side of the country rather than the other side of the street. I guess they're no more violent than we were, but at least we were getting some exercise and fresh air while living out our most savage fantasies. I guess the one upside is that it's a lot harder to cheat when playing video games, so at least kids like Steve will finally learn fair play. It's a catch 22 situation, but I'll take a cap gun and some fresh air over a controller and a TV screen any day.

Just don't make me play with Steve.

You Thought Your Teachers Lived At School

Remember when you thought your teachers lived at school? Although it sounds silly as an adult, kids around the world still think this to be true, just like you did when you were young.

From your point of view, it made sense that they lived at school. After all, you never thought of your teachers as having lives of their own, or even being real people. You held them in an almost mythical regard, because they held so much power over you. They controlled when you woke up, when you ate, what time you went home, and even when you went to the bathroom. They had more control over you than anyone you had ever encountered, and they didn't seem to fit into society the way the rest of the world did. They held special positions in a special place, and for some reason you assumed they never left that place.

If you were like me, not only did you think your teachers lived at school, you also thought they were all married to the principal. That's because all the teachers at my school were women, and the principal was a man. In my world, if adults lived together, it was because they were married, and since my teachers and the principal lived at school, I logically assumed that they were married to each other, just like my parents.

I think that most kids assumed this, but we never talked about it. That's because there was no reason to. You never talked about the fact that the sky was blue, so why would you talk about your teachers living at school and being married to the principal? That was just the way it was, and no one ever questioned it.

Eventually, however, you were forced to start reconsidering that notion, when cracks and flaws started appearing in your theory. One day, you may have seen your teacher at the grocery store. What was she doing leaving school? They didn't do that. Or maybe you saw your teacher out with another man. Did the principal know? Would he fire her if he found out she was cheating on him? Another time, your teacher may have mentioned something about her children, but as far as you knew, her students were her children, so who was she talking about? All these things made you start to wonder if you were wrong about your teachers, and before long your paradigm was shattered.

Of course, if you had thought about it more carefully, your theory could have been shattered much earlier. After all, chances are the janitor at your school was also a man. What was his role in the arrangement?

Was he married to one of the teachers too, or was he the principal's lame friend who just hung around and didn't have any women of his own? Also, if your teachers lived at school and never came or went, why was the parking lot always full of cars. In order for your paradigm to survive, you had to isolate and omit certain factors, but since doing so made everything more sensible, you were willing to do it, though you couldn't ignore the evidence forever.

Eventually the truth came out, and it was truly a shock when you found out that not only did your teachers and your principal not live at school, they weren't even married to each other. In a way, it was disheartening to find out that your teachers had lives and spouses of their own, but it also made you see them as people and helped you to appreciate them in a way you hadn't before. That realization marked a major change in your life and in your way of seeing the world, and it also signaled the end of a genuinely naïve phase of your life. While you still believed in Santa Claus, the Easter Bunny, and possibly the Tooth Fairy, at least you didn't believe in something as stupid as your teachers living at school anymore.

That was for babies!

A Pet Died and the Grief Was Unbearable

When someone you love dies, the pain can be unbearable. When a goldfish or a caterpillar dies, it can also be unbearable, but only for a child. When you were a kid, the size of the pet you lost had no impact on the amount of grief you felt. You experienced the same sense of loss for your caterpillar as you did for your hamster, budgie, dog or cat. The only difference was the length of time you felt that grief, and how quickly you were able to get over it.

There was definitely a hierarchy of sorrow related to pet deaths, which basically followed the rule that the bigger the pet, the longer the grieving process. The pain you felt was still as deep, it just didn't last as long for a caterpillar as it did for a dog. Basically, the length of time you grieved for a pet was directly related to the amount of effort it took to replace that pet. For example, replacing a caterpillar was easy. All you had to do was go out to the garden and find a new one. As a result, your grief was deep, but short-lived. If a fish died, your heartache lasted a little longer, because you had to wait until your parents could drive you to the pet store to get a new one. The same was true for gerbils and hamsters. You experienced a terrible sense of loss, but it immediately subsided once your parents said you could get a new one and you promised them that this time you wouldn't suck your hamster up in the vacuum because you thought he'd find it fun.

Now, fish, gerbils, and birds were one thing, but when a dog or a cat died, that was the biggest loss of all, because those animals were special. I can't speak for cats, but dogs really are man's best friends. They love you in a way that no one and nothing ever has. They love you unconditionally, no matter how dirty, stinky, depressed, drunk, or whatever else you are, and they're not easy to replace. They are replaceable, though, it just takes a lot longer than it does for a fish or a bird because dogs and cats cost more. On top of that, your parents were probably the ones who got saddled with all the responsibilities that a dog or cat came with, so they weren't exactly chomping at the bit to get a new one. If you bugged them enough though, they eventually gave in and got you a new dog or cat, which they immediately regretted because once again they were the ones doing all the work.

      Losing a pet was always hard, no matter how big or small, because you loved them all the same. Whether it was a fuzzy caterpillar you had found in the garden or the family dog who had been there for you since before you could crawl, the loss of a pet was always met with heartbreak. As I conclude this section,

I am reminded of the wise words of Yoda in *The Empire Strikes Back*, when he famously said to Luke, "Judge me by my size, do you?" Just because a pet was small, it didn't mean your grief was when it died. After all, Yoda himself was quite small, and I was devastated when he died. I'm sure I'm not the only one who was deeply upset by his onscreen passing, and if Yoda's death didn't get you in *Return of the Jedi*, I doubt any of you made it through *E.T.* without bawling your eyes out.

You Had Water Fights

Today, water fights are socially irresponsible. When you were a kid, they were a summertime staple.

Water fights were one of the best things about childhood, and like most things in life, they experienced an evolution over time. When I was four or five, the only water pistols that existed were those tiny plastic ones you bought from the toy store for a dollar or two. The great thing about those little guns was that they kept water fights fair. That's because they were the only water pistols that existed, so everyone was fighting on even terms.

Those pistols were great. Most of the time, they were a see-through plastic colour, and they always seemed to have a leak somewhere. You didn't have any other options though, so you didn't complain. You loved those water pistols, and for some reason you also loved drinking out of them. I don't know why, but while waiting behind a bush to ambush a would-be enemy, I always drank from my water pistol by squirting it into my mouth, using up all my ammo in the process. For some reason, that water tasted better than any other water, even hose water, and that was saying a lot. With the advent of adult knowledge, I now realize that it was probably all the harmful toxins in the plastic leeching into the water that gave it that unique taste, but at the time, ignorance was bliss. Of course, loving the taste of that water also meant that by the time my enemy showed up, I had very little ammo left, but it didn't matter, because most of the time the kids I was playing with had done the same thing, and it was back to the fill station for both of us.

Besides water pistols, water balloons were an integral part of water fights. They had a few downsides, however. One, they hurt like hell when you got hit with them, and besides making you wet, they often made you cry. Two, they were so hard to fill up, tie, and hit someone with without breaking that you rarely did any damage. Three, chances are you were trying to fill and tie water balloons before you could even tie your shoes, so when you gave up on trying to tie a proper knot after dousing yourself several times, you just chased someone with the balloon and squeezed water in their direction in a vain attempt to get them wetter than you'd already gotten yourself.

In addition to water pistols and water balloons, there was one other weapon that children employed on the battlefield, and it had no equal: the garden hose. Now, every kid knew that using the hose was cheating, though it didn't stop people from doing it. The hose area was supposed to be like an oasis in the desert, a neutral zone, where no one was allowed to squirt each other, and its only purpose was supposed to be for refilling empty water guns. Even though this rule was revisited at the start of every water fight, someone always broke it and turned the fill station into their own Armageddon dispenser. On my street, it was always one of the big kids who did that just to be a jerk, and just because they could.

As a result, every water fight started and ended the same way. The little kids, the group to which I belonged, thought that this would finally be the time we would beat the big kids, and it would also finally be the time the big kids wouldn't cheat by turning the hose on us. So just like always, it was the big kids versus the little kids, and from the very beginning, there was no way in hell we were going to win. That's because even though we outnumbered them at least two to one, they had bigger, more powerful water guns than we did, and they could hurl water balloons like liquid artillery with their big kid strength. On top of that, they always found ways to cheat, whether it was dumping buckets of water on us at the hose stations, wrestling our water guns out of our hands and turning our own weapons against us, or using the hose to soak us into oblivion. As a result, every water fight on my street ended with the little kids soaking wet, crying, and vowing never to play with the big kids again.

Of course, the next day we were knocking on their doors and challenging them to another water fight, big kids versus little kids. We had forgotten our vow to never play with them again, but we hadn't lost the determination to win because we thought that maybe this time would be different. Maybe they wouldn't cheat, and we would finally taste the sweet victory that was a lifetime in the making. Sadly, that never happened. They always cheated, we always lost, and the cycle repeated itself over and over until one day the big kids finally became too old to play with us anymore, but as life would have it, we suddenly realized that we had become the big kids and found ourselves being challenged to water fights on a near daily basis by a bunch of annoying little kids who wouldn't leave us alone. We figured that if we gave them a thorough enough soaking and made life miserable for them, they would eventually give up and go away, but just like when we were their age, they never did.

You've got to admire that kind of tenacity.

You Played Tee-Ball

Tee-ball was the greatest sport ever invented, because anybody could be good at it. It was the one game where even if you didn't have a shred of athletic prowess, you could still excel. All you had to do was hit that little rubber ball off that plastic stand and run for your life. Even if you weren't good enough to hit the ball, all you had to do was hit the stand and knock the ball off, and people would still cheer for you. It was the ultimate self-esteem booster, and that's why when you were a kid it was your favourite sport in the world.

Those were the good old days, when the bar was set so low. As a result, self-worth was at an all-time high. No matter how much you sucked, you could still get on base. You didn't have to worry about striking out, because it was impossible, and everyone on your team was as uncoordinated as you were, so the playing field was completely level. It was the only time in your life that sports would ever be like that.

In tee-ball, making it to first base was almost guaranteed, even if the ball only rolled two feet from the stand. Sometimes it even rolled backwards, but you could usually still get on base because the back catcher, who was three feet tall, was wearing gear designed for someone twice their size and they could barely move while wearing it. In addition, the mask they were wearing was way too big and kept falling down over their eyes, so even if the ball was right in front of them it took them awhile to find it. When they eventually managed to find the ball and try to make the out, it didn't matter, because they couldn't throw far enough to reach first base anyways, and by that time, you'd usually made it there, even if you were a slow runner. Regardless if your hit had been a line drive or lousy, setting foot on that sandbag always felt incredible and made you feel like the athlete of the year.

That was the fun part of tee-ball – being up to bat. Being in the outfield was boring because nobody could hit the ball that far. I recall most kids just standing around watching the clouds, or lying down in the grass and looking at bugs, and then the coach yelling at them to get up because we had a "heavy hitter" coming up to bat, which meant he could hit the ball about six feet instead of the standard four. Really, the players in the outfield were pretty much on vacation, but that was ok. We liked it that way.

Another reason tee-ball was great was that there wasn't much difference in skill level between the players on your team. Sure, the coach's son was usually better than everyone else, probably because the coach made him practice on his off days and was hoping he'd make the major leagues, but for the most part, the majority of your teammates were pretty middle of the road. They could hit the ball most of the time, though they still suffered the occasional mishap when the pressure was on and all they could hit was the stand, they usually got on base, and were good for scoring a run or two each game. Of course, every team always had a few duds just to even things out. Those were the kids who could only hit the stand. They struggled to get on base and they were the only ones who never scored a run because they moved like sloths struggling to get their day started. Those were the kids who always got the trophies for "Most Improved Player" or "Biggest Heart" because they were awful, but kept on trying, either through sheer persistence of will or from total ignorance of their ineptitude. As terrible as they were, even they sometimes managed to get on base and received thunderous applause when they did, but that was the true beauty of tee-ball: no matter how bad you were, it always made you feel great.

I think a lot of people would have higher self-esteem today if they could have played tee-ball their whole lives. It's almost a shame that people had to graduate to baseball, where the stakes and the expectations were so much greater. It's a shame we had to start putting more and more pressure on ourselves as we got older. Adult life is filled with so many pressures that it's wonderful to think back to a time when we could be awful at something and still get all kinds of accolades for it. Maybe we should apply our childhood expectations of ourselves to our adult lives and let the world know to start expecting a whole lot less from us. It worked when we were kids, so maybe it will work now.

Who knows, maybe we'll even get a trophy for it.

You Had a Lemonade Stand

Lemonade stands, the summer time staple of kids from small towns and those who grew up on quiet suburban streets. If you made a lemonade stand when you were a kid, it was probably your first foray into the business world, and also probably your first failed money making scheme. But that doesn't mean you didn't have a blast doing it.

Now, the term "lemonade stand" is a bit generous. Back then, we had all seen fancy wooden lemonade stands with nicely painted signs in comic books and on TV, but we knew that our stands weren't going to look anything like those. Instead, they consisted of a TV tray or a small table, a couple plastic chairs, and a piece of paper with the word "Lemonade" written in crayon, hopefully spelled correctly.

Your storefront may have been low budget, but your expectations for success certainly weren't. When you first conceived of the idea, I think it was an almost universal notion that before long, you'd be rolling in dough and running a thriving business, making more money than you'd ever imagined. Before you even poured your first cup of lemonade, however, you had several things working against you that you were too young and inexperienced to think about.

For starters, the only way you could actually run a lemonade stand was if you lived on a quiet street where your parents felt it was safe enough for you and your friends or siblings to set one up in the first place. That meant that there wasn't a lot of foot traffic passing through, which was your primary customer base, so right off the bat your lemonade stand was going up against improbable odds. With virtually no potential customers, your start-up was doomed to fail, but since you had no idea about things like customer acquisition and consumer demand, you went ahead and set that stand up anyways.

In addition to a total lack of customers, you also started your business in the hole because the lemonade you were selling wasn't actually yours. It had been provided to you by your investors, who in this case, were your parents. In the real world, which you fortunately weren't operating in, you would have had to sell enough lemonade to repay your parents for the can of frozen concentrate they had given you before you saw even a penny of your own profit, and with no customers to sell to, that wasn't going to happen. Fortunately, investor returns weren't on your radar, which was good, since that would have spoiled all the fun.

Economics and logistics aside, you were happily out there manning your lemonade stand, certain you were going to succeed. Your business model may not have been sound and you may have already been in the hole, but you were determined that before long, word would spread about your fancy lemonade stand where a cool, refreshing cup of lemonade could be had for only a dime. You knew it was only a matter of time before hordes of thirsty customers came come flooding to your stand, so you patiently sat and waited. And waited. And waited some more, because nothing was happening. In fact, the only people drinking the lemonade were you and your friends who were running the stand, because no one was coming by and you were starting to see the flaws in your plan.

Now, it's not to say that no one was coming by at all, because if you had nice neighbours, they had seen you out there waiting patiently at your little plastic table and had taken pity on you. They bought a glass or two and proclaimed that it was the best lemonade they had ever tasted, but that was it. Crowds of thirsty customers weren't lining up at your stand the way you had envisioned, and while you thought you would be filling your piggy bank with cold hard cash, you only had a few nickels and dimes to show for your hard work. It was the first, but not the last time that life didn't live up to your expectations, and you had to wrestle with the knowledge that sometimes you just can't win, no matter how certain of success you may have been.

You had tried your best, and failed miserably. It was a bitter pill to swallow, but that was where the beauty of being a kid came in, because that bitterness was quickly washed away, most likely with the lemonade you still had left over, and replaced with something sweeter.

Within an hour of your business going under, you and your friends were on to something new. You were catching bugs and frying ants, playing hide-and-go-seek, or choreographing tricks for a neighbourhood bike show you planned to sell tickets for (to the same people who had bought your lemonade, of course). Your short-lived feelings of failure had quickly been replaced by an intense focus on whatever you were doing in the moment, and you never gave another thought to your botched lemonade business.

Adults would have handled that debacle totally differently, dwelling on it for days and really letting it get to them. They would have gone over their mistakes time and time again, wondering what they could have done differently, and all their friends and family would have heard about it. It would have taken days, weeks maybe, for an adult to pull themselves out of that chasm of disenchantment and failure, whereas kids never entered that chasm in the first place. They instantly moved on to something new, and because of that, they were happier.

That was one of the best things about being a kid. You had the ability to fail and immediately get back up, dust yourself off, and either try again or move on and never look back, fully immersing yourself in the present moment and giving all of your attention to what was in front of you rather than behind. You weren't thinking about the mistakes of the past, and you weren't worrying about the challenges of the future – you were just being in the moment, and it was an incredible way to live your life.

Didn't someone write a book about that for adults and become a multi-millionaire? We already knew that as kids. Maybe we should have been writing books instead of building lemonade stands. Of course, we could barely spell "Lemonade," so I'm not sure how successful our publishing career would have been.

Probably about the same as our lemonade stand.

You Got Stung By a Bee

Getting stung by a bee was an awful part of childhood. It was one of those things that you thought only happened to other kids, not you. In the back of your mind though, it was your biggest fear. You'd wake up thinking, "What if today is the day?" It was like getting chicken pox or breaking your arm. You knew people it had happened to, but so far you had been spared.

You were glad for that, but there was this morbid curiosity about getting stung that made you wonder about it. What exactly did it feel like? How much did it hurt? You tried to get people to describe it to you, but no matter how good their explanations were, it never truly conveyed the experience. Like falling in love or having an orgasm, it was something you had to experience yourself in order to understand.

Your first bee sting, and every bee sting after that, seemed to come out of nowhere. One minute you were playing with your friends, laughing and giggling, and the next, you were feeling a pain unlike anything you had felt before. It was as if someone had grabbed your skin with a pair of pliers and pinched it as hard as they could, ripping through your flesh in the process. As you looked down for the source of that pain, you heard the tell-tale "bbzzzz" and saw the black and yellow perpetrator flying away, and suddenly, you knew you'd been stung.

If it was a bee that stung you, you felt some relief in knowing that you'd be in pain for a while, but the bee would die a slow, agonizing death, and that evened things out a little. If it was a wasp, you felt no such relief because you knew that nothing was going to happen to it. Wasps are like the astute criminals of nature who keep committing crimes and going unpunished; there's no justice for a wasp sting, and they live only to torment.

Truth be told, it didn't much matter whether it was a bee or a wasp that stung you. What mattered was that you had been speared by what felt like a harpoon, and from that moment on, your life would never be the same. You had joined the inestimable host of kids who had been stung and lived to tell about it. In a way, it was like getting a battle scar that you could brag about. Later on, you could exaggerate the size of the bee, at which point another kid would claim that they got stung by a bigger bee, so you'd change your story to make yours even bigger, until it got to the point where the bee was so big that even the most gullible kid wouldn't believe your story. But bragging rights would have to wait. First, there was the life or death matter of getting adult attention and putting a Band-Aid on that mortal wound.

To let your parents know you needed immediate first aid and a possible code three evacuation to the hospital, you did what every kid does when they get hurt: you covered the sting with your hand and started screaming at the top of your lungs. Almost instantly, your parents came running out of the house, worried someone had been hit by a car, because the way you were screaming sure made it sound that way. Then they saw you, slowly walking towards them, Frankenstein-like in your movements, your hand covering the part of your body that had been stung, eyes closed and shrieking, hot tears streaming down your cheeks, and they knew immediately what had happened.

Your parents rushed you into the house while the crowd of anxious kids outside who had been with you during the attack fervently discussed whether or not you were going to make it, or if your arm or leg would have to be amputated. Then, they would start telling stories about the time they got stung, and how the bee that got them was at least 10 times bigger than the one that stung you, and they hadn't even cried.

Inside, your parents immediately set to work fixing you up. A bee sting wasn't like a scraped knee or a bruise. It required special treatment: an onion rub,

Sting Stop, a couple Band-Aids, and probably some ice cream. That was the good part about getting hurt as a kid - it was usually followed by some kind of treat, which doesn't happen when you're an adult. The only treat you get when your older is if your medical insurance covers the cost of your injury, and frankly, that's not as tasty as ice cream, although far more helpful in the long run.

Once you had been patched up, you lay down for a couple hours and watched TV while your parents periodically checked on you to make sure you hadn't slipped into a coma and died. Chances are that after all the crying you had done, you may have fallen asleep, and when you woke up you were a changed person. Your mettle had been tested and you had lived to tell the tale, one that would be grossly exaggerated for the rest of your childhood.

Although the size of the bee that stung you and your immense courage in the face of danger would be the first greatly embellished story you would ever tell your friends, it certainly wouldn't be the last.

You Could Eat a Popsicle Without Feeling Sexual

For me, this was a long time ago. I don't think it's a coincidence that as people begin to mature and become aware of things like nutrition, sugar intake, and diabetes, they also become aware of the fact that eating some foods can resemble a sex act. The most obvious example of this, of course, is eating a popsicle.

Whenever I eat a popsicle now, I always feel like people are looking at me funny and judging me.

"Look at that guy. Look what he's doing, eating a popsicle like that. Doesn't he know what that looks like? Come on buddy, there are kids around!"

As a kid, I never felt self-conscious about that. I could just eat a popsicle and enjoy it. I didn't question my sexuality, and neither did the people around me. The only thing I worried about was finishing my popsicle before it began to drip all over my hands and I turned into a human beehive, since the only things that liked popsicles more than I did were the bees and wasps that never let me eat one in peace.

Yes, the days when you could eat anything you wanted and not think twice are long gone. I can barely shop for cucumbers and carrots today without feeling slightly insecure, and corn on the cob is off the list completely. It's a different world now, and it makes me miss the old days when we were too busy enjoying ourselves to even think about being self-conscious.

Oh well, the one upside is that most of the foods that make us feel this way are actually awful for us to ingest. For example, I'll never eat another Twinkie in my life, and that's something my body will thank me for in the long run. I'll still eat a popsicle from time to time though…as long as nobody's watching.

You Had a Remote Control Car

Everybody remembers their first car. Some people had a Volkswagen, some people had a Honda, and some people even had a Mustang. For most of us though, our first car was a K-car, and I don't mean a Chrysler. I mean a K-car, because it was a remote control car that you bought from Kmart.

Growing up, every kid on my block had a remote control car, and they were all exactly the same. They looked like an off road version of an Indy car that had been lifted, given knobby tires, and taken steroids. They had this mean look to them, with aggressive styling, pin striping along the body, a souped-up spoiler above and behind the tinted cockpit window, and a stream-lined front bumper, which came in handy on a regular basis. The only difference between them was the colour. You could have either red or white, which meant you really had to pay attention to keep track of which car was yours in the middle of a drag race with all the neighbourhood kids.

Back then, those cars were the coolest thing you could own. Any kid who didn't have one was immediately dropped down a few rungs on the social ladder, and while the other kids raced, did tricks, and jumped their cars off plywood ramps, the kids without were forced to stand on the sidelines and stare with green-eyed envy until they finally got a car of their own.

Eventually, nearly every kid on my street had a remote control car, and we drove those things like lunatics. We crashed them into each other, we sent them flying off ramps, we even took them off road. Well, we drove them over people's lawns and through their gardens, but in our eyes, that was still pretty impressive.

Back then, it seemed like our cars could do 100 mph. In reality, it was probably only about five, but that's not what it seemed like to us. We knew we were in control of high end racing machines, and we were proud of our driving skills. We felt like we could do anything with our cars, and to show off just how cool we were and how well we could handle them we drove them like maniacs, just like real grown-ups with real cars.

We were all eventually humbled, however, when we crashed our cars because we were driving them like idiots, just like real grown-ups with real cars. I have never totalled a car in real life, but I did smash up my remote control car quite terribly. It happened when I was showing off to my friends and sent it flying off a jump. I miscalculated the trajectory and the car hit the jump at an angle. As a result, it flipped over as it was flying through the air and landed on its back, right on its shiny red spoiler. In one dreadful moment, my spoiler and my pride shattered in unison.

After my crash, I was never the same behind the remote. I had lost my nerve, and I didn't do the crazy stuff I used to do to show off and get attention. I was more cautious, more reserved. I had pushed my limits and paid a heavy price, and because of that my racing days were over. Fortunately for me, all the other kids eventually mangled their cars too, so I wasn't the only one driving around at slow speeds with a fractured body kit or a busted fender. It was unspoken, but you could tell that we all felt the loss of pride and self-assurance that we had before we wrecked our rides. We had been so haughty, so certain of our skills, but flown too close to the sun on remote control wings, and as a result the era of remote control cars tearing up the neighbourhood came to an end.

It was a somber day on the block when the last kid wrecked his car. We knew that a wonderful phase of life had come to an end, a phase where we, and our cars, had seemed indestructible. It was probably the first moment we realized we were mortal. As a result of our dangerous driving, we had destroyed something that had been a part of who we were. Thanks to our carelessness, that part of us was gone forever because we couldn't afford to buy new cars, and our birthdays and Christmas were still too far away to consider getting replacements.

    The day the last kid wrecked his car was the day the sun set on a golden era of my neighbourhood. We were left with nothing but memories of what once was, though we still held hope for a brighter future. Fortunately, that brighter future was just around the corner, because Nintendo had just been released in North America, and within a month or two, none of us would ever think about our remote control cars again. Well, not until our parents kicked us out of the house to get some exercise and we found ourselves thinking back to the good old days when we raced cars for real, not just in video games. But by then, that seemed like a lifetime ago.

Someone Told You, "If You Touch It, You Take It"

When I was a kid and my grandpa took my brothers and I to buy candy at the corner store, or "The Chinaman's shop," as he called it, he had one simple rule: "If you touch it, you take it."

So one day, I touched every candy in the store – and then he spanked me.

Just kidding. He didn't spank me, but he did cuss me out something awful on the walk home.

But what did he expect saying something like that to a kid in a candy store?

Saturday Mornings

Adults love Saturday morning because it's one of the only days they can sleep in, and they know they don't have to go to work that day. Kids love Saturday morning because it's devoted entirely to them, and when you were a kid, you loved it for the same reason.

Saturday morning was the best time of the week. Not only did you not have to go to school, the whole morning was dedicated exclusively to you. There were amazing cartoons on almost every channel, and sometimes there were so many good cartoons on that you had to watch two at once. You were constantly flipping back and forth between channels, trying to follow the storyline and catch the action of each one. It was an overdose of excitement and the greatest morning to be alive. It was also perhaps the one time you and your siblings got along for more than two minutes without a fight breaking out, because no one wanted to risk having cartoons taken away.

The only thing that made Saturday mornings better than they already were was spending them at your grandparents. I don't know about you, but when I stayed at my grandparents, it was like staying at a five star hotel. Unlike your mom and dad, your grandparents were always awake before you were on

Saturday morning, and by the time you rolled out of bed in your pajamas, they already had the TV on and were making breakfast for you. They served you that breakfast in front of the TV and waited on you hand and foot while you filled your face with bacon and eggs, pancakes and cereal, hot chocolate, and anything else you wanted, and they did it all with a smile.

As an adult, you can't get that kind of service anywhere. Even if you pay for room service at an expensive hotel or go to a restaurant with the most attentive wait staff in the world, it's just not the same. That's because your grandparents did it for love, not money, and that made all the difference.

Yes, there was nothing better than Saturday morning when you were a kid. You didn't have to go to school, and you could watch amazing cartoons all morning. It was a blessing for your parents too, because since you were preoccupied all morning, it meant they actually got to have some peace and quiet and enjoy themselves too. Come to think of it, they might have been the only people who liked Saturday morning better than you, but for an entirely different reason.

You Rode Your Bike Everywhere

When you were a kid, there was one form of transport that dominated all others, and that was your bike. The great thing about bikes was that everyone had one. It wasn't like when you first got your driver's license and only certain people could drive; with bikes, everyone was game. They came in all shapes and sizes, and each one was unique to its owner. Some kids had brand new bikes. Some had hand me downs. Some kids even had trikes, but it didn't matter. As long as you had wheels, you were as cool, except of course if you had training wheels, but even then you were considered an up and comer.

Your bike was everything to you. It was your first status symbol, and the first thing you ever owned that you were proud of on a materialistic level. It was also your first babe magnet. You showed off as much as you could on your bike. If you liked a girl in your class, you knew that nothing would impress her more than cruising by her on the way home and pedaling as fast as you could, or if you really wanted to show off, standing on your seat, or maybe even popping a wheelie. Even if that girl never talked to you for the whole year, deep down, you knew she was digging you and your awesome bike.

Besides giving you a superb way to show off, the other great thing about bikes was that they were never just bikes; they were whatever you wanted them to be. They were motorcycles, speeder-bikes, fighter jets, tanks, horses, anything your imagination could conceive of. That's why no bike ride was ever just a bike ride; it was an adventure every time.

Riding bikes was an exhilarating part of childhood because not only did you wildly exercise your imagination while you rode, your bike also gave you your first taste of freedom. It was on your bike that you pushed the limits of where you were allowed to go and found amazing new places you never knew existed, since it could take you so much further than your feet ever could. Your bike took you into the great unknown beyond the end of your street, and returned you safely home after each grand adventure.

As adults, we don't have anything that brings us close to the sense of adventure and freedom we had when we rode our bikes. I mean, when was the last time you pretended your car was a fighter jet and you started swerving all over the road and making machine gun noises as you weaved through traffic in an intense combat simulation? I understand why we don't do that in our cars, but it illustrates my point about the lack of excitement in our lives.

Maybe we should do ourselves a favour and start leaving our cars at home and get back on our bikes again. Sure, it will take longer to get everywhere and other adults will think we're crazy when they see us zipping through traffic making weird noises, but who cares? Let them sit in their traffic jams and get stressed out on their killer commutes. At least we'll be having fun, and maybe even discover some wonderful new places in the process. I for one am going to go pump up my tires…maybe I'll see you out there. Oh, and if I do and I'm pretending to shoot at you with an imaginary machine gun mounted to my handle bars, feel free to shoot right back.

You Got New Shoes and Could Run Faster

If Olympic athletes really wanted to win gold, they wouldn't waste all their time training. Instead, they'd just buy a new a pair of shoes on race day and run faster than they ever had before. To an adult, that may sound ridiculous, but when you were a kid, you knew that nothing made you faster than a new pair of shoes.

Remember when you bought a new pair of shoes, and as soon as you put them on you could run 10 times faster than you could before? There was something about new shoes that granted you temporary super powers. Suddenly, you were like The Flash, racing everywhere at top speed. You were challenging your friends to foot races and beating them all. You were so confident in your abilities that you even tried to convince your parents to try to race you with the car, which they declined, likely for fear of running you over in the process.

That feeling of super human speed was amazing. When you tried new shoes on in the store, you could feel the power inside them. In fact, you could barely contain it. You had to fight the urge to break into a top speed sprint up and down the aisles, and you knew that if you didn't get those shoes off soon, there was a chance you would run right out the front door and all the way home.

Buying new shoes was always an exciting experience. Not only did you look cooler, you also knew that there was no way the ice cream man would ever get away from you again. Your newfound speed gave you confidence you never dreamed of, and it lasted a long time. Just long enough, in fact, for you to get another new pair of shoes, at which point your speed would increase yet again, and you would be even faster than before.

Back then, the fact that new shoes meant you could run faster was common knowledge among children. Like so many things you once knew with certainty though, you eventually stopped believing in the power of a new pair of shoes, but with good reason. That's because if your theory was correct, it would mean that adults would be running everywhere at 100 miles an hour, since they had owned more new shoes than anyone, except of course for your grandparents, who you never saw sprinting anywhere. That meant that either once you reached a certain age, new shoes lost their ability to make you run faster, or it was all in your head. Both concepts were disappointing to reconcile.

Although it's funny to look back on now, when you were a kid you were convinced that new shoes made you faster. Imagination was everything to you back then. That's why being a kid was so awesome. New shoes meant new powers, and dressing like a super hero made you a super hero. The world was whatever you believed it to be, and as long as you kept that fertile imagination of yours healthy and alive, you thought you could do anything.

Who knows, maybe new shoes really did make you faster because you believed they did. Perhaps that's the power of the human imagination: if you believe it, you can do it. Of course, that's the same reason why thousands of awful singers audition for American Idol each year and expect to win it big, only to have their dreams crushed on national television, so maybe that theory is not so accurate after all. Oh well, it was fun while it lasted.

A Cardboard Box Was The Greatest Toy

Forget Furby. If they had marketed big cardboard boxes for Christmas one year, they would have been the top seller. There is no greater toy for a kid than a cardboard box, and every child knows it. That's why when a baby gets a present, he or she doesn't care about what's inside, they just play with the box and ignore the rest.

When you were a kid, the best thing about a cardboard box was that it could be anything you wanted: a boat, a spaceship, a castle, you name it. Whatever your imagination could conjure up, that box could become, and it provided endless entertainment. How much fun did you have just sitting in a box pretending you were blasting off into space or roaring around the track at the Indy 500? If you were like most kids, the answer is a lot.

The only thing better than one cardboard box was multiple cardboard boxes. When that happened, your imagination could stretch even further. Now, instead of a locomotive, you could have a whole train. Instead of a spaceship, you could have a space station.

When I was about eight years old, my dad brought home a bunch of fridge boxes. My brothers and I took those boxes and turned them into a castle, complete with a working drawbridge. Our entire basement was taken up by those boxes, which we had cut to shape and taped together, and it was the coolest "toy" we ever had. It was so cool that word of our cardboard castle spread around school, and all kinds of kids used to come over to play in it. Of course, I use the term "castle" loosely. The only castle-like feature about it was the drawbridge that we could raise and lower with some string we had taped to the doors, but to our powerful imaginations it was a mighty fortress.

We spent hours, days, weeks and months in that castle before our parents finally insisted on having their basement back to working order. It was a sad day when our castle came down and its impenetrable cardboard walls were put to the curb, but even now, 25 years later, I have amazing memories of just how much fun a few kids and their imaginations were able to have with some simple cardboard.

The difference between now and then is that I know if you gave me a cardboard box today, I would just recycle it. Anytime I buy a big appliance or something that comes in a box, I never get the urge to sit in it and play space anymore, or tape a bunch of them together to try to recreate that castle from my childhood. I guarantee you though that if I was still eight years old, those boxes would still be in my house and I'd be having the time of my life pretending to be an astronaut or a train conductor. Of course, if I was doing that today my mental health would be in question and I would never be able to hold down the job that helped pay for those appliances in the first place. At least I can donate them to the neighbourhood kids; it'll give them a chance to stretch their imaginations.

Ok fine, it'll save me the hassle of breaking them down for recycling, but it's still for a good cause.

You Got Indian Burns

I suppose these days, the politically correct term for these would be "First Nations Burns," but when you were a kid you just called them Indian burns, a name that was only partially accurate. I never knew what the "Indian" part had to do with anything, but I certainly understood where the "burn" came from. That's because when someone gave you an Indian burn, your arm felt like it was on fire and you experienced a pain unlike anything you'd felt before.

When someone asked if you wanted an Indian burn, it sounded innocent and kids had a way of really selling you on them.

"Come on, you gotta try it! Everyone else has," they'd say.

Not wanting to be left out, you immediately agreed to let that person treat you to an Indian burn, and as soon as that rotten kid had a hold of your arm and was twisting your skin in two different directions, you wished you had been smart enough to see it coming, even though that little voice in your head had told you not to do it. That was probably the first time in your life you wished you had listened to your intuition, and it would be a lesson you wouldn't soon forget.

Being tricked into getting an Indian burn was a terrible experience. You always felt like a fool and a victim at the same time, and the other kids all pointed and laughed at you afterwards, even though they had all fallen for the exact same trick.

Feeling ashamed and in a lot of pain, you sauntered off and tried to think of some way to make yourself feel better – and that's when you saw another unsuspecting kid who had yet to fall victim to an Indian burn. Wanting to pass the torch of indignity onto someone else, you approached them and asked if they wanted an Indian burn, because all the other kids were getting them. When they said yes, you gave them the hardest one you could, and now the tables had turned. You had gone from victim to perpetrator, and it felt great. Your target, in turn, would then do the exact same thing to some other unsuspecting sap, and that's how Indian burns spread like wild fire across the playground until every kid in school had had one.

I'm not sure if kids are still dolling out Indian burns on the playground today. Not only could they get in trouble for being a bully, the penalty might be increased for cultural appropriation, so the dreaded Indian burn might actually be a thing of the past. I guess there's an upside to PC culture after all.

You Played Violent Games in Elementary School

Dodge Ball. Chicken. Red Rover. Nowadays, most of these games have been outlawed by schools because of the safety risks they pose, but when you were a kid, they were loved by all.

Looking back, I think the main reason teachers made you play those games was because it was the only way they could get back at you for all the stress you caused them. For example, if a kid was getting on their nerves and they physically accosted that child, they'd be fired, but if they happened to "accidentally" peg that kid in the face with a dodge ball, hey, that was just gym class.

Pain and injury, although usually minor, seemed to be part of your daily reality back then. It seemed that no matter what you were doing, there was always some kid who got hurt. They took a dodge ball to the face, or sprained their wrist in Red Rover, or twisted an ankle during a two-person relay, yet day after day, gym class after gym class, you kept playing those games. Being a kid in gym class is a lot like people who volunteer to go to war. They know that there's potential for injury, even death, but they think it's going to happen to someone else. That's why you lined up against the gym wall without question or protest while kids whipped balls at you at 50 mph, why you linked arms with the person next to you as the biggest kid in class charged at you from across the field and nearly tore your shoulder out of its socket as you tried to stop him, and why day after day, you exposed yourself to flying dodge balls aimed directly at crotch level.

Back then, you loved those games, and your teachers loved making you play them, yet they're games you never play as an adult for one simple reason: they hurt. Show me one adult who wants to have stinging dodge balls whipped at them at high speed while wearing minimal clothing or have people twice their size charge them at full speed while they try to stop them dead in their tracks, and I'll show you someone who needs their head examined.

As an adult, you don't do those kinds of things anymore because you consider things like welts, groin injuries, and pulled shoulders, and how all of those can be avoided. If there's even the slightest risk of injury, you're able to foresee it and do whatever you can to avoid it. When you were a kid, it was the complete opposite; you didn't think about anything and had no forethought whatsoever. You loved every minute of those dangerous games, and you never entertained the idea that you could be put down by an errant ball or pulverized by a kid the size of a dump truck because no matter how brutal those games were, they were still better than doing fractions.

That says a lot about math, doesn't it?

You Never Washed Your Gym Strip

As an adult, I can't wear a shirt for more than a day without needing to wash it. Like most guys, I tend to get sweaty, and that's on a normal day when I'm not doing anything too vigorous. If I'm actually doing something intense, like exercising or playing sports, the shirt that I'm wearing is being peeled off my body as I'm walking in the front door and going straight into the laundry because it's sweaty, stinky, and I'd be crazy to wear it again without washing it. You're probably not that much different from me - you wouldn't dream of not washing your exercise clothes before wearing them again, because you'd reek to high heaven. So how come when you were a kid, you could go a whole year without washing your gym strip and still not stink?

I will never understand how as a kid you could wear your gym strip day in and day out, keep it in a bag at school, never wash it, and still have it smelling fresh at the end of the year. Did you not sweat back then? Or maybe everybody stunk, since no one else washed their strip either, but if that was the case your teacher probably would have said something, because a classroom full of stinky kids would have been too much for them to handle. They never did though, and therefore, I am under the impression that you simply didn't stink back then, no matter what you did.

I'm sure that if the teachers didn't make you take your gym strip home at the end of the year you would have just left it at school for the following September. The only time you would have had fresh strip was when you outgrew your old threads and had to buy new clothes for gym. Barring that, you could have finished your entire elementary school career without ever washing your strip, because frankly, you didn't see the point.

I guess if kids ran the world, people would save a lot of money on their water and electricity bills, since no one would ever do laundry. However, society would be a very stinky place, since laundry day would only happen once a year. As often as I've favoured the way we operated as children, this is one case where adults have the right idea. I would never want to go back to the way things used to be, except for the not stinking part - I'd take that any day.

Oh, and it would be nice having someone do my laundry for me again.

You Learned How To Play Rock, Paper, Scissors

When you were a kid, learning how to play rock, paper, scissors was a major turning point in your life. Not only was it a fun game, it was also an effective way to settle any argument or decision that had to be made. To this day, the game is used by people around the world to make important decisions. In fact, when the Allies were dividing up Europe after World War II, rock, paper, scissors was used on countless occasions, although the history books often leave that fact out.

Rock, paper, scissors was a great game, until my little brother had to ruin it by inventing the laser gun. One day after losing several consecutive rounds, he came out with this new super weapon, which according to him obliterated everything else in the game. As if that wasn't bad enough, he would always break out the laser gun *after* I had already won with conventional weapons, so every game after the inception of the laser gun went like this:

Both of us: Rock, paper, scissors!
Me: My rock crushed your scissors!
Little Brother: Laser gun!
Me: What?

Little Brother: Laser gun! Laser gun blows up rock.

Me: There is no laser gun.

Little Brother: Yes there is! It's a secret weapon I invented. I win!

After the laser gun came out, the game quickly descended into chaos, and rock, paper, scissors became punch, kick, scream until my parents came and broke up the fight, then banned us from playing the game for the rest of the day.

I'm sure I'm not the only person who went up against someone who cheated by bringing illegal weapons into what was supposed to be a low-tech game, but once someone started bringing in non-conventional weapons, you couldn't play anymore. Although it was infuriating at the time, in hindsight the people who came up with the idea for laser guns and other dominant weaponry were actually quite brilliant. I mean, who doesn't want to bring a laser gun to a rock fight?

Time Went Slower

The older you get, the faster time goes. For example, an hour to an adult is no big deal. If you have to wait an hour for something, you'll grab a coffee, watch some TV, maybe do a few chores, and before you know it, that hour is up. When you were a kid, an hour was an eternity! Besides months and years, it was the longest measure of time that existed. If you had to wait an hour for something, it was the adult equivalent of waiting an entire day, because when you were young, time went so much slower than it does today.

When you were a kid, didn't everything seem to take longer and last longer too? Days passed slowly and summers lasted forever. Christmas Eve made time feel like it was crawling through molasses, and on Christmas morning, those hours between 4:30 am and the time your parents finally agreed to get out of bed and let you open presents seemed like a life sentence.

You had a much different sense of time back then. That's probably because you were less busy and you had few, if any, important things occupying your time. You spent your days playing with toys, hanging out with friends, splashing in puddles, jumping in leaf piles, and never, ever being concerned about time, because you always had more than you needed.

That's simply not the case today. As an adult, times moves too quickly. You're so busy with the million little things that occupy your life that you never seem to have enough time for anything, especially if it's fun. If you have an hour to fill you don't think, "What am I going to do?" the way you did when you were a kid, you think, "Only an hour? That's not enough time to do anything!" and you pick the most important of those million little things and try to do one or two of them.

As a kid, an hour didn't mean an opportunity to accomplish an overwhelming list of tasks, or lie down for a short respite from your busy life; it meant a very long time that you had to wait for something, whether it was the end of school, your favourite show to come on, your parents to take you somewhere you wanted to go or pick you up from somewhere you didn't want to be. No matter what was on the other side of that hour that you had to wait for, it always took forever.

Perhaps the one place an hour seems to take as long for adults as it does for kids is in church. There is no longer hour in the world than the one you have to spend sitting in those hard, unforgiving pews, staring at the clock and trying to pay attention to what the pastor is saying. It's the one place where time hasn't changed, and it takes forever whether you're five or forty-five. Maybe it's all part of the spiritual experience, but who said church has to be an hour, anyways? I didn't see anything about that in the Bible. Couldn't we get the whole thing over with in 15 minutes? You come in, say a few prayers, sing a song or two, hear a quick sermon, have your sins forgiven, and then get out of there. Express church: it needs to be looked into, but in the meantime, it will remain the great equalizer of time for old and young alike.

Without a doubt, time speeds up as you age. Nowadays, summers come and go in the blink of an eye and every time you turn around it's Christmas again. I yearn for those endless childhood summers, where not only did time move slower, it was filled with so much joy and happiness that arose from the simplest of things: playing with friends, riding bikes, or sitting on the sidewalk and sucking on a popsicle on a perfect summer day that seemed like it would never end.

Yes, time is flying by and you never seem to have enough of it now, but there's one upside to this otherwise disheartening phenomenon: at least your unpleasant experiences are over faster. After all, remember how awful it was when you were grounded for a whole week? Back then that was insufferable, but nowadays it would be no big deal...though hopefully you're not getting grounded as an adult. If you are, time passing quickly is the least of your problems.

You Got To Stay Up Past Your Bedtime

This was one of those rare childhood events that only happened once in a blue moon. It was usually tied to some special occasion, like a wedding or a birthday, or something on TV that was educational or entertaining enough for your parents to bend the rules.

In my house, the only thing on TV good enough to warrant a late bedtime for me and my brothers was a Charlie Brown special, and that's because my parents loved it more than we did. Charlie Brown had been a beloved part of their childhood, and for that reason they wanted it to be a part of ours too. My brothers and I were thrilled about that, because we would have watched anything to stay up later, but it just so happened that we fell in love with Charlie Brown too, so everyone was happy. I'm sure you got to stay up late for similar reasons, and it wouldn't surprise me at all if Charlie Brown was that reason. Or maybe you were more of a Garfield or a Muppets family. Either way, getting to stay up past your bedtime was always an exciting event.

As wonderful as it was getting to postpone your bedtime, it was also stressful in a way. You couldn't fully enjoy the novelty of staying up late because you worried that at every commercial break your parents would finally decide you had stayed up later than you should have and they would bring the fun to a sudden end. Still, it was an exhilarating experience to burn up the midnight oil, often until the wee hours of 8:45 pm, or even nine o'clock. The world looked different in that darkness, didn't it?

Besides giving you a glimpse into the mysteries of the nightlife, getting to stay up late was also something that earned you bragging rights at school. Just like your age and the kind of bike you rode, every kid knew every other kid's bedtime, so when you got to stay up late you boasted about it the next day.

Of course, never wanting be outdone, any time you had been allowed to stay up late, coincidentally, some other kid had been allowed to stay up late too, and later than you, they claimed.

You'd be at school and say something like, "My parents let me stay up 20 minutes

past my bedtime."

Hearing that, another kid would go, "Yeah, well my parents let me stay up 30

minutes past mine!"

Then another kid would best you both by saying, "Big deal! My parents let me stay

up an extra half an hour!"

And then you'd both go, "Wooooah!!!!" knowing you'd just been humbled by your match, though clearly not your math.

You Played with Lego

Perhaps the most iconic childhood toy that has ever existed is Lego. It was universally loved, and whether you asked for one or not, chances are you received at least one set in your lifetime. It was a toy unlike any other, and not just because you had to build it yourself.

At one point in your life, there was probably at least one Lego set you really wanted. It was the gift you desired above all others, and if you were lucky, you got it either for Christmas, your birthday, or maybe even an excellent report card at the end of the year. When you got that set you wanted so badly, you were ecstatic, but unlike every other toy, you couldn't just open it up and play with it. First you had to build it, and by you, I mean your parents.

That was the irony of getting Lego as a gift. You were never the first one to play with it; your parents were, and they didn't even want to. They had to though, because you had no idea how to follow the instructions. Your parents must have cringed every time you opened a gift and it was Lego because they knew that it meant hours of unwanted labour for them. As if they didn't already have enough to do keeping a family afloat, now they had to build your massive castle, or pirate ship, or space station.

To this day, I have visions of my dad sitting at the kitchen table resentfully building the enormous Lego castle he and my mom had bought me for Christmas, his frustration manifesting in a furrowed brow and a short fuse as he dug through piles upon piles of little pieces, searching for the right one.

Of course at that age, I had no idea that he had better things to be doing with his time than building Lego, and I only aggravated him further by constantly checking on his progress and asking why he wasn't finished yet. It was imperative that I played with that set immediately, so I went into slave driver mode and irritated the hell out of him until he built it for me.

I think that the most frustrating thing for your parents about building your Lego wasn't that you forced them to do it or that it caused them unnecessary stress, it was that after they spent hours putting it together while ignoring more pressing matters, you didn't even play with it; you just sat there and looked at it.

But that's how you "played" with Lego. You looked at it, but you didn't touch it, and your friends couldn't touch it either. After all, you had spent all that time manipulating your parents into building it for you, the last thing you wanted to do was risk breaking it. It was much safer to just put it on the shelf and look at it while preventing anyone from actually enjoying it.

I remember my friend Steve had the coolest Lego sets imaginable, and he never once let me touch them. He just had them up on a shelf in his room, and every time I went over to his house it was like going to the museum: I could look, but I couldn't touch. That upset me to no end, but deep down, I knew where he was coming from. After all, when Steve came over to my house, I did the same thing to him.

Lego was such a weird toy because of that. You desperately wanted a particular set, but once it was built, all you did was look at it. On top of that, Lego on the box always looked infinitely more exciting than Lego in real life. That's because the Lego on the box had been digitally rendered with an artistic background, the characters suspended from mid-air, and the whole picture was like a movie poster for some amazing action movie. When you finally got your Lego built and set up, it looked nothing like that. It was almost anti-climactic, but not quite, because we're talking Lego here, and even if you couldn't play with it, it was still one of the coolest toys you could have.

Even though your set didn't look as exciting as it did on the box, your imagination quickly took over, and pretty soon you were creating something even better. You put the figures in cool poses, made elaborate set ups, and once you had everything looking perfect and exactly the way you wanted it, you put it high up on a shelf so that neither you nor anyone else could touch it. That was partly because you wanted to enjoy the visual fruits of your labour, and partly because you didn't want anyone smashing it, unintentionally or not.

It was also because your dad had told you that was the last Lego set he was ever going to build, and although you didn't fully believe him, you didn't want to risk it.

There was one downside to Lego though, and that was when you lost a piece, especially if it was a one of a kind part. that you couldn't replicate or substitute. There was nothing more frustrating than that, and you had no choice but to search for that one tiny, pivotal little piece until you found it because you couldn't go forward without it. You turned on every light in the room, ran your fingers delicately through the carpets, and even brought out a magnifying glass to see if that would help.

Remember how you freaked out if your parents tried to vacuum the carpet when a critical piece was missing? That was always cause for alarm. Typically, they were good about not vacuuming until you had found that missing piece, but ironically, they were usually the ones who found it by stepping on it and wondering what could possibly be lodged in the carpet that would hurt so much. You yourself had stepped on enough pieces to know just how painful it could be, so at least you could empathize with them. Come to think of it, that was probably one of the first and only things you could sympathize with your parents about, since you couldn't relate to any of the other difficulties they had to endure. But stepping on Lego? That was something you could bond over.

Despite the irritation to your parents and its limited playability, as well as the excruciating pain when you stepped on it, Lego was a childhood staple that almost everyone enjoyed, and like so many other facets of your own childhood, it remains a favourite among children today. Like video games and Hide-and-Seek, Lego is timeless, and it also seems to be tied into the Karmic cycle of life. If you loved Lego, you're going to want your kids to love it too, but that means you're going to have to build it for them, at least until they're old enough to figure out how to do it themselves. It might be worth it though, since it will take you back to the days when you had Lego sets of your own. As a bonus, you can even play with it when they're not around, and by play with it, I mean set it up and look at it, but never touch it. That would just be crazy.

You Never Got a Sore Back

When I was a kid, I thought adults who got sore backs were pathetic. Today, I am one of those pathetic adults who gets a sore back from time to time, and if you're like me, you know how useless you are when that happens. At least as this age you can sympathize with someone who's put their back out, but that wasn't the case when you were a kid.

When you were young, you didn't understand how having a sore back could render someone so useless, let alone how you could even get a sore back in the first place. That's because you had never had one, and you simply couldn't relate. You'd had cuts, scrapes, boo boos and bee stings, and you understood why those could put you down, but a sore back? Come on, those adults were just being wimps and you knew it.

To you, it seemed like your parents equivalent to when you faked sick, and since you were the master of such deception yourself, you could spot another faker a mile away, or so you thought. As a child, I can vividly remember walking past my dad in the living room, who was lying on the ground writhing in pain and asking him what was wrong.

Between clenched teeth, he said, "My back's out!"

Totally confused, I responded with, "Well, you'd better put it back in and get off the floor, because dinner's not going to make itself."

That was the level of sympathy I had, because I couldn't relate to what he was going through. I couldn't understand how a sore back could cause someone so much pain and make them so unfit for duty. Back then it was a totally mystery, but like everything else in life I couldn't previously relate to, one day it happened to me and I finally understood just what my dad had been going through.

One Sunday in the fall, I decided to plant 20 cedar trees in my backyard. I figured it would be a quick job. How long could it possibly take? Dig a few holes, shove the trees in, water them well and be done in time for dinner. I calculated it could be done in no time.

Wanting to get them in the ground before I lost the daylight, I worked like a mad man to dig the holes, wrestle them into place and plant them all by myself, a task which required an exorbitant amount of bending, lifting, and reaching, while working against time and rushing to finish.

It took the whole afternoon, but I finally got it done. However, once I had planted the trees and had everything cleaned up, I knew I had over exerted myself, though it wouldn't be until the next day when I found out just how badly.

The next day at school (I'm a teacher, not a student), I could feel I had tweaked my back, and I thought it would be a temporary inconvenience that would quickly pass, but that's not what happened. As the day wore on, I felt more and more pain in my lower back. When the bell rang to signal the end of lunch, I started walking up the stairs to unlock my classroom door, when all of a sudden it felt like someone was literally folding me in half as I found myself doubled over on the stairs, my feet planted on one set of steps and my hands two steps above them.

I was in incredible pain. I felt paralyzed, and was literally frozen in place. As streams of students began to shuffle up the stairs, I was stuck in the middle of the stairwell, bent over in the most embarrassing position and breathing hard through clenched teeth, feeling both the pain of a strained back and the humiliation of being caught in such an unfortunate position at such an unlucky time.

As I craned my neck to seek out a sympathetic by passer or a helping hand, I saw only irritated faces staring back at me, and I recognized that look. It was the same one I had given my dad so many years ago as he lay on the floor of the living room, while I stood stared at him with contempt and wondered how the man I had previously admired so much could be rendered so useless and frail because of a simple sore back.

It was at that moment that life had come full circle, and at last I understood what my dad had been going through all those years before, though it was too late to offer my sympathies or do anything to help him. There is no doubt that the countless number of bewildered students who saw me bent double in the middle of the stairs will have a similar epiphany one day, but not until they too hurt their backs doing something seemingly mundane and realize just how fragile they really are. Until that time, I will remain in their memories as the weirdest teacher they ever knew.

Oh well, I guess it's nice to be remembered for something.

You Had Indoor Lunch at School

Outside, it was pouring rain. All morning, you had stared outside your classroom window and wondered if come lunch time, you would be forced out into that cold, wet world with its muddy fields and slippery playground equipment, only to come back inside soaked to the bone and be forced to suffer through an afternoon of soggy shoes and itchy, wet feet. The closer it came to lunchtime, the more apprehension you felt. You crossed your fingers, you desperately hoped for it, and if you believed in God, you prayed. And then it happened. Just before the lunch bell rang, the principal came on over the loudspeaker and addressed the whole school.

"Attention, boys and girls. Please pardon the interruption."

And then he waited an eternity to say what you desperately hoped was coming next. He took a breath, and hesitated, like he was contemplating whether he was making the right decision or not, as if lives hung in the balance. And then, he soberly spoke them, the magic words that every kid was on the edge of their seats waiting to hear.

"It's looking very rainy and wet outside. Because of the weather, and the field conditions, today will be an indoor lunch hour."

And then you and every other kid went crazy. Kids screamed. They threw up their hands for joy. They hugged and high-fived like a baseball team who had just won the World Series, all because they got to stay in the classroom instead of running around outside for 45 minutes.

There was nothing like an indoor lunch hour at school. Maybe it was because it happened so rarely, or because it meant that the bullies couldn't come after you, or because you got to hang out on the carpet with your friends, drawing pictures, playing games, and actually being able to relax and enjoy school for once. Or maybe, just maybe, it was because there was a quiet, cozy feeling about getting to stay inside your classroom while it was pouring rain outside and you got to play a game with the person you liked, both of you knowing you had a crush on each other without ever saying a word about it, but just enjoying the silent, unspoken affection that flowed between the two of you.

Whatever it was, those indoor lunch hours were special. To this day, kids around the world still celebrate with reckless enthusiasm when the principal comes over the loudspeaker and takes a lifetime to say those six magic words: "Today will be an indoor lunch." And while the kids celebrate, the teachers grit their teeth and brace for the longest lunch hour of their lives, while once again contemplating whether or not early retirement is worth the reduced pension.

You Got a Homework Package on Vacation

There are many things that can ruin a great vacation: illness, lost luggage, natural disasters. However, none of these are as awful as having to complete a homework package you got from your teacher, especially when you left it all until the last minute.

A homework package on vacation was kind of like when Voldemort's face was attached to the back of Professor Quirrel's head in *Harry Potter*. Quirrel knew it was there, but he didn't want to acknowledge its existence.

No matter how much fun you were having, that package was always in the back of your mind going, "You didn't forget about me, did you? I'm not going to do myself you know."

As if coming home from vacation wasn't hard enough, having a huge pile of homework waiting for you made it that much worse. In order to try to avoid this, you always told yourself a big lie.

"I'll do it on the plane!" you'd say.

Or in the car, or on the boat, or on whatever mode of transportation you were taking. This always sounded like a great idea. The problem was, you knew you were lying to yourself (and your parents), but it was better than acknowledging the bitter reality that when you got back home, a huge pile of nasty homework would be waiting for you. No kid in history has ever done homework on the plane. In fact, if you were like most kids, you didn't even bring your homework with you. After all, why spoil a perfectly good vacation with schoolwork? Even your parents couldn't fault you for leaving it at home. They understood, and they were happy to be spending time with you as a family doing fun things rather than getting stressed out about how much harder math had become since they were kids.

Despite the wonderful time you were having on vacation, that homework package was always lurking. The closer you got to going back home, the more you thought about it. Like an evil shadow, you couldn't get rid of it. You knew there would be no choice but to eventually do it, and it was a terribly unpleasant feeling, a sick churning in your guts.

Knowing that your homework was waiting for you was the worst part of coming home. Forget the fact that your holiday was over and you had to go to school the next day, you had a 50-page pile of work to get through, and it was eight o'clock at night. Talk about stress. Why did you always think the package would be so much smaller than it actually was? That was just another bold-faced lie you told yourself to feel better about the situation.

"It will be ok," you'd say. "It's just a few math sheets, some geography, a couple science questions. No big deal, it'll take ten minutes."

But it was a big deal, and it didn't take ten minutes, and four hours into it you had barely scratched the surface. You were stressed out, crying, and now your parents were frazzled too, because not only did they have to come back from vacation, unpack, do laundry, and get themselves ready for work the next day, now they also had to help you with your homework, so it ruined the last of the vacation for everybody.

Those packages were awful for everyone involved. Even your teacher was unhappy when they finally got it returned to them because now they had to mark it. Clearly, we all would be better off if homework packages had never been invented. Why are schools still issuing them anyways? Why don't they just say, "You know what? While you're gone, we're not going to do anything important. We're going to learn about the salmon life cycle, do a few fraction lessons and memorize the countries in South America. Honestly, it's nothing you can't look up on the Internet when you get back, so just enjoy your trip and don't let me ruin it with homework."

Of course, kids nowadays really do have the option of getting all their answers online, whereas we actually had to work for ours. On second thought, maybe we should keep those packages around so kids have to suffer a little, just like we did when we were their age. It's only fair.

You Buried Pets in the Backyard

Does size matter? It certainly does, especially when you're deciding on a final resting place for a family pet. If you're like most people, your first experience with death was through the loss of a pet, whether it was a dog, cat, bird, hamster, goldfish, or anything else. Even though you knew that your furry, feathery, or floating little friends weren't supposed to live as long as you, it was still heart breaking when you lost them. The funny thing about being a kid is that your heart could break just as much for a hamster as it could for the family dog. It wasn't the size of the pet that mattered, it was how much you loved it that made you so sad. The only reason the size of your pet mattered was because it was the determining factor in deciding whether or not it could be buried in the backyard.

There was a set of unwritten rules that regulated how pets were buried, a kind of hierarchy, if you will. Fish were usually flushed down the toilet, while gerbils, rabbits, and birds usually got a shoebox and a proper burial in the garden, complete with a grave stone, which was often quite literally a stone inscribed with a Sharpie or a homemade wooden cross made from popsicle sticks. Dogs and cats were too big for the backyard, according to your parents, but if you could have buried them there you would have, because you knew they would have wanted it that way.

If your family was anything like mine, you eventually had a sizable pet cemetery in your backyard. My family had so many pets laid to rest in the garden that every time we went to entomb a new one, we had to make sure we wouldn't accidentally dig up one we had previously buried. Our backyard was like the elephant graveyard for small pets. There weren't any elephants, but there were a lot of budgies, rabbits, guinea pigs, and even a few wild birds that had flown into the windows and broken their necks. If the zombie apocalypse included animals that would rise from the dead, my backyard would have been ground zero.

When you lay a pet to rest and your biggest concern is digging one up you have already buried, that's a pretty good sign that maybe you're not cut out to be a pet owner. It's a dangerous world out there, especially if you're a furry or feathery little creature that small children find adorable, as they can easily forget just how fragile you are, or accidentally murder you with the best of intentions. Sadly, I think most families go through several incarnations of these types of animals before they finally wise up and either stop buying pets altogether, or invest in something more durable, like a cat or a dog, which can't be buried in the backyard due to legality issues...and because there's no room left.

Trampolines Were God's Greatest Gift

Forget fire, the wheel, and the lever: the greatest technology ever bestowed upon mankind is the trampoline – or at least we thought so when we were kids. Back then, trampolines were legendary, and so was every kid who had one.

When you were young, you never met a kid who didn't love trampolines. That's why rebounders were always the favourite station in gym class; they were as close to a trampoline as most of us could get. Despite their rarity though, there was usually at least one kid in your class who had a trampoline. Once you found that out, your main goal in life became making friends with that kid so you could go to their house and jump on their trampoline, and you did whatever you could to get that invite. You shared your snacks, picked them first in gym class, and even did their art projects for them while they enjoyed center time. You stooped to any level to get invited over to their house, because you knew in your heart that it was worth it, and that you were doing the right thing.

After weeks and maybe even months of sucking up to them, you finally got invited to their house, and you were ecstatic. It was the adult equivalent of being madly in love with someone totally out of your league and begging them to go out with you until they finally caved in and gave you a pity date, but you were simply grateful for the opportunity.

Before the play date happened, you had visions of going to your new friend's house and jumping on the trampoline for hours, laughing, bouncing, and having the time of your life. You pictured a perfect experience that couldn't be spoiled by anything. Unfortunately, the reality of what awaited you was far from what you were expecting, and that's because of one thing: siblings.

When I was in grade two, I found out a girl in my class, let's just call her Jenny, had a trampoline, so I spent months sucking up to her to get invited to her house. I couldn't wait to go, but as soon as I got there, I immediately wished I was back home. That's because before I even stepped onto the trampoline, her older brother ran out of the house and jumped on before me, and I'll never forget the look on his face. It was the first time I saw what could be described as a maniacal look on someone's face. He was staring at me and laughing in a way no one had before, how Scut Farkus from *A Christmas Story* stared at Ralphie every time he bullied him. It was terrifying, and nothing had even happened yet. But it was about to.

As I cautiously stepped onto the trampoline and started timidly bouncing, her older brother watched me carefully, like he was studying my movements for some reason. All of a sudden, he jumped as high as he could, timing his descent so that he landed just before I did and double bounced me 10 feet in the air.

I shrieked in horror, begging him to stop, which only encouraged him further. It was the bully scene from a *Christmas Story* playing out in real life, her older brother laughing like a madman while I begged for my life. I was on my hands and knees trying desperately to crawl to the edge, but every time I got close he bounced me back to the middle where I was helpless to defend against his relentless double onslaught. It only ended when his mom eventually heard my cries for help and came out to see what was the matter and made him put a stop to it, but that was the last time I ever went to Jenny's house to jump on her trampoline.

With Jenny's house no longer an option, I knew that if I wanted to jump on a trampoline again I would have to find some other lucky kid who had one. To my absolute surprise, that lucky kid turned out to be me.

I don't know what kinds of parental strings we pulled or what kinds of empty promises my brothers and I made, but somehow we talked our parents into getting a trampoline. That trampoline actually wound up being one of the best investments they ever made because it got us out of the house, and we never fought while we were on it because we didn't want to have it taken away as punishment, so it was win-win for the whole family.

Once we had a trampoline, we became the most popular kids in the neighbourhood, and even the adults used to come over and bounce on it. We soon found that you could do everything on a trampoline. We started having birthday parties on it, sleepovers, water fights, you name it. If you could do it anywhere else, you could do it on a trampoline, and we did. There was something about doing things on a trampoline that just magnified the joy of everything, and sometimes, there was nothing better than just hanging out with your friends on a perfect summer day, lying on your back and watching the clouds drift slowly overhead while the trampoline cradled you like a baby in a bouncy polypropylene blanket.

Besides actually going swimming, there was nothing better to do on a hot summer day than putting water on the trampoline or setting up a sprinkler underneath it. The way the sun sparkled off the water, turning it brilliant shades of gold and silver as you and your friends bounced to your hearts' content under a perfectly blue summer sky was a magnificent sight. On some trampolines, you could even put dish soap on them and make your own slip and slide, which always led to two things: full body slides across the trampoline, and someone flying off the edge and being catapulted onto the grass. You know what the funny thing about that was? Back then, it didn't even hurt.

Without a doubt, trampolines were God's greatest gift to children, and any kid who was lucky enough to have a trampoline was God's greatest gift to other kids. Hopefully you got to experience the thrill and the excitement of trampolines when you were younger, because as adults who get sore backs, they're one more part of life we can't enjoy anymore. Oh well, at least we can watch our kids have fun on them, and hope to God they don't go flying through the fence or catapulted into the neighbour's yard, or worse, have one of their friends injure themselves and be sued by their parents. Again, all things we never had to think about when we were kids. Don't you miss those days?

You Had to Use a Phone Book

I haven't used a phone book in over a decade, and it's safe to say I'll probably never use one again. That's because we don't need them anymore. Today, finding a phone number is easy. You just ask your smart phone to look up whatever number you need, and it does it instantly. Life wasn't always so simple, however, because for most of our childhood, we had to rely on that most hated of all books: the phone book. Back then, if you wanted to look up someone's number, the phone book was your only option, and it was terrible for many reasons. First, it was huge. It was the size of four encyclopedias glued together, and twice as heavy. It was so big, in fact, that your family had an entire drawer dedicated to it in the kitchen. Just getting the book out of that drawer was a major hassle in itself, and that was the easiest part of the ordeal. Second, there were hundreds of thousands, if not millions, of numbers in that book, and you had to find just one. Third, you had no idea how to actually use the phone book, so the whole task became that much more complicated. There were blue sections, yellow sections, white sections, and all you wanted was to find the name of your friend, whose name wasn't even in the phone book because they were listed under their parents' names. Talk about a needle in a haystack.

After the monumental task of actually getting the phone book out of the drawer and scouring the blue and yellow pages, only to realize your friend's name and number weren't there, you finally got to the white pages, where things started falling into place, sort of. Unlike the other sections, the white pages had a list of last names that seemed like they could be real people, not pet stores or plumbers or pizza shops. Now came the next problem though: not knowing the names of your friend's parents, which you needed in order to pin down the right number. At that point, sometimes you just had to guess what their names might be, and that usually meant a few wrong numbers before you finally found the one you were looking for. If you knew your friend's address, that helped, but if you or your parents were calling for an initial play date that was information you didn't necessarily have, and the only way to find the right number was through the guessing game, or as adults called it, trial and error. If you were persistent, you eventually found the number you wanted, but not until you had invested a lot of time and energy and talked to a few irritated strangers.

Growing up in the phone book era was an entirely different experience than what we're used to today. Back then, if you wanted to be friends with someone, you had to earn it. You could have easily given up when you saw how difficult it was going to be to find their number, but you didn't. You persevered, because the person on the other end of that number waiting to be called meant something to you, and you were willing to work for their friendship. Maybe that's why many of us are still friends with the people whose numbers we had to look up in the phone book. Those were friendships that were won the hard way, and once we'd gone through the trouble of actually finding that person's number, we nurtured that friendship, if only because we couldn't be bothered to keep looking up new people's numbers all the time. Either way, it was worth it in the end.

There Was Only One Way to Save a Video Game

There was a time long ago, before memory cards, hard drives, and auto save, when there was no way to save a video game. You should have been able to save them though, because video games were impossibly hard back then. For example, I played hundreds of Nintendo games in my youth and only ever beat a handful of them because they were just that challenging, and their difficulty was amplified tenfold by the fact that you had no way to save your progress. That was ok though, because you figured out a save feature of your own; it was called leaving the machine on all night.

Back then, you didn't know what a power bill was. You also didn't know what an electrical fire was, or that a melted Nintendo would permanently damage the new flooring your parents had just put in. All you knew was that the only option you had to save your game was to leave the machine on all night and continue playing the next day. Unfortunately, it was never quite that simple.

When you left your Nintendo, or your Sega, or whatever system you had on all night, there were two concerned parties: you, who only cared about saving your progress, and your parents, who cared about things like electricity bills and fires. You had no knowledge of either of those things, while your parents had no appreciation of how hard it was to beat level eight in Super Mario 3, let alone how hard it was to even get to that level in the first place. They also didn't understand how important video games were to you. Video games weren't just a part of your world, they *were* your world, and beating a beloved game was one of the most fulfilling things you could do back then. In fact, beating a certain game was probably the only life goal you had at the time, and you worked hard to achieve it. You knew how much dedication and commitment was involved, and once you had made significant progress towards your goal, you weren't about to throw in the towel and call it quits just because it was time to go to bed. The stakes were too high. You had already spent the entire day raging at the TV and battling past endless bosses, and you needed a way to continue from where you left off. Since there was no built-in save feature, you did the only thing you could: you left the machine on and went to bed, knowing that your progress would be saved and that tomorrow you could pick up from where you had left off.

  The next morning, you woke up, had breakfast, and then rushed back to your game system to continue your quest for glory. As soon as you saw the machine though, your heart fell into your stomach, because the first thing you noticed was that the little red button that glowed when it was on was mysteriously dark. Seeing that button ominously dark was an atom bomb dropped into your guts, because as a child, someone turning off your game system was one of the worst thing that could happen. When it did, you lost it like only a child could.

You immediately dropped to your knees and began screaming at the top of your

Lungs."NO! NO! NOOOOO!"

From the other room, your parents came rushing in, terrified you had been

injured. "What is it!? What's wrong!?"

Then you turned to face them, the most likely perpetrators of that unspeakable

crime, and screamed, "SOMEONE TURNED OFF THE NINTENDO!" after which

you fell to the ground, clutching your head and curling up into the fetal position,

unable to process the incredible tragedy that had just befallen you.

And then your parents just stared at you, watching you heaving and writhing on the ground, and wondered if other peoples' kids were as crazy as you before giving you most matter of fact answer they could.

"Of course we did. It was going to start a fire."

But you didn't care. The house could have been burning down around you, and you would have burned with it if it meant beating a certain game. After all, once you had achieved the pinnacle of childhood success, what more could you ask from life?

But your house never did burn down, because your parents were smarter than you were, and they knew that in the grand scheme of things, having a place to live was more important than beating a video game. So, after several minutes of shrieking, crying, gasping for air, and feeling your world collapse around you, you did the same thing you always did when that happened: you sat down, turned the machine back on, and started all the way back at level one. And you repeated that process over and over and over again, until one fateful day, you finally beat that last boss through sheer grit and determination...or you got a Game Genie.

You Loved The Sears Catalogue For One Reason

For adults, when the Sears catalogue came out each year around Christmas time, it was a chance to browse new household items, clothes, and anything that might be on their wish list. For young boys all across North America, it was their best chance of seeing a nipple.

We loved the Sears catalogue. We cherished the Sears catalogue. And every year when it came out, we scoured it for that most elusive of all female body parts. We knew that with the plethora of bra ads and bra models, there had to be at least one nipple that had slipped past the censors, and we examined those catalogues like forensic scientists trying to find one. I even caught my older brother using a magnifying glass one day, though he would never admit it.

Probing the Sears catalogue for nipples may seem outlandish today, but when we were kids, it was our only option. That's because we were the pre-Internet generation, and our access to nudity was almost non-existent. For many of us, our only recourse was a National Geographic, but that wasn't the kind of nudity we were looking for. As a result, the Sears catalogue was our best bet, and a constant winter companion.

The truly great part about the Sears catalogue was that you never had to feel like a pervert, or even hide what you were doing. Sure, you didn't look at the underwear ads at the kitchen table, but if your parents did come into the room while you were checking it out, you just flipped to the toy section. It was the safest and softest form of pornography on the planet. After all, no parent could fault their child for looking at the toys they wanted for Christmas, and man, did you love looking at toys!

To this day, I wonder if my parents knew what I was really doing when I was absorbed in that catalogue. Kids are never as clever or sneaky as they think they are, and parents always seem to know a lot more than their kids think they do. I will venture this: my dad knew what I was doing, because when he was a kid he probably did the exact same thing. That's why if I have kids and see my own son obsessively gawking at such a catalogue, I'll know what he's up to. I'm sure it will bring a smile to my face, just like it did when I was his age and finally got to see a nipple for the first time. Move over, Playboy; the Sears catalogue was all we needed.

Things at the Dollar Store Cost a Dollar

Last week I went into a store called "Dollar Surprise." The surprise was that nothing cost a dollar. Today, the term "Dollar Store" is misleading, because there is no such thing as a dollar store anymore. They should be called the "Dollars Store," because things there cost dollars, plural. At least stores like "Dollar Plus" and "Loonie and Toonie Town" are more honest with their names, but you'll still need more than a buck or two to buy anything. That's because today, nothing at the dollar store actually costs a dollar, but it used to.

I can't remember the last time I walked into one of those stores and actually paid a dollar for something. It probably wasn't since I was a kid, and I bought a cap gun for a dollar. That was a bargain of a deal for such a cool toy, and that cap gun provided me with endless hours of entertainment and countless games of cops and robbers, until that fateful day I thought it would be a good idea to spray some WD40 in the cylinder to help it cycle faster, and it exploded in my hands, nearly taking a couple of my fingers with it. That was the most epic start, and simultaneous end, to a gunfight in my neighbourhood's history, though it left me with a fear of aerosols for years to come, as well as the need to buy a new gun. Fortunately at only a dollar a piece, I could easily afford a replacement, just as soon as I did my chores and got my allowance for the week.

Back then, the dollar store was an awesome place for a kid because you could afford anything there. Literally everything cost a dollar, and those stores had the greatest assortment of candy, toys, water pistols, guns, and anything else you could lay your greedy little hands on. Real dollar stores were a magnificent part of childhood that has gone the way of the dodo, and they're now a forgotten relic of a bygone era, when there was still a little truth in advertising.

Kids today aren't living in the same economic dreamland, and you can't buy anything for a buck anymore. Everything is more expensive, and that includes having fun. As a result, there are barely any kids today running around the streets, fueled by copious amounts of cheap candy and shooting each other with cap guns that they bought from such a store. Instead, they're sitting inside on their X-Boxes and PS4's that their parents bought them, blasting each other away in the digital world. Sure, you were just as prone to simulated gun violence as they are, but you did it for a lot less money. At least you got some exercise while you were doing it too, unlike today's kids, who just stare at screens all day and the only part of them that's in shape is their fingers.

Do I sound like an old man now? Oh well, it was bound to happen eventually.

You Got People Presents You Wanted

We've all done it, and we're not proud of it. At least once in our lives, we all bought someone a birthday present we knew they didn't want because we wanted to play with it at their party. I truly believe that we did this in the hopes that the person we were buying the gift for would hate it so much that they would just tell us keep it. It was an absolutely selfish act, done by an absolutely selfish person, and at the time, it seemed like a brilliant idea.

This scheme wasn't fool proof, however. You knew that the birthday boy or girl would know what was going on, because when you were on the receiving end of this swindle, you always knew it too. After all, it's not like you hadn't told people what you wanted. Sometimes, you even told people the exact toy to get you, and if everyone followed the instructions, you could have an entire collection of something by the end of the day. For example, on one of your birthdays you may have told people to get you Ninja Turtles toys, or Barbies, and you had made a list of which friend would get you which figure. If everyone followed the plan, you could have the entire team or group assembled, complete with bad guys to fight (well, not if you were asking for Barbies), and maybe even a vehicle or two.

Unfortunately, there was always someone who screwed up the plan, and sometimes it was you.

I'll never forget the year when I was in grade six and got invited to Jacob Werther's birthday party. Jacob was kind of dorky, and hugely into Star Trek. He had invited about a dozen kids from class to his party, and each of us had been given specific instructions on which Star Trek figure to get him. I was supposed to get him Data, and my friend Craig had been tasked with getting him Wharf. Well, Craig and I went to the toy store, found the exact figures Jacob had asked for, and as we were standing there with his birthday wishes in our hands, the gifts we knew would make him happy and really make his birthday, we looked one shelf over and saw something we had never seen before, something 100 times cooler than the geeky Star Trek figurines we were holding.

They were called "Exo Squad", and they were essentially robotic war machines with human pilots you could put inside of them. They were awesome, and instantly Craig and I dropped the Star Trek figures and picked up the Exo Squad toys, practically drooling over them. They were the same price as the Star Trek figures, infinitely cooler, and since both of our birthdays were still months away, we knew that the only way to play with them sooner rather than later was to do something slightly devious. We exchanged a glance, and we both knew what the other was thinking.

"Should we?" I asked.

"I'd be happy to get this as a present," Craig reasoned.

"Sounds logical to me."

With that, we both walked up to the counter with Jacob's presents, something we both knew he didn't want, but we didn't care. As long as we got to play with those toys at his party, it would all be worth it.

On the day of Jacob's party, Craig and I showed up with the rest of the kids from class and did the usual party things. We played games, ate pizza, had birthday cake, and then it was time for the best part of all: opening the presents.

Now, Craig and I knew there would be some slight awkwardness around this time, but we were ready for it. After all, we figured we couldn't have been the only people to deviate from Jacob's ultra-specific list, but as present after present was opened, and Jacob shrieked with joy each time he held in his hands the exact toy he had asked for from each person, Craig and I began to get a little uncomfortable. Maybe we had underestimated just how much Jacob liked Star Trek. After all, the whole party had been Star Trek themed. Jacob was wearing the Spock ears he got from his parents, the Star Trek shirt he got from his grandma, and we could clearly see the Star Trek phaser he got from his uncle sitting in the corner of the room. On top of that, the plates, napkins, and cups had all been Star Trek themed; even the cake had the Star Ship Enterprise painted on with icing. But it was too late to do anything about it now.

With all the other presents unwrapped and Jacob's birthday wishes nearly fulfilled, it was down to the last two presents: ours. As Jacob took my present in his hands, he held it with a skeptical curiosity. It certainly wasn't the shape of the others. He turned my present over and shook it, trying to determine just how far off the mark I had landed. He then held it up to his ultra-sensitive Vulcan ear, listening. I don't know what he was looking for, but the more he handled that present, the more I saw his forehead start to wrinkle and the doubt begin to build in his mind. He lowered it towards the floor, his lips pouting upwards in a quizzical fashion, and very slowly, in very non-kid like fashion, began to peel back the wrapping paper. He could already tell that his birthday dreams weren't going to be realized, and I think he was trying to delay that crushing disappointment for as long as he could while attempting not to look completely ungrateful for the unwanted gift he was now opening.

You would think he was unzipping a body bag to make a positive identification of a loved one the way he peeled back the wrapping paper ever so slightly just to get a peek at the disappointment that lay beneath. When he had finally unwrapped it enough to see what it was, his reaction would have made you think I had put a shrunken head in there or something.

"No!!!" he screamed. "This isn't what I asked for!!!"

He threw the present to the floor, sending it careening across the carpet and into the wall. Then he grabbed Craig's gift and ferociously unwrapped it, only to be wounded a second time, this time deeper than the first, as he realized that his Star Trek crew would not be down just one important bridge officer, but two.

As I sat there watching Jacob throw a fit and then burst into tears and begin to sob, I couldn't help but feel like the world's biggest jerk. I had known exactly what he wanted, the precise thing that would have made him happy, but had selfishly chosen my own happiness over his. All the other kids sitting in the living room stared at me accusingly, knowing full well why I had bought him the Exo Squad toy instead of the Star Trek figure he had asked for. I tried to feign innocence, but what I said next didn't help my cause.

"Open it; let's play with it."

Jacob had managed to get his sobbing under control by that time, one Spock ear slightly askew, and as he looked up at me with those tear-streaked, reddened cheeks, he said four words that let me know he understood exactly what I had done, and that he wouldn't play my game.

"I'll open it later."

That was kid code for, "Screw you, buddy." I had played my hand, and so had Jacob. If he couldn't play with the toy he wanted to on his birthday, there was no way in hell he was going to let me do it, either. Touché.

Although that moment was incredibly awkward, fortunately, it didn't last long. While Craig and I sat in the corner with the unopened Exo Squad toys, Jacob set his new figures up in various poses and began making them talk to each other about things none of the rest of us knew about, since he was the only Star Trek fan there. By that time, the party was winding down, and parents had started to arrive to pick up their kids. As I took my goodie bag and left Jacob to play with his nearly complete Star Trek collection, I reflected on the day's events. Although it was only birthday presents and toys we were dealing with, that day had taught me that being selfish and putting my desires above those of others didn't always pay off. I saw how giving selflessly was a source of true happiness for all, while being selfish, and even deceitful, never worked out for anyone. I saw how appreciative Jacob was to those who had given him what he had truly wanted, and how those giving him the gifts looked almost as happy as Jacob did to be receiving them. I also saw how crushed Jacob was when I had done something so obviously selfish, and felt a deep sense of shame and regret as I realized that I had been the one to spoil Jacob's birthday. Well, it was Craig's fault too, let's be fair.

It was a valuable lesson that I learned at a young age, and I'm sure I'm not the only person who experienced something like this. For many of us, such an event was our first experience with the golden rule: "Treat others as you would like to be treated, and they'll do the same to you." In our case though, it was "Give your friend the toy they asked for, and they'll do the same for you." Either way, it was an important lesson, one we should still be applying to our lives today, except probably not with toys anymore.

And Jacob, if I ever get invited to one of your birthday parties again, I promise to get you exactly what you ask for. Also, do you still have those Exo Squad toys kicking around? I would love to give those a whirl.

You Faked Sick

Faking sick is probably one of the only things you did in childhood that you still regularly do today. The only difference is that now you fake sick with your boss so you don't have to go to work, but when you were a kid you faked sick with your parents so you didn't have to go to school. The end result is still the same though: getting a day off from somewhere you don't want to be and having an excuse to lie on the couch and watch TV all day.

Like today, you likely faked sick when you were a kid more than you were actually sick. It was probably one of the first deceitful things you began to do on a regular basis, but if it meant that you didn't have to go to school, being deceptive every once in a while was just fine. Most kids had an arsenal of vague, easily faked, yet hard to identify symptoms that they suffered from every time they wanted to stay home from school, and each individual had a certain routine they liked to follow to try to fool their parents.

Personally, I was a big proponent of starting to fake my symptoms the night before so that I would have something to build on in the morning and wouldn't be starting from scratch. Before I went to bed, I'd start complaining about some ailments my mom couldn't simply rule out with a thermometer: a headache, a stomachache, dizziness, a general sense of just not feeling well. I would start this routine about an hour or two before bed and lie on the couch not moving very much, looking incredibly lame and pulling out the "sick voice" that always accompanied these Oscar winning performances. I'm certain that every time I did this, my mom knew exactly what I was doing, and as time went on, less and less sympathy came my way, but that wasn't about to stop me from giving it my best. After all, it was either act sick and put on a phony voice for a few hours and get to stay home, or go to school and do math. Obviously, the choice was easy.

When I really needed to go the extra mile to convince my mom I was ill, I employed what I thought was the smartest move in kid history. I would head into the bathroom and lock the door, then empty the laundry bucket. Then, I'd fill it with water, and once it was about a quarter full, I'd shut off the tap, wait a minute, and then begin to make puking noises. As I was doing that, I would pour the water from the bucket into the toilet to make it sound like I was throwing up. In my mind it was a brilliant maneuver, but to my mom, my deception was as transparent as cellophane. That's because she could hear me running the bathtub and filling up the laundry bucket prior to me pretending to throw up, but that was something that never occurred to me back then. Unfortunately, this trick didn't once fool my mom, but that didn't mean that I stopped doing it every time I needed to pull out the big guns. It was the grand finale of my performance, the ace up my sleeve. I was certain that if she wouldn't buy the headache, stomachache, dizziness, and the general just not feeling well, she'd have to be duped by the fake throwing up routine, but she never was.

To her credit, she let me stay home enough times that I had complete faith in my acting ability. Even though I knew deep down that she didn't believe me, I figured my performances must have been good enough to create a shred of uncertainty in her mind, just enough to give me the benefit of the doubt, and that was good enough for me. And every day when I was curled up on the couch watching cartoons while my brothers were slaving away in school, all that effort was worth it.

Until someone brought me a homework package.

You Stayed Home From School Because You Were Actually Sick

Sometimes, getting to stay home because you were actually sick was better than when you were faking it. That's because when you were actually sick, your parents doted on you hand and foot, unlike when they knew you were faking it and gave you the cold shoulder so as not to encourage that kind of behaviour in the future. When you really were sick, your parents pulled out all the stops: pudding, chicken noodle soup, tea, hot chocolate, movies, video games, hot water bottles, the steamer, anything you wanted. It was like being at a five-star resort, and your parents were the amazingly attentive hotel staff you never had to tip.

Most of the time, actually being sick was awesome. In fact, it was one of the great pleasures of being a kid. Never in your life did your parents give you so much care and attention, especially your mom, and the sicker you were, the better they treated you. Not only did you get to watch cartoons all morning and miss school, you could lie on the couch all day and wait for them to come back on again at three, and no one said a word about it. There was no way you could get away with that under normal circumstances.

The only part about being sick that wasn't fun was when cartoons ended and adult TV came on. After *The Price Is Right*, which was like the transition point between kids shows and adults shows, it was all downhill. I remember thinking how boring adults' lives must have been based on the types of shows that were on during the day: *People's Court*; *Days of Our Lives*; the news. I always assumed my mom watched TV all day when we were at school and my dad was working, but she told me that wasn't the case. After seeing how boring daytime TV was, I started to think that maybe she was telling the truth.

That time between 11am and 3pm was the hardest part of the day. There was nothing good on TV, and you had no choice but to lie on the couch and wallow in misery. I don't know about you, but trying to make it through that awful cartoon drought made me feel like a dying man crawling through the desert. I knew that there was an end to it, I just didn't know if I'd make it there alive.

On the other hand, there was nothing better than falling asleep on the couch sometime after lunch and waking up just before 3 o'clock. You had missed the worst part of the day, cartoons would be coming on shortly, and if you had siblings, they would be home soon so that you could enjoy their company, or rub it in their faces that they'd had to go to school while you lay on the couch and ate pudding all day. Of course, this is where karma could get nasty, because even though you had been lying in the lap of luxury and watching cartoons while they had slaved away at school, now the situation might be reversed because of the same thing that ruined your sick days when you were faking it: the dreaded homework package.

You Chose Friends Based On Their Toys

Little kids are the most materialistic people on earth. If you don't believe me, just remember back to the days when you chose your friends based on the toys they had. After all, whenever you heard that someone had a new video game or toy that you wanted to play with, didn't you suddenly decide that person should be your friend and immediately schedule a play date with them? I know I did, and like everything else we've talked about, I know I'm not the only one.

Although you had decided to reach out and make a new acquaintance, your motivations were questionable. You didn't care about spending quality time with them, and you probably didn't even like them that much. In fact, if you'd had it your way, they wouldn't have even been there when you went to their house. You would've preferred to simply go there, play with their toys, and then leave without cleaning up, but you couldn't, so you pretended to like them instead.

Deep down, you knew what you were doing was wrong. You were using them for what they had and your interest was purely materialistic, but the reward was worth the price. There was an element of guilt associated with what you were doing though, and you realized that your selfish actions might hurt their feelings if they discovered your true intentions, but that didn't stop you. After all, if you weren't going to take advantage of them for selfish reasons, some other kid would, so it might as well be you. Like Johan Bruyneel said to Lance Armstrong regarding the Tour de France, "[You] might as well win."

Sometimes, even if the person you were taking advantage of knew you were only interested in them for their toys, they didn't care because they loved them just as much as you did, and now they had the opportunity to play with them with someone else. This usually happened when someone had a whole collection of cool toys, like Batman, Ninja Turtles, or Transformers. I'm sure you could include Barbie in that list, though I don't know for certain, since my only experience with them was limited to making Barbie and Ken lie on top of each other and have sex in her bed (was it just me who did that, or was that normal?). Anyways, sometimes the person you were taking advantage of had so many toys that it was actually better having two people to play with them, because now the good guys could fight the bad guys, characters with working guns could shoot each other, and action figures with movable limbs could kick and punch each other to your hearts' content, or until their limbs snapped off.

In rare circumstances, using someone for their toys actually turned into real friendship, and in those cases you were doubly blessed. Not only had you made a new friend, your new friend also had the coolest toys; it was like winning the lottery twice. However, because you didn't want to have to share those toys with anyone else, you made sure not to tell anyone at school just how cool your new friend actually was. For your sake, it was better for your friend's social status to stay low. In fact, you might have even spread a little dirt about them, just to keep other kids from coming over to their house and getting in on the fun.

While friendships sometimes formed as a result of your selfish materialism, other times you realized that you had nothing in common with the person you were taking advantage of and that it was wrong to keep using them for their possessions. Whether or not this made you stop hanging out with them was a different story though. Depending on how awesome their toys were, you may have been willing to put aside your morals for an entire school year, or at least until Christmas or your birthday, when you could get those same toys for your very own.

Whether true friendship formed or you realized you were stooping to a level you never expected of yourself, you always learned something from those situations. Either you learned that you should look past material possessions when deciding whether to be friends with someone, or that there was something immoral about using people for their belongings, and it was something you shouldn't do. It would probably take you awhile to apply the latter lesson, but eventually, using people for material gain became something that most of us outgrew. I say most of us, because when you look around, it's clear that some people never stopped exhibiting that kind of behaviour. If you want proof, just look at the hot blonde hanging out with the overweight rich guy who's 20 years older than her and driving a cool sports car, or the cheerleader who dumped the high school football captain and married the nerdy computer programmer for his money. But hey, you never hear those guys complaining, so everybody wins.

You Felt You Were Getting Old

There was a time in your life when you felt that celebrating your next birthday would practically qualify you for a senior's discount and place you mere inches from your deathbed, and that was just before you turned 10.

Do you remember the mental and emotional turmoil you experienced in the days leading up to your tenth birthday? You were about to stop being a kid, and there was nothing you could do about it. To make matters worse, all the adults in your life emphasized how old you were getting, just to drive the point home even further.

"Double digits!" they'd say. "You're not a kid anymore," as if you needed reminding. "Pretty soon you'll be too big to go on the playground!"

What horrible news. As if you weren't suffering enough with your own worries, adults were now compounding that misery with affirmations that you were indeed getting old, and for some reason, took it upon themselves to begin listing off all the wonderful things you wouldn't be able to do anymore: no more going in the play place at McDonalds; no Ball Room at Ikea or Chucky Cheese, no more kiddie rides at the fair; pretty soon, you'd even be too old to go trick or treating

– talk about a world you didn't want to live in! Your life was falling to pieces, and you were powerless to do anything about it.

Turning 10 was your first milestone birthday, and the first time you entered a new decade of your life. At the time, it was scary. You felt like you were about to leave your childhood behind and enter a phase of life you weren't at all prepared for: junior high, high school, girlfriends, boyfriends, dating, things you knew nothing about but would soon be thrust into the middle of.

The bittersweet part about how you felt back then was that you were right. Once you hit those double digits, puberty wasn't far behind – well, for most of us – and pretty soon, your world would change completely. Sleepovers wouldn't be about toys and pajamas anymore, they'd be about Playboys and porno cards, or talking about who you had a crush on. You'd start to question your undying faith in Santa, the last of the ill-fitting religious holiday figures, and you'd even start to tell yourself that maybe you should start cutting back on the candy, since you knew it wasn't good for you. You spent a great deal of time fretting about what was about to happen, and in the end, it turned out like it always did: the things you feared so much came and went, and nothing really changed. Well, not overnight at least.

Over time, so slowly and gradually that you didn't even notice, you did start to change, but not in the way you thought you would. Little by little, you stopped using your imagination the way you did before, and suddenly you found yourself walking most of the time instead of running everywhere at top speed. You found yourself trading the imaginary world for the material, and you almost never played with sticks anymore, unless you were pestering a sibling.

Those changes were so slow to take hold that you didn't even notice they were happening, the way you sometimes don't notice that the leaves have changed colour until they've fallen from the trees. It wasn't until you looked back and saw the metaphorical leaves on the ground that you went, "Things are different now."

Yes, things are different now, and they'll continue to change for as long as you live, but so long as you can look at all the beauty that the world has to offer, life can still be as wonderful as it was when you were a child and in love with the magic of the world. And anytime a birthday is around the corner and you feel that you're getting too old, just remember that you've felt like that every single year since you turned 10, and life turned out alright, didn't it?

You Rented a Game System

As a kid, nothing made a weekend more exciting than renting a game system. The anticipation was incredible, and it was all you could think about in the days leading up to it.

Renting a game system always followed a predictable cycle. Friday afternoon was filled with excitement and anticipation, and when you actually got the system, the rest of the day was sheer bliss. You spent the entire afternoon playing on that system that was infinitely superior to the one you actually owned, and you and your friend, or your siblings, or whoever you were playing with, were having the time of your lives. You played into the small hours of the morning and happily went to sleep knowing that system would be waiting for you when you woke up.

Saturday morning was awesome, because you woke up and immediately started playing video games again. You spent the morning working your way through the game and were still having a blast. By Saturday afternoon though, you were starting to get stressed out because you couldn't beat a certain level, and you had been playing for six straight hours.

It was usually around that point that your friend had to go home, and your parents started telling you that you needed to take a break and get out of the house, which you were eventually forced to do. When that happened, you spent the entire time thinking about how you could beat that level, and as soon as your parents let you come back inside, you started playing the game again with a renewed determination and ferocity.

By Saturday night, you were aggravated beyond belief that you were still stuck in that same spot, and at that point, video games were no longer about having fun – they were about beating that damn level, even if it meant staying up all night, which you did.

By Sunday morning, you hated video games. There was nothing enjoyable about them anymore. They were just stressful, and you were actually looking forward to returning the system to the store because it had completely taken over your life. You barely went outside, you hardly slept, and you interacted with other humans as little as possible, unless they were playing video games with you. Instead, you just sat on the floor two feet from the TV for hours on end, and that had turned you into a raging lunatic. The only people who were looking forward to getting rid of that game system more than you were your parents, because they had to deal with the monster you had become as a result of it.

The moment your parents told you it was time to pack up the system and return it to the store was a moment of deliverance for you. Finally, you could return to normalcy and begin functioning as a human being again, but it wasn't easy. You were physically and emotionally exhausted from playing video games all weekend and getting little to no sleep. On top of that, you still had to do your chores and the homework you had put off in order to play those video games, and the thought of school the next day was already weighing heavily on your mind. At that moment, life sucked, and it was all because of video games. You swore you would never rent a game system again, or at the very least, would regulate yourself better the next time. You knew you were lying to yourself, but it still made you feel better to pretend you had learned your lesson, even though deep down, you knew you wouldn't change a thing.

Despite the inevitable stress that came with it, renting a game system was one of the best things you could do back then. No matter how old I get, I'll always remember how wonderful it was to share those times with friends and family. I'll also remember how I couldn't beat *Jurassic Park* for Sega Genesis no matter how many times I rented it, but it still made for some of the best memories of my childhood...even if I did get eaten by a dinosaur.

Your Parents Walked In Front of The TV During Video Games

Speaking of video games, wasn't this the most annoying thing in the world? Now, as I mentioned already, your parents didn't understand how important video games were to you. If you were like a lot of kids, boys especially, your life revolved around video games, while your parents' lives centered around trying to raise a family and keep food on the table. They didn't have time to think about video games, let alone play them. This meant that when it came to priorities, there was a massive divergence between you. That disconnect was the source of many quarrels, but there was no greater conflict than when they walked in front of the TV at a critical moment in a video game.

The worst part about that was that they always picked the most awful time to do it, like when you were fighting a boss or trying to land on some slippery little platform that required the dexterity of a brain surgeon to pull off, and it always happened the same way. You'd be sitting on the floor, two feet from the TV, entirely focused on your game. You were one with your game, and the outside world didn't exist, until your mom walked in front of the TV and started vacuuming and you lost your mind.

"MOM!!!!!!!!!"

"What? What's wrong!?"

"YOU WALKED IN FRONT OF THE TV!!!!!!"

And then your mom just stood there and stared at you, totally confused as to why that was a problem. That made it even worse, because she wasn't moving and she was continuing to block your view, so you freaked out even more.

"GET OUT OF THE WAY! I'M GOING TO DIE! I'M GOING TO...AUGH! I DIED!!"

At that moment, your mom wished she'd never had children, and not for the first time. I don't know how parents deal with that kind of stuff. Their child, who they're giving their lives for, is screaming at them because they're trying to clean the house and they stood in front of the TV for less than five seconds, and suddenly, it's the end of the world. If it was socially acceptable, that might have been one of those times your parents would have driven you out to the middle of nowhere and left you there. If you made it back home, it was meant to be and all would be forgiven, but if you never came back, that's the way it was supposed to go, and they'd be fine with that. Of course, your parents weren't allowed to do that, so instead, they just had to accept the fact that their child was a complete lunatic and tell them that if they want to vacuum the house themselves, they were more than welcome to, but if not, they'd better pause their game for 10 seconds while the vacuuming was being done.

Faced with the prospect of briefly pausing your game or doing house chores, you always chose the first option, but not without a whole lot of hateful thoughts directed at your parents. You felt that having to put your game on hold so they could do parent stuff was a total inconvenience, and deep down, you felt that your parents had no manners or respect. The funny thing is that your parents felt the same way about you, and in this case, they were right. After pausing your game for what felt like an eternity, even though it was really only 10 seconds, you got right back to playing your game and carried on with your carefree day, while your parents continued cleaning and doing countless other things to keep you alive, so that you could continue to be totally unappreciative and freak out at them for the simplest things, like walking in front of the TV while you were playing video games. Who said parenting isn't rewarding?

You Had Sleepovers

Sleepovers were a quintessential part of childhood. They are likely the source of some of your most cherished memories, something you can look back on and remember with sincere fondness. Of course, I'm talking about the kind of sleepovers you had when you were a kid, when all the fun was innocent and childish, not the kind you had when you were older and you got too drunk to go home, or someone passed out on your floor. You probably had fun at those sleepovers too, but it was a different kind of fun, and they were a lot less magical too. When you were a kid though, there was nothing more fun than a sleepover.

When you were little and first started having sleepovers, they had a lot of parental involvement. All you had to do was convince your parents to let you have a sleepover, and they did the rest. They phoned your friend's parents, arranged a drop off and pick up time, took you there, made sure you had everything you needed, and off they went, leaving you in the capable hands of your friend's parents. If you were lucky, you would be invited for dinner, and that usually meant pizza or hamburgers and some kind of awesome dessert. After that, you and your friend got to watch your favourite movie, or head to the video store to rent one. During the movie, you ate popcorn, drank pop, and played with each other's toys, since you'd brought some of your own. After that, you put on your pajamas and went to sleep in your friend's room. The next morning, you woke up bright and early, possibly to a pancake breakfast, and immediately picked up from where you had left off, playing with each other's toys or heading outside to romp around the yard and play with the neighbourhood kids. Sometime later, your parents would pick you up, remind you to say thank you to your friend's parents, and whisk you back to your house, where your wonderful, carefree day continued.

Those sleepovers were great, but they were nothing compared to the ones you had when you got a little older. Those sleepovers were where the real memories were born. Once you reached the age of about 10 or so, you developed a newfound sense of independence, which permeated into your sleepovers. While you had relied on your parents to do all the legwork when you were younger, now you were the one calling the shots and arranging all the details. The only thing you needed from your parents was permission, which didn't always come as easily as you wanted it to, but if you twisted their arm and made enough promises you both knew you'd never keep, you could usually talk them into it, despite them knowing you would be a total grouch the next day.

After you had arranged the sleepover with your friend and cleared it with both your parents, you headed to their house and looked forward to an awesome night. Many elements of those sleepovers were similar to the ones you had when you were younger. For example, you typically got invited for dinner, which still usually involved pizza or hamburgers. You also frequently rented a movie and watched it together, and depending on your age, you may still have played with each other's toys (I'm thinking Star Wars, Nerf, or Starcom here). Besides those factors, however, these sleepovers were quite different from the ones you had when you were younger, and that's because of what came after.

The main difference was that now, you really didn't do much sleeping. You and your friend stayed awake long after everyone else had gone to bed, and that probably had something to do with the two-liter pop you had been drinking, or the fact that your night centered around playing video games with the intention of beating whatever game you were playing, which meant you often played until the sun came up. Yes, there was no better time to beat a video game start to finish than at a sleepover with your friend, and many Nintendo, Super Nintendo, Sega, and PlayStation classics were beat on such nights. *Streets of Rage* or *Double Dragon*, anyone?

Now, this next section probably only applies to the males reading this, but besides pizza, movies, video games and pop, there was one other essential element that made for a classic sleepover, and that was nudie magazines. For most of us, this meant something classy and elegant, like a Playboy, the next step after the Sears catalogue. By our early teens, most of us had managed to get our hands on our very own Playboy, and we had various means of obtaining them. Maybe you stole one from your older brother or your dad, or raided the big kids' fort in the woods where they kept a bounty of such sophisticated literature. If you were like me, you found the Chinese corner store where they sold nudie magazines to kids, and you daringly purchased your own, feeling a mix of pride and shame as you did. No matter where or how you got them though, having a Playboy or some other brand of adult magazine always made for the best sleepovers. It added an element of excitement that you couldn't get with anything else, and usually you and your friend each had a magazine of your own and you could trade. As an adult, you would never want to hang out in a sleeping bag with your friend next to you as you both looked at porno magazines, but back then it was par for the course.

Despite the allure of those magazines and the excitement of seeing a naked woman in something other than a National Geographic, they couldn't hold your attention like video games. That's why the Playboy part of your sleepover only lasted 45 minutes or so, and before long you and your friend were back to trying to beat the game you rented. In fact, video games were almost always the bookends of your sleepovers. There was something so addicting about them, and you knew that two minds, or really, two sets of hands and two player co-op, had a much better chance of beating a game than you did on your own, and that's why you literally stayed up until the crack of dawn playing them. That, and the fact that the game was usually a rental and had to be back at the store the next day, so you wanted to get your money's worth.

After a night like that, where you may have literally stayed up until the sun was peeking over the horizon, you were a total write-off for the rest of the weekend. You were grouchy, crabby, and exhausted, just as your parents had forewarned, but it was worth it. You'd had an amazing night with one of your best friends and enjoyed every minute of the time you shared, and though you didn't know it at the time, had created memories that would last a lifetime. Heck, maybe you even beat the game you were playing.

The time in your life when you had sleepovers was a wonderful part of childhood you can never recapture because you've changed too much and come too far from where you were. At least you can look back on those times with fond memories though, and remember all the fun and excitement you used to have doing something as simple as spending a night with your friend, sharing the things you loved, and laughing the night away. To my friends who shared those experiences with me and gave me so many wonderful memories to look back on, thank you. Oh, and Craig...do you still have my Playboy?

TVs Were Normal Size

Twenty years ago, the terms "big screen TV" and "smart TV" didn't exist. There was only one type of TV: it was called a TV. Yes, there were different sizes, but for the most part, a TV was just a TV.

Today, that's not the case. Now, our TVs don't just play shows and movies, they also play music, go on the Internet, record shows when we're not around, and even program themselves. If you believe conspiracy theorists, our Smart TVs are even spying on us! Talk about a technological revolution, where the things we used to watch are now watching us. It's *1984* all over again.

TVs have come a long way, but perhaps the greatest change is in their size. TVs today are monstrous. They are bigger than some people. Currently sitting in my living room is an 80-inch TV. It's bigger than anything I could have imagined as a child. In fact, it is bigger than most children. It's even bigger than most adults. At it greatest measurement, it is six feet, six inches across. That means I have the equivalent of an NBA basketball player mounted to my wall, so that I can watch NBA basketball. Isn't that ironic?

If someone had told you as a kid that one day TVs would be bigger than people, you wouldn't have believed them. That's because when you were younger, TVs just didn't come that big. If you wanted to clearly see what was going on in a video game or your favorite show, you had to sit right in front of the TV because of its small screen size. Today, you never sit mere inches from the TV, because you don't have to. If you did, your view would be worse, because you wouldn't be able to see the whole screen. You'd just see one tiny little section, and you'd be forced to move back to a viewing distance that your grandparents, who always warned you not to sit too close, would be proud of.

The ironic part about TVs getting bigger is that people's homes are getting smaller, so there's a real mismatch happening. Previously, I had a TV that was 51 inches. That TV was over four feet in diameter, in a room that was only eight feet wide. That means my TV was literally half the size of my living room, but that's normal nowadays. In fact, it's almost rare to walk into someone's house and see a TV under 40 inches. If you do, you look at it and go, "What's wrong with your TV? I can barely see it."

Back in the day, it just wasn't so. TVs were a normal size, and the only times they stood out was if they were giant, which you only saw if you went to a rich person's house, or very tiny, which was much more the norm. If this trend of increasingly gargantuan TVs continues into the future, your current big screen will seem laughable in comparison, much like the TVs that you grew up with are now. One or two generations from now, your great grandchildren will wonder how you ever got by with so little as they watch TV on screens the size of houses. Of course, if the trend towards smaller houses also continues, they won't be able to fit those TVs in their homes anymore, so I'd say you're better off today than they'll be in the future. I guess it's a happy medium.

Your Chores Felt Like Slave Labour

Your parents cooked, cleaned, paid bills, went to work, cleaned the house, mowed the lawn, washed the car, did your laundry, ironed your clothes, helped you with homework, drove you to sports, threw you birthday parties, bought you presents, taught you how to ride a bike, fed you, clothed you, bathed you, and if they asked you to take the garbage out, you thought it was slave labour.

Every time your parents asked you to do something, your response was always, "What am I? Your slave?" as you sat there watching them make lunch for you, demanding that they cut the crusts off your sandwich and cut it into triangles, because you wouldn't eat it otherwise. The hypocrisy of those moments must have been astounding to your parents, but you felt completely justified in your stance. After all, you hadn't asked to be born, and if they didn't want to clean up after you, maybe they shouldn't have had kids.

Of course, the only reason you thought that way was because you were impossibly selfish back then, and had no idea just how much your parents did for you. That's because they worked so hard to make your life run like a well-oiled machine, and you never heard them complaining about it. Meals were made, bills were paid, and a roof was kept over your head, while you remained completely oblivious to the incredible sacrifices your parents made on a daily basis to make it so. You had no idea how hard they worked to keep you alive, and as a result, you didn't appreciate anything about it.

In fact, it wasn't until you became an adult and had to start doing everything on your own before you came close to realizing just how much they did for you back then, but by that time, it was too late. You couldn't go back and make up for what a selfish, rotten kid you were, and you couldn't take back all the mean things you thought about them either.

In life, you can never go back; only forward. And for your parents, you better believe that there's a great deal of satisfaction in knowing that. That's because they know that one day, if it hasn't happened already, you'll have kids of your own, and they'll pay you back for every ounce of bad attitude you gave your parents when you were young. So at the end of another exhausting day, when you barely have the strength to open your eyes and you ask one of your children to help clear the table, they can look up from their delicious home made meal, which they didn't lift a finger to help prepare, look you square in the eyes, and go, "What am I? Your slave?"

You Got Mad When Your Parents Bought Neapolitan

As a kid, nothing made you happier than when your parents told you they'd bought ice cream. And if you were like me, nothing made you angrier than when they told you it was Neapolitan. In my family, every time my parents came home with that flavour, this is how the conversation went:

Parents: We got ice cream!
Me: Yeah! What kind?
Parents: Neapolitan!
Me: Why!!?!

I hated Neapolitan, and with good reason. That's because it was the best flavor, chocolate, mixed with the two worst flavors, strawberry and vanilla. It wasn't just me who felt that way; hating Neapolitan was an almost universal phenomenon among children, because it always felt like a rip off. If you don't believe me, think back to what every bucket of Neapolitan ice cream looked like after a week in your freezer, and you'll remember a consistent trend. The chocolate was completely gone, while the vanilla and the strawberry remained virtually untouched. Once the chocolate had been devoured, that derelict bucket of ice cream sat in the freezer for months, until the last two flavors were covered in frost and someone had to finally choke them down or throw the bucket away in hopes of getting a better flavour the next time around.

Since my parents did the grocery shopping, they usually picked the flavours. Every time they were left to their own devices, they always bought Neapolitan, even though they knew we hated it, and my dad's reasoning was always the same.

"I like strawberry!"

Every time he said that, I always thought the same thing.

"Then buy strawberry! You've got a job, you can afford it! Buy a small container of strawberry for yourself, and a big tub of chocolate for the rest of us normal people!"

The thing that always drove me over the edge was when I caught my dad, the self-proclaimed strawberry lover, eating the chocolate. I would actually challenge him on it, because I thought his behaviour was totally out of line. I'd come home to find him eating a big bowl of that precious chocolate ice cream, and I'd lay into him like a parent who had just caught their kid smoking pot.

"Hey! What are you doing putting that in your mouth! Put that spoon down right now, mister!"

At that point, my dad would just stare at me as he enjoyed his well-deserved ice cream, take another bite, and hit me back with the most logical but infuriating response he could.

"I paid for it."

He was right, and I knew it, but still, it irked me to no end. If he loved chocolate so much, why didn't he just buy chocolate? Despite my formal protests, he wasn't about to let anyone, least of all his spoiled children, tell him how to eat. In fact, I'm sure he took some degree of pleasure in those exchanges. It was one subtle way he could get back at my brothers and I for all the hell we regularly put him through as a parent, and deep down, I think he loved getting caught eating "our" ice cream.

I think the real reason my parents always bought Neapolitan was because they knew it was the only way that ice cream would last for more than a week in our house. Once the chocolate was gone, my brothers and I wouldn't touch it, and that gave my parents the ability to do something they never could with greedy children at home: eat delicious desserts at their own pace, rather than having to gorge themselves in a frantic effort to get some before it was gone. I know my parents weren't the only ones who employed that tactic, and I have to hand it to them: it was a brilliant maneuver.

Neapolitan ice cream was a source of controversy in my family for years, and there's a good chance you faced similar tribulations in your own family. Whether those problems were related to ice cream flavours, cereal, or the type of soft drinks your parents bought, grocery day could be a great blessing, or a terrible curse. Of course, back then, most of us were too young and spoiled to simply appreciate the fact that we had groceries in the first place, so making a big deal out of nothing was par for the course.

Getting the wrong ice cream flavour seemed like a colossal problem when we were kids, but in retrospect, it was nothing. It was but a mosquito bite on the spectrum of life's problems, but we treated it like a mortal wound. Isn't life often like that, though? The things we think are monumental issues in the moment become laughable with the passing of time, and the gifts of hindsight and contemplation make life's little complications seem ridiculous in retrospect. Learning to laugh at our struggles and look at old problems with new perspectives is a wonderful gift, and a sure sign of the acquisition of both wisdom and maturity. And just think, it all started with ice cream.

Chicken McNuggets Were Purple and Grey

There was a time in your life when chicken McNuggets were purple and grey, but you never noticed. You know why? Because that's what chicken McNuggets looked like, and they were delicious, so nobody complained. Sure, you'd heard all kinds of horror stories, like they were made by throwing whole chickens into a blender and scooping out the gooey remains, or that people sometimes found beaks and feet in them, but none of that mattered to you. You loved the way they tasted, and all you cared about was getting your BBQ sauce or your little packet of honey that came with your Happy Meal and enjoying your McNuggets, and life was good.

Then one day, McDonalds did something that made you question what exactly you were eating when you were mowing down those delicious McNuggets. They came out with an ad campaign advertising all white meat McNuggets, and suddenly everyone went, "It's already white, isn't it?"

After that, people started looking at their McNuggets carefully between bites, and examining the texture and the colours, and all of a sudden, they realized that those McNuggets they'd been eating for so long hadn't actually been white, as they'd assumed. Instead, they were a purple and greyish colour, and that kind of put a damper on McNuggets for a lot of people. I know it did for me.

The all white meat campaign was a terrible idea for McDonalds. The world used to love McNuggets, despite the revolting rumours. If McDonalds had never drawn attention to the unholy colour of the meat inside its McNuggets, no one would have noticed, and more of us would still be eating them today. That's one example where honesty in advertising wound up hurting the company, but I'm sure McDonalds has learned from its mistake and will never tell the truth about its products again. Does that mean we'll never get a solid answer to the potato milkshake theory?

Political Correctness Wasn't a Thing

I hate political correctness. I'm afraid to say anything nowadays, for fear of insulting some minority group that I didn't even know existed. Political correctness has made it hard to even have a conversation with someone today. You can't use terms that everyone knows, and you always have to pause a conversation to try to think of the most up to date word for any group who has a different skin colour than yours.

For example, you're not supposed to call black people black anymore. They are African American, or African Canadian, or African whatever, despite the fact that 99% of the black people in the Western world have probably never been to Africa, and will never go. Indian people are now called South Asians, as well. South Asians? I assumed South Asians would be people from South Korea, or southern Japan or China. Political correctness makes everything so confusing. If people from India are called South Asians, then what are Chinese people called? Orientals? That's probably the wrong term too, but I just don't know what's right anymore. Back in the day, political correctness wasn't a thing, and it made life so much easier.

Take my grandpa's generation, for example. Their conversations were really efficient, because they didn't spend time thinking of the most up to date term for a group of people who weren't even around to hear them talking, much less get offended by their dialogue. While not always accurate, their exchanges were effective, and everyone always knew exactly who the other person was talking about. A Native American was an Indian. A guy with a turban was a Hindu. A Chinese person was a Chinaman, and so on and so on. They had one term for each race, and while not always precise or flattering, it really sped things up. The best part about it was that everyone was fine with it, and no one got offended because they felt like they were supposed to. I admire that, and I'd love to be able to go back to those times, if only for simplicity's sake.

Frankly, I think we've gone too far in the wrong direction with political correctness, and we should all just agree that we won't be upset by whatever term we're called, as long as it's not blatantly insulting or offensive. I'll be a white guy, you be a black guy, you be an Indian, you be Chinese, you be whatever the heck you want, and we'll all be a whole lot happier. It'll make life so much easier, and in the end, isn't that what we're all striving for anyways?

You Broke Your Parents' Mold

For a brief period in your life, your parents were the model for everything you did. You wore the same clothes as them, you listened to the same music as them, you had the same haircut as them, and so on and so on. You were basically a mini version of your parents, inside and out. Then one day, it all changed.

For each of us, the moment that inspired us to break away from the molds our parents were creating for us came at a different time and for a different reason. For some, it might have had something to do with the first time they saw their parents in a spandex one piece gearing up to go for a bike ride or a run. For others, it was the time the kids at school made fun of them for listening to Phil Collins or Cream. Or, maybe it was the time they wore black dress shoes with shorts, because their dad did, and then looked around at all the other kids who were wearing runners and thought to themselves, "I'm different."

The moment you realized that not everything your parents did was cool and that you shouldn't completely mold yourself in their image was life changing. It marked the beginning of you creating your own unique persona in the world, which if you were like most people, was one that aimed to look the complete opposite of your parents.

Once you abandoned your parents as your personal branding agents, you had to turn to others for guidance. So who did you look to for inspiration? The coolest people you knew: your peers. Almost overnight, your life and your look changed dramatically. You started getting mushroom cuts, wearing "No Fear" T-shirts, and wearing clothes that were ten sizes too big. You had found your look, and you'd set yourself apart from the rest of the world by looking exactly like everyone else your age. Yes, you'd finally become unique, and it was empowering.

In your own mind, you thought you were awesome. Your parents, however, in their spandex running suits and high-waisted mom jeans, thought you looked ridiculous, but the feeling was mutual. It was probably the first time in your life that you experienced a generation gap, and you experienced it on a quantum scale. This departure from your parents' tastes and styles usually happened around the age of nine or ten, and by twelve, you wanted to be as different from them as possible. This was also around the time you started walking ten feet in front of them in public, as you didn't want to be seen with them because you thought they were embarrassing. They probably felt the same about you, but, being the mature and understanding parents they were, they never said a word. They let you get your stupid haircuts and wear the exact same clothes as everyone else, because they wanted to let you make your mistakes and learn from them.

Like most things in life, you probably learned that lesson after it was too late to do anything about it, as that moment likely came when you looked back at your high school yearbook photos from the previous year and went, "I thought that was cool? What was I thinking?" Unfortunately, you seemed to repeat that process every year, didn't you?

That's the funny thing about life. No matter what you're doing or what you're wearing, there usually comes a time when you look back and think, "Really? That's what I was doing? That's what I thought looked good?" So in a way, you haven't changed that much from your pioneering formative years. The style you're rocking today that you think looks great will one day become the subject of ridicule for your future self, and you'll wonder how you ever left the house with any self-respect. But that's life; you're always awesome in the moment, but incredibly uncool in hindsight.

Oh well, there's nothing you can do about it, except wait until you get old and stop caring about how you look and how you come across to others, and then, you'll have nothing to worry about. Especially because by that time, all the younger generations will look like idiots to you and you won't care if the feeling is mutual. You'll have settled on the final expression of who you are, and you won't give a damn about anything. That sounds great, doesn't it?

Your Pet Went To The Bathroom Indoors

As an adult, if your pet goes to the bathroom in the house, you clean it up right away. That's because if you don't, no one else will...especially your kids. How do you know this? Because when you were a kid, you never cleaned up a mess your pet made. Instead, you did what every kid on the planet does, which was to pretend not to see it and wait for your parents to clean it up.

No matter how obvious a mess was back then, you pretended you didn't see it, even if there was no way you could get inside your house without walking right past it. For example, when my dog made a mess inside, she always went in the middle of the entranceway, the room that every member of my family passed through when they came home. Despite the fact that you couldn't miss it unless you were blind, my brothers and I always pretended we didn't see it, and carefully stepped around it and went about our business like nothing was wrong, rather than taking responsibility and cleaning it up ourselves.

When you were a kid, you did the exact same thing, but as adults, we have to ask ourselves why we did that. The simple answer is that that's just what kids do. They're selfish, lazy, and smart enough to know that if they ignore something long enough, eventually, someone else will deal with it. That someone else, of course, was your parents.

Your parents would come home after a long day of work, loaded down with groceries, stagger into the house, and sometimes, step right into that mess that had been sitting there for hours while you watched TV and played video games. Then, they'd freak out and ask, "Why didn't someone clean up this mess?", to which your response was always, "What mess?"

And so, regretfully, angrily, and cursing the day they ever said yes to letting you get a pet, your parents cleaned up the mess, because they knew no one else was going to. Once again, you had dodged a bullet, and you took great pride in being able to avoid responsibility so well, especially a responsibility as gross as that.

Unbeknownst to your parents at the time, your poor behaviour was actually being positively reinforced by the fact that they always cleaned up the mess, even though they knew you'd seen it. Since your trick worked every time and your parents always wound up cleaning it up themselves without ever really calling your bluff, you knew you could keep getting away with it forever, and so you did. You were willing to sit in a room with a piece of dog pooh in the corner for hours, days, weeks even, if it meant you didn't have to deal with it. To you, that was a better alternative than cleaning it up, but to an adult, that was simply unacceptable, which is why they dealt with it right away.

Yes, when we were kids, the combination of our ability to watch TV next to a pile of feces and our total lack of responsibility kept us from ever cleaning up any messes our pets made indoors. Now, however, as adults who have pets and kids of our own, our lives have come full circle, and we're on the receiving end of this unacceptable behaviour. But that's life, and sometimes life stinks. In this case, literally.

You Made Prank Calls

Thanks to the advent of Caller ID, prank calls are almost impossible to make today. When you were a kid, they were the funniest things you could do.

Making a prank call to a stranger was probably the first delinquent thing you ever did. It was the first time that you knew you were doing something wrong on a social level, and that someone else was going to suffer as a result. It was something that you knew you shouldn't do, but the temptation was so overwhelming that you went ahead anyway, dialled a random number, and made a prank call that you thought was absolutely hilarious.

My first prank call went something like this:
Me: "Hello sir, this is Sears appliances. We just wanted to ask, is your fridge running today?"
Random stranger: "Yes, I think so."
Me: "Well, then you'd better go catch it!"

Then I hung up, and my friend and I laughed ourselves into oblivion. We thought that was hilarious, and back then, it was. At the time, it was cutting edge comedy, and as we hung up the phone, we could only imagine the person on the other end fuming with rage, knowing they'd fallen victim to the best prank call that had ever been made.

Unfortunately, since you got such a kick out of it, doing one successful prank call made you want to do more, because of the adrenaline rush and the entertainment you got from it, so you began pranking more and more people. Sometimes your friends even became the target of your devious new hobby. Did you ever phone your friend's house and pretend to be the school principal, or the police, and ask to speak to your friend's parents about something they'd done? That would really get them going.

Of course, the fact that you were 10 years old and didn't sound like a school principal or a police officer took a lot of the credibility out of your attempted hoax, but sometimes putting on a fake voice, even if it was bad, was enough to throw your friend off and give them a good scare.

As much as you loved making prank calls, there was a downside to them, and that was when they happened to you. Then, they weren't so funny anymore. The worst kinds of prank callers were the people who just kept on phoning. Every time you hung up, they phoned again, and usually they didn't even say anything. They just sat on the other end of the line in total silence, or made strange noises into the phone, and that incensed you to no end. To make matters worse, there was no way to track them down. All you could do was threaten them, but when you did, you could hear them snickering and giggling on the other end of the line. You knew that as soon as you hung up, they were going to call back right away and continue to torment you, and there was nothing you could do about it. It was one of the most infuriating things you could experience, but thankfully, a solution was on its way, although it would spell the end of prank calls for everyone.

Prank call anonymity couldn't last forever, and it didn't. Eventually, people started getting call display, and that signalled the death of the prank call era. It was a slow roll out at first. Maybe only one of your friends had it, but you always found out the same way. You prank called them and launched into your spiel about being Constable So and So from the local police department and you wanted to talk to their parents about something they had done, but instead of getting a panicked reaction from them like you normally did, this time there were a few seconds of silence, and then your friend calmly, though with slight hostility in their voice, said, "Yeah, I know it's you. I can see your number. We've got call display."

And then you were like, "You have what?"

"Call display. It's this new thing. It shows me the number of who's calling. I know it's you."

That dropped an atom bomb right in the middle of your prank calling paradise, and this time, you were the one who was panicking in stunned silence, barely able to comprehend this latest turn of events.

Caller ID was the beginning of the end for prank calls. Nowadays, they are impossible to make. You just can't do it. Everyone has call display. Even the most basic cell phones and landlines have call display, so you can't get away with those calls anymore. In fact, now the tables have turned, because instead of you phoning someone to prank them and having your fun ruined by call display, now the person you're calling can just look at the display, see your number, and not answer the phone because they don't want to talk to you. The game has been completely flipped around, but no one's having fun anymore.

Like so many things that have been and gone, pranks calls were a wonderful part of your past, as long as you were the one making them. However, in the immortal words of Robert Frost, "Nothing gold can stay," and the advent of caller ID marked the demise of pranking friends and strangers alike. Now if you want to get in on a good prank, you're forced to watch YouTube videos of other people pranking total strangers. Of course, the funny thing about those videos is that the people making them are usually adults, not kids. Perhaps they're the same people who used to call your house endlessly and just breathe into the phone. I guess pranking people is something they never grew out of. I wonder why that is? Maybe none of their friends had caller ID.

Your Family Had a Swear Jar

There was a time when all of the males in my family, except my older brother, who to this day I've never heard swear, went through a period of unnecessary, uncalled-for foul language. For some reason, we all started swearing excessively, and it was a trend that needed to be curbed. To counteract our vulgar language, it was decided that our family needed a swear jar. When you got caught swearing, you had to pay a penalty, and at the end of the month, we'd use the money in the jar for a family treat, like going for ice cream. Now, this seems like a strange proposition, since you would think that the more you swore, the more money there would be for ice cream, but no kid wants to pay for their own treats, and they especially don't want to pay for someone else's, so it's not like we were going to start swearing more in order to get a bigger payout at month's end, since we'd be the ones financing it.

The swear jar worked on the same premise as speeding tickets, where if you got caught breaking the law, you had to pay a fine. As research has shown, however, speeding tickets are not an effective deterrent for reckless driving, and the swear jar wasn't successful at eliminating our profane language either. The reason it was so ineffective for my younger brother and I was because we didn't have any money. You can't get blood from a stone, and you can't get money from kids who don't have jobs, so guess who the only person who could actually pay into the swear jar was? That's right: my dad.

My poor dad. He worked his butt off for our family and gave us everything he could, and he got the short end of the stick in everything, including the swear jar. It's not to say that my younger brother and I never paid; we did, it's just that we only had enough money to pay a few times, and after that our coffers were bare. My dad was the only one with the financial capital to continue cussing, so while my brother and I had been bled dry, he had to keep coughing up for every offensive word he spewed.

To make matters worse, we didn't let him get away with anything, since we knew what the money was going towards. My brothers and I suddenly became the worst snitches who had ever lived, and our dad had to pay up for every "hell," "damn," and "frig" that came out of his mouth. Sure, "frig" wasn't a swear, but it sounded close enough to the F word to count, so we were on top of it.

At the end of the month, the swear jar had done its job, and everyone was happy. My younger brother and I had greatly reduced our cussing, and my mom was proud of herself for having come up with such a brilliant plan. My dad had curbed some of his language too, though it had never been that bad in the first place, and my older brother, who probably had a hand in orchestrating the whole thing, had enjoyed weeks of tattling on anyone who cussed in order to maximize his profit, and at the end of it all, we got to go for ice cream and spend time together as a family. And to think, we owed it all to profanity.

P.S.

To the dads out there who give their all for their families, you truly are wonderful people. You make the world a better place just by being who you are, so thank you to all of you. Especially mine.

You Dressed Like Everyone Else

Fashion trends come and go, but you can probably remember a time in your life where one style of clothing, or even a brand, dominated all others, and for a little while, all the kids your age looked exactly the same. Whether it was mushroom cuts, baggy sweaters, or ripped jeans, there was no shortage of short-lived fads that we experienced back then. I remember a lot of style trends growing up, but the one that sticks in my mind the most, and the only one I ever jumped on the bandwagon with, was "No Fear."

In case you're unfamiliar with "No Fear," it was a clothing company that had inspirational, and usually cocky, sayings etched onto its T-shirts. For example, their T-shirts had sayings like, "You Miss 100% of the Shots You Don't Take," "You Let up, You Lose," and the ever popular, "Pussy, Chicken," which depicted a rooster and a cat locked in a stare down, calling each other those names.

Those T-shirts were a sign of the times, and of cool kids everywhere. I myself got in on the trend, though just before it faded, and my shirt read this: "Second Place Is the First Loser." You know what was ironic about my shirt? I was the second guy in my grade to get it.

Despite that, I thought I was pretty cool in my No Fear shirt, and if you had one, you did too. We all looked exactly the same, and we were totally in style, possibly for the first time in our lives. It was a big moment for many of us. Unfortunately, that moment only lasted as long as it took for the cool kids to start wearing another brand, because they didn't want to be seen wearing the same shirts as everyone else.

That's what really killed the No Fear trend. It was when everybody, and I mean everybody – even the teachers – got on board with it, and suddenly you couldn't tell the cool kids from the nerds. When that happened, they had to jump ship and find another brand in order to separate themselves from the nerd - I mean the herd.

That's how fashion goes, though. One minute, something's all the rage, and the next, you find it at the Salvation Army when you're buying clothes for a retro party and thinking about how stupid you looked back then. It's funny to think about all the crazy fashions we had when we were kids. From stupidly huge glasses, to full tracksuits, to No Fear shirts, we really had a great thing going. We looked like idiots, yet thought we were the coolest people around. That's the beauty of life, though. You're always awesome in the moment. It's only when you look back that you realize how ridiculous you were, but as the old saying goes, "Don't look back. You're not going that way."

People Could Smoke Everywhere

It wasn't that long ago that people could pass a security check, safely stow their overhead, and then light up a cigarette on an airplane. Today, doing that would mean a minimum $5000 fine and possible jail time. Back then, it would mean they were sitting in the smoking section.

Remember when people could smoke in restaurants? Restaurants used to have two sections: smoking and non. It was completely normal for patrons to light up a cigarette or two with their meals. No one considered it rude, as long as that person was in the smoking section. Sure, it was unpleasant if you were a non-smoker on the border, but it was something you put up with, because that's just the way it was. If you tried to light up in a restaurant today, you'd be the star of a "People Are Idiots" compilation video on YouTube.

Things certainly have changed over the years. Not that long ago, smokers were treated as equal citizens who had the right to smoke in public, albeit they often had to indulge their deadly habit in a designated area. Nowadays, they're looked down upon as a sub-class of society that non-smokers want nothing to do with. That's why non-smokers banded together and made smoking illegal almost everywhere you go: airplanes, restaurants, the bus, the beach, bars, you name it. What used to be a smoker's paradise burned up in a cloud of second hand smoke, and suddenly, smokers had almost nowhere left to light up and breathe in their deadly carcinogens.

The world must be a terrible place for smokers today. Where I live, in Vancouver, Canada, you can't smoke anywhere. If you light up at the beach, you'll get a fine. If you're smoking within six meters of an air intake or close to the doors of a business, you'll get dirty looks and be asked to move along by security. And forget smoking in the woods – you'll burn the forest down and be labeled an eco-terrorist!

Yes, life is certainly rough for smokers today, what with the fines, the dirty looks, and the threat of being put on a no fly list. With all the hassle smokers have to put up with, you'd think they'd simply choose to quit, but that doesn't seem to be the case. If you're a smoker, you'd probably love nothing more than to be able to build a time machine and go back to the early 90's, when you could smoke anywhere you wanted. That would be great, wouldn't it? I'd think quitting would be easier than building a time machine, but I don't have experience with either, so it's not my place to say. Good luck to you though, whichever path you choose. In the meantime, the rest of us non-smokers will be enjoying our time on smoke-free outdoor patios and beaches, where instead of second hand smoke, we can focus on more pressing matters, like trying to avoid skin cancer and irradiated ocean water. Isn't modern life great?

You Didn't Have To Wear Deodorant

When you were a kid, you could run around all day getting dirty and sweaty, only take a bath once a week, never wear deodorant, and miraculously, still not stink. As an adult, if you even break a sweat, you start to smell, and if you're only bathing or showering once a week, you're offensive to all. In addition, if you don't wear deodorant, you are shamed and ostracized, though maybe without being aware of it. When I was a kid, however, I didn't even know there was such a thing as deodorant. Then, when I got a little older, say 12 or 13, I'd heard about it, but I never knew you had to wear it. I thought deodorant was only for stinky people, and since I wasn't a stinky person, I didn't wear it.

Guess what happened with that? I got to grade 8, and someone in my math class kept saying, "Man, who forgot to wear their deodorant? Somebody stinks!" But it couldn't have been me. I didn't need to wear deodorant. As I'd said before, deodorant was for stinky people. But guess what? I had become the stinky person without even realizing it, and without deodorant, I would stay the stinky person. It was an unsettling, uncomfortable revelation that had been brought to my attention as a result of my ignorance and poor social awareness, but in the end, I'm glad someone pointed it out. I'm sure I'm not the only person who this happened to, and undoubtedly, everyone knew someone who hadn't gotten the message about deodorant that the other 99 percent of the population had. It was the only time in my life I'd been a one-percenter, and much like today, the rest of the world resented me for it.

Fortunately, although stinky, some friends proved their mettle in this difficult and odorous time. I would like to thank my friend James Louis for having the courage and the kindness to pull me aside after class and politely suggest I invest in a stick of Right Guard. Had he not had the audacity to do so, to this very day, I might still be the stinky guy with BO riding the bus or hanging out at the library, completely oblivious to his own offensive odor, simply because, much like I used to, he believes deodorant is only for stinky people, and that's not him.

Parents, do your kids a favour. When they hit that certain age and they start to stink, buy them a stick of deodorant and save their social standing, won't you? Though I love and admire my parents deeply, I still have a hard time figuring out why they let me go on being the stinky kid, when I obviously needed an odourvention. Oh well, at least my friend had the heart to tell me. Thanks James, I owe you one.

You Called Someone You Liked For the First Time

You know what I love about cell phones? Knowing that when you call someone, you're only going to have to talk to that one particular person. When you were young, you didn't have that luxury. If you called someone's house, you never knew who was going to answer the phone: the person you wanted to talk to, their brother or sister, their parents, someone who didn't speak English – it could have been anybody.

For most of your childhood though, it didn't matter who answered the phone when you called someone's house, because you were usually just phoning to make an innocent play date. When it did start to matter, however, and matter a lot, was when you started calling people because you had a crush on them. That's when calling someone's house and talking to other people became a big deal, because you had to run the parent gauntlet – or worse – the sibling gauntlet. Calling someone you liked for the first time was already intimidating, and having to potentially talk to their whole family before you finally got the person you wanted only made it that much worse.

There was nothing more nerve wracking than calling someone you had a crush on, especially the first time. It wasn't a simple process, either. It's not like you just picked up the phone, dialed their number, and had a great conversation. No way. First, you had to build up the courage to even decide to call, and that could take days. Once you'd finally psyched yourself up and had committed to making that call, you had to actually go through with it. That was a gut wrenching experience; you could literally feel your heart beating faster, your breath getting shorter, and your whole body tensing with anxiety as you picked up the receiver and started to dial that number, terrified of what awaited you on the other side.

Fortunately, you didn't have to make those calls alone. You always had a friend backing you up for that first call, pushing you along and telling you there was nothing to be afraid of, even though you knew they'd be just as terrified as you were if the roles were reversed. Having your friend's support was crucial, and because of it, you were eventually able to make that call, after several aborted attempts, of course.

How many times did you dial someone's number, let it ring once, panic, and then slam the receiver down before anyone could pick up? Didn't you always feel like the person on the other end knew it was you who had done that, even if they didn't have caller ID? That only made things worse, because now you had to call them again, and you were worried that the person would ask if you'd just called, and you'd have to lie and say no. It took an already daunting ordeal and magnified it tenfold. Given all that, it's a miracle any of us ever got together.

Remember when the phone rang five or six times and no one picked up? That was always a mixed blessing. On the one hand, you were happy because you'd had the courage to call, but you were also relieved that no one had picked up. At the same time, however, you knew that you'd eventually have to go through the whole process again, and next time, you'd probably have to talk to someone. In a way, it was like someone on death row getting their execution date pushed back. They must feel some sense of relief, but at the same time, they know it's still going to happen, so there's really nothing to get excited about.

When you eventually worked up the courage to call again and someone actually picked up, one of two things happened: the person you liked was home, and you talked to them, or they weren't, and you were given the difficult choice of either leaving a message, or simply remaining anonymous. Neither option was pleasant. If you left a message, you knew that whoever took that message was going to know exactly what was going on. Suddenly, a strange boy or girl they'd never heard of was calling the house, asking to talk to their son or daughter. This always raised red flags for parents. Who was this mysterious person, and what did they want? If you left a message, you knew you'd be the subject of conversation that night at dinner. If you didn't, you were just some weirdo who didn't have any confidence or manners. There was really no way to win in those situations.

If you did decide to leave a message, you had to play the waiting game, which was equally as nerve wracking as making that first call, if not more so, because you were no longer in control. Every time the phone rang, your heart skipped a beat, and you listened intently as your parents, or whoever had answered the phone, spoke with the mystery caller on the other end of the line. Was it a routine call? Was the tone and conversational style of your parents normal, or was something slightly off – a hint of confusion, or a noted change in their tone of voice. If there was, you knew that call was for you, and you had to go through with it. It was too late to back out now, and there was nothing to do but take that phone and heed the call of destiny, even though you were terrified.

Like most things in life, the scariest thing about that first phone call was what you imagined about it. Once it was happening, you realized, "Hey, this isn't so bad. I'm talking to the person I like, and it's awesome."

Even if the conversation was laboured, which it usually was, you were happy that you had put yourself out there and taken a risk, and one way or another it was paying off. You pushed yourself to do something you were afraid of, and as a result, you established a rapport with your crush. For the two of you, there was nowhere to go but up...at least for awhile.

Despite the fear and anxiety you felt about calling someone you liked for the first time, when you finally summoned the courage to do it, it was so much easier than you had imagined. Life is often like that. The things that you're afraid of aren't so scary once you're doing them, and the distressing scenarios you create in your mind never match what actually happens. That's why calling someone you liked when you were a kid taught you one of life's more beautiful lessons, and as an adult, you should remember how much courage you used to have when you were young. Sure, you were afraid, terrified even, but back then you constantly pushed yourself to do the things you were afraid of, and it always paid off in the end.

As adults, I think that all too often, we stop taking those kinds of risks. We stop putting ourselves out there, and we let our fear get the best of us. Because of that, we often never even try, and as a result, we never win like we used to. We never get to celebrate those victories, those rare and precious moments when we put it all the on the line and actually come out on top. But we should. We should keep doing things we're afraid of, because we used to do that on a regular basis, and life was wonderful because of it. If we never did something that seemed dangerous or daunting, none of us would have ever learned how to ride a bike, or play sports, or even walk down the stairs. Often, I think we need to take a lesson from our younger selves, who were so much braver and more willing to risk than we are now. After all, that courageous kid you used to be is still a part of who you are, still very much alive inside of you. So if there's something you're dying to do but are afraid to try, just remember the courage you used to have, and do it. While you're at it, call someone you like for the first time. You'll be glad you did.

You Had a Walkman

At one point in your life, there was nothing cooler than having a Walkman. It was a portable status symbol that said, "Hey everybody – I'm awesome." No matter how nerdy others thought you were, if you had a Walkman, you were cool and you knew it.

Walkmans were amazing. They were cutting edge devices that let you walk around with a soundtrack to your life. Of course, some Walkmans were better than others. For example, if you cheaped out, your Walkman didn't have a rewind button, only fast forward. Saving twenty or thirty bucks to forego a rewind button seemed like a good idea at the time, but you quickly realized that was a mistake that you would regret for as long as you owned that Walkman.

Unfortunately for me, that was the kind of Walkman I bought. It wasn't a Sony or a Panasonic, but some knock off brand, like a Panavonix or a SYNO. If I had known what a hassle it was going to be to have to flip the tape over and fast forward it, then flip it back and see if I had fast forwarded enough to rewind the other side to the place I wanted, I would have happily paid the extra twenty bucks for one with a rewind button. It was too late to change it now though, and since I couldn't afford to buy another one and Craigslist didn't exist yet, I just had to suffer.

As with all new technology, it wasn't long before something even more innovative came out that would replace the Walkman, and that was the Discman. Once Discmans were available, you could finally listen to your music with ease. With the press of a button, you could find the exact song you wanted. All Discmans came with both a scan forward and a scan back button, so being a cheap skate was no longer going to ruin your listening experience, but trying to do anything other than standing perfectly still while you listened to your music would.

That was the downside of Discmans. Listening to music on them was easier, but only if you weren't planning on going anywhere. On the other hand, Walkmans were great for taking to the gym or going for a run. You just threw in your favourite tape: MC Hammer, Vanilla Ice, Phil Collins, or whoever it was you were listening to back then, stuck your Walkman in your pocket, and off you went. The tape would play without a problem and keep you entertained throughout your entire workout. With Discmans, that just wasn't the case. If you threw in a CD and wanted to listen to it, you were pretty much forced to stay exactly where you were. They were great for listening to music while you did homework or relaxed, but the minute you tried to get up and go somewhere, your musical experience was over. Oh, and forget trying to fit those early models in your pocket. You had to carry them like a dinner tray!

Remember when they came out with those fancy anti-skip Discmans that could scan 20 seconds ahead of the part you were listening to in order to prevent your song from skipping? That feature worked great – for about 20 seconds. After that, you either had to sit down or stand still, and you often had to make the choice between standing still all day, or going without music.

Although Discmans were superior to Walkmans in a stationary setting, Walkmans still reigned supreme for people who liked to move and actually do things while listening to music. There were benefits to each system, but neither was perfect. Then one day, the MP3 player came along, and that changed everything. Suddenly, we went from being able to listen to one tape or CD, to being able to listen to hundreds, if not thousands of songs on a single device that didn't skip and could both fast forward and rewind. It was the dawn of a new age, and we were in digital music Heaven.

With the advent of MP3 players, we said goodbye to the Discman and the Walkman. We also said farewell to what used to be a highly regarded status symbol, because pretty soon, everyone had an MP3 player. It wasn't just the cool kids anymore.

In spite of their massive popularity, however, I don't think anyone ever felt as cool with an MP3 player as they did with a Walkman or a Discman. Maybe that's because by the time MP3 players came out, we were older and had moved on to different status symbols, like cars, clothes, and attractive partners. Or maybe it was because suddenly, everyone had an MP3 player, whereas before, only a hip minority of people carried Walkmans. Whatever it was, something had shifted, and today you barely see anyone without an electronic device, although smartphones have replaced Walkmans, Discmans, and MP3 players all together.

Despite the endless benefits of smartphones, Walkmans and Discmans still had one advantage over modern technology, and that was that we could be plugged into our devices and still remain vaguely aware of the world around us, unlike the technocrats of today, who could be at ground zero of the Zombie Apocalypse and not even notice it because they're lost in their screens. Oh well, if you're going to get eaten by a zombie, at least you can take some great selfies while it's happening. Maybe you'll even have time to upload a few before you turn. Now that would be a Snapchat story worth following.

No One Had a Cell Phone

How did we ever get by without being able to text someone and tell them we'll be there in two minutes? It seems incomprehensible now, but not that long ago, almost no one had a cell phone, yet the human race still managed to survive.

Although cell phones didn't exist, people still had wireless communication devices – they just weren't as high tech. Some people had pagers, but only the most important people: doctors, paramedics, secret service agents, etc. However, they couldn't communicate with their pagers. All they could do was know that someone wanted to talk to them, and unless they were at home, had to find a payphone and call that person back. That was as advanced as it got, but back then it was cutting edge.

As time moved on, technology continued to improve. First, we got the car phone, which no one needed, but some people bought because they wanted to seem cooler than they were. Then came the massive cell phones that looked exactly like the ones radiomen used in Vietnam, and many of the people who used to have pagers traded them in for these monstrous new cell phones. Over time, those cell phones got smaller, cheaper, and more readily available, and once the smartphone was invented, suddenly everyone on the planet had one. Once that happened, life became very different from how it was before.

Suddenly, cell phone conversations became more important than holding a conversation with the person in front of you. Texting replaced talking, and people traded the real world for the virtual. All types of new trends developed, like texting and driving, which replaced drinking and driving as the number one cause of traffic related fatalities, though for some reason, people still seem to think it's ok to do. In addition, it somehow became totally normal for people to take naked pictures of themselves and send them to people they liked, something no one ever did before cell phones came along, likely because taking nude photos of yourself, having them developed at the photo lab, and then mailing them to someone was just too much work, and also would've been considered really weird at the time. The world changed seemingly overnight, and all at once, people went crazy. But not long ago, it wasn't like that at all.

Only a decade or two ago, no one had cell phones and we got along just fine. We didn't text, we didn't tweet, and we didn't snap or sext, yet we somehow managed. If we wanted to talk to someone, we phoned them, or sought them out in person, unlike today, where most people choose texting over talking, and a conversation that should take two minutes takes an hour. We also didn't used to freak out when an unknown number came up on our call display and wonder who the heck was trying to get a hold of us, or what kind of scam we'd just been targeted for. Heck, for a long time we didn't even have call display! We just boldly picked up the phone like a normal person and had to deal with whatever came our way, and we were better for it.

In addition to the way we communicate, cell phones have also changed the nature of dating. Have you ever looked at two people on a date and seen them both texting? That's the sign of a bad date. Back in the day, people didn't have that option. If you were on an awkward date, you had no choice but to ride it out or climb out the bathroom window of the restaurant. We had to be a lot more resourceful back then, and sitting through terrible dates really helped us to develop a type of resiliency that people just don't have today.

Despite the negative impact on our social interactions and a few other downsides, like having more dangerous drivers on the road, there are, admittedly, many upsides to cell phones that we could have benefited from in days gone by. For example, they're great in emergencies, or for getting directions. You can find anything you want at the touch of a button, and friends and family are literally at your fingertips. Why learn to read a map when Siri can do it for you, and even tell you exactly how to get there, though she could give you a little more warning when you need to take an exit ramp off the freeway. And of course, everyone knows that the best thing about cell phones is the ability to avoid anyone you want in public. Nowadays, if you see someone coming towards you who you don't want to talk to, all you have to do is whip out your phone and pretend like you're having a conversation, and that person will walk right past you. It's a great way to avoid unwanted social interactions, unless of course, your phone rings at that same moment. When that happens, it can get awkward, but hopefully by that time you've put enough space between you and the person you wanted to avoid, and you can just keep walking down the street as if nothing happened.

Yes, despite the fact that cell phones have severely retarded face-to-face interactions and relegated us to a bunch of tweeters and texters, with some sexters thrown in the mix, there are just too many upsides to ever be without them now. Maybe as technology gets better though, we can aim for some kind of happy medium between proper communication, common sense, and maintaining the art of conversation and social interaction. Of course, as I'm writing this, I'm reading about people in their 30s and 40s who are making Pokémon Go their number one priority in life, and with virtual reality imminently poised to enter the market place and the human experience, such hope may be futile. I wonder if we'll use our cell phones to ignore people in the virtual world as well? I guess we'll find out soon enough, and I'll see you there...unless I'm taking a call, that is.

There Was No Internet

Doesn't it blow your mind that not that long ago, we didn't have the Internet? Now that we have it, we can never go back to living without it, because life simply wouldn't work. We do everything online: we bank, we shop, we talk, we even date. It's mind blowing just how much the Internet has enmeshed itself into our lives, yet just over 20 years ago, it didn't exist for most people.

What did we even do in the days before the Internet? It's hard to imagine a world without it, but for a major part of your life, that was your reality. Your life was so much different, and in many ways so much more difficult, although you never noticed it because you didn't know what you were missing. For example, remember when you had to do a school project and the only place to find information was in books? That meant you had to drive all over town going to different libraries, wasting entire days just trying to find one particular book so you could find out what the climate of Australia was like, or what Koala bears ate so that you could do your school project. It was a colossal waste of time, but since you didn't know any different, it was just the way it was.

Whether it was doing a school project or looking up a phone number, finding information was infinitely more difficult without the Internet. Nowadays if you want to look something up, you can do it in five seconds. 20 years ago, it could have taken five hours to find that same piece of information. In fact, you could have spent all day searching for something and still not have found it, and you just had to try again the next day or give up entirely.

Kids today don't know how good they have it, but you can't tell them that. That's because if you tell them that there was no such thing as the Internet when you were their age, they'll look at you the same way as if you told them dinosaurs existed when you were a kid. To them, a world without the Internet is inconceivable, but when you were a kid, that's just how it was. If you had a school project to do, you checked out more books than you could carry from the library. If you wanted to date someone, you had talk to them in person. And if you wanted to spend your day looking at pornography, you had to build a fort in the woods and go there with your friends, not just look it up on your smart phone while you're in the bathroom or on the back of the bus.

Yes, it was a different world before the Internet came along. Maybe in some small way it was better, but that's only because you didn't know what you were missing. Now you literally have the world at your fingertips, and it's amazing. From talking to people on the other side of the planet, to learning new languages, to accessing information you never would have been privy to in days gone by, you can do anything you want online. Unfortunately for some, that just means looking at excessive amounts of pornography, but hey, everybody needs a hobby.

You Had Cameras With Film

Taking pictures used to be so much harder than it is now. Today, most of us don't even own cameras; we own phones that have cameras built into them, and those cameras are infinitely better than anything we used to take pictures with. We don't need film, we don't need to take our photos to the lab, and if we don't like the way one turned out, we just take it again until we finally get the perfect picture. These are luxuries we didn't use to have, and digital cameras – I mean cell phones – have dramatically improved the art of taking pictures in so many ways.

To start with, you could never just take a camera out and go shoot something; you also had to have film, and film was expensive. Plus, you only had a limited amount of pictures you could take before your film ran out. That meant that every picture you took had to be worth it, and when you started nearing the end of your roll, you always had to consider whether a moment was photo worthy or not.

You'd stand there going, "How many pictures of a sunset do I need? Just one? One should be good. I hope it turns out..."

In addition to having to carefully consider each picture you took, you also had to wait forever to actually see your photos. I might have a bad memory, but I seem to remember sometimes having to wait up to a month for film to get developed. You had to wait for your parents to take it to the store, drop it off, pay for it, wait for it to get developed, bring it home, unwrap it, and finally, after weeks of waiting, you could look at your vacation pictures. Despite the wait, looking at newly developed pictures together was always a fun family thing to do. That way, your parents could look at all those beautiful sunset pictures you and your siblings ruined by making stupid faces and sticking your tongues out, and look back on all the other wonderful things you did as a family too. Of course, the classic North American family photo was taken at a place like Disneyland, with the entire family wearing Mickey Mouse ears and being festooned from head to toe in Disney memorabilia...and at least one kid sticking their tongue out.

 Of course, everyone remembers that the worst thing about taking pictures with film was that you never knew how the pictures were going to turn out until it was too late to take another. You just had to hope for the best, and there were no second chances for people caught making unintentionally ugly faces or blinking at the moment of truth.

You know what the most limiting part of film cameras was? Erotic pictures. Back then, 99% of people never took an erotic picture, unlike nowadays, when the first thing someone does when they get a new phone is take a naked picture of themselves. That didn't happen back then because you knew that someone else was going to develop that film, and you didn't want the guy in the photo lab at London Drugs or K-Mart to show them to his buddies working there.

He'd be developing your roll, see your crazy picture, and call his friends over going, "Hey guys, look at this! This guy took a picture of himself buck naked in front of the mirror, flexing his muscles and making the stupidest face I've ever seen…what a loser!"

You didn't take those kinds of pictures back then because you couldn't stand the embarrassment of knowing that the entire lab staff would see what you were doing, and there was always the chance you'd lose your ticket stub and have to describe some of your photos to the technicians in order to claim them.

"Yeah, hi there, I lost my ticket stub, but I had a bunch of photos of my kid's soccer game, my son's graduation, a couple of my dog playing fetch, oh, and a bunch of me in front of the mirror buck naked and flexing."

"Oh, you're that guy? Got 'em right here." And then the technician would call out to the other people working there, "Hey guys, check it out – it's the naked guy!"

No one wanted that to happen, so no one took naked pictures; at least not with film. That's what Polaroids were for.

Despite their many downsides, film cameras weren't all bad. Maybe the best thing about them was that there was no such thing as selfies back then, and people weren't as narcissistic as they are today. No one took selfies with film cameras, because selfies are hard to take, and no one had that much film, money, or time to waste trying to get a good one like they do today. Personally, I think the world was a better place because of that.

Yes, there were pros and cons to the pre-digital age of photography. You didn't have the luxury of taking a hundred pictures to get the perfect one, or never having to wait for film to get developed, but I would say that as a whole, society had a lot more class back then. People weren't quite so narcissistic, and it wasn't a normal thing to send naked pictures of yourself to someone else, only to later find them on the internet. We'll have to wait and see what the future holds for photography and print images, and no doubt we'll one day look back at our current technology and wonder how we ever got by with such primitive tools, but that's part of being human. What amazes us today will seem like stone age technology in 20 years, and future generations will be unable to fathom how we ever got by as they're watching holographic movies and teleporting themselves to their friends' houses, talking about how primitive their parents' generation was. Don't feel bad though; the same thing will happen to them one day too, because the circle of life never stops spinning.

You Went to the Video Store

Thanks to the advent of digital technology and illegal downloading, what was once a staple of life for our generation is now only a memory of a bygone era. Fortunately though, anyone who grew up before the Internet was invented will still remember the thrill and the excitement that only going to the video store on a Friday night could bring.

When you were a kid, video stores were everywhere. In every town and city across the western world, you could always find a video store. Sometimes it wasn't even a whole store, it was just a section of another store you could rent videos from, like in a small town corner store, but it was still wonderful for the people who lived there and those visiting from out of town who wanted to stay inside and cozy up for a night. No matter how big a city or how small a town, there was at least one video store, and it was always the most popular spot on a Friday night – except for maybe the liquor store.

On Friday nights, everyone in town went to the video store. It was a sure-fire plan to kick-start your weekend that was fun, exciting, and social. If you couldn't think of anything else to do, renting a movie was always your go to, as it was perfect for so many occasions: hanging out with friends; a first date with that special someone; or a family night incomplete with popcorn and soda. The video store provided high quality entertainment for a variety of social functions, and it was the cornerstone of your weekends.

Going to the video store was only slightly less exciting than going to the movie theatre, and it was a heck of a lot cheaper. On top of that, you were guaranteed good seats. Although seeing the movie you wanted wasn't a sure thing, that aspect added an element of uncertainty and exhilaration. It was its own unique feeling, one that kids who rent movies from iTunes and Amazon will never experience. They'll never know the thrill of the hunt that we did, which made our movies that much more exciting to watch.

After all, if you wanted the latest popular release, it took skill, tact, and careful planning. You couldn't just stroll in at 6:30 and expect that blockbuster to be waiting on the shelf for you. You had to have a plan and some strategy. Maybe your dad was going to get off work early and roll by the store around three o'clock to make sure he got that movie before anyone else did. Or, maybe you were old enough that you could sprint to the store as soon as school let out and get the most popular video game that every other kid in town was after, or perhaps you'd thought even further ahead than that and had reserved it the day before.

There were several clever ways to make sure you got the movie or game you wanted, and there was nothing more satisfying than actually having it in your hands, paying two dollars to rent it for the weekend, which at the time seemed like highway robbery, and taking it home with you knowing you had beat the odds and gotten exactly what you wanted.

Whether you were with your family, your best friend, or that special someone, there was a distinctive, special feeling of going to the video store that we can't experience anymore. Even though online streaming is great, and much more convenient, it doesn't have the same magical quality that renting movies from the video store did. There's no thrill to it, no excitement, and you can't spend an hour walking up and down the aisles and holding hands with the person you like, browsing for a movie you both know you're not going to watch anyways. Sitting on the couch and sifting through ITunes just isn't the same. There's no build up, no risk, and hence, no reward. Maybe it's the same way people feel when they meet someone off the Internet and decide to Netflix and chill on a first date, without ever getting to know each other or taking the chance of meeting someone in person. I've never done that though, so maybe I shouldn't judge. Personally, I'd rather take my time getting to know someone as we leisurely peruse the aisles of the video store, but I just can't do that anymore, since there are no video stores left. But if I could, I would. Call me old fashioned I guess.

People Had Sex in Movies and You Thought It Hurt

I can't be the only kid who watched people having sex in movies and thought, "Wow, that must hurt."

That was my primary reaction to sex on screen.

My second reaction was, "Why do people do that?"

There didn't seem to be anything fun or pleasurable about it. They screamed, they grunted, they made the kinds of noises kids only made when they got hurt, so why were they willingly subjecting themselves to something that sounded so awful? You'd think that if they liked each other, they'd avoid the whole thing altogether, but apparently not. As a kid, I just couldn't figure it out. Then I hit puberty, and everything changed.

After that, I spent the better part of my teenage years desperately hoping that one day someone would have sex with me, and I could make those same weird noises I used to wonder about as a kid. The activity that used to seem so aversive and painful had become my primary goal in life, one that I hoped I would achieve if I managed to get really, really lucky, or some girl got really, really desperate. I was willing to settle for either.

Sex had gone from being something I couldn't understand to something I wanted more than anything I had desired before...except for that Lego Pirate set I asked for for Christmas one year, but relatively speaking, that was a lot easier to get.

You Lived Off Pizza Pops

The exact numbers vary between sources, but there is a large percentage of the population who survived their teenage years by eating nothing but Pizza Pops. They were a staple that helped you through that tender age when you didn't know how to cook and you were too lazy to learn. You also couldn't afford real pizza, so Pizza Pops were the next best thing. They were the greatest lunch, dinner, after school and late night snack ever invented, and like a good friend, they were always there when you needed them, provided your parents remembered to buy them.

As a pre-teen or teenager, you were hungry all the time, but since you didn't know how to cook and you didn't want to learn, this resulted in a serious dilemma. Fortunately, Pillsbury had the answer. If you were like me, you'd come home and eat two, three, maybe four Pizza Pops after school, and that was just a snack to tide you over until dinner, which if you were lucky, was also Pizza Pops. Growing up in a house with three boys, the only way my parents could keep a steady supply of Pizza Pops available was to buy them at Costco, and even then, our freezer had to constantly be resupplied. If it hadn't been for Pizza Pops, my brothers and I may have starved to death, or at least suffered from serious malnutrition, which is ironic, since eating too many Pizza Pops probably could have led to the same condition.

Nowadays, you would never try to live off Pizza Pops unless you found yourself in some kind of survival situation. That's because as an adult, you're likely more health conscious than you used to be. You're more careful with what you eat, and you consider things like nutritional value and health benefits, or detriments, before you put something in your body. As a teenager, however, thoughts like that never crossed your mind, and on top of that you never seemed to put on weight no matter what you ate, so you didn't have to be as stringent with your diet. Even if you had considered those things though, Pizza Pops were so delicious and so convenient that you would have kept eating them anyways. In fact, the only reason you stopped eating them was because you eventually got a part time job and were able to afford real pizza. If that hadn't happened, you probably would have kept eating them for the rest of your life, or at least the rest of your teenage years

Pizza Pops were one of an infinite number of life's little phases. At the time, you thought they were the best thing that could ever happen to you, but eventually you moved on when you found something better, whether that was a healthier snack, or as I said before, real pizza. When you look back on what you used to think was perfection, you are often baffled at what you settled for. Whether it's Pizza Pops or a relationship, when you find something better, you know you have to leave the past behind and move on. Of course, trading Pizza Pops for a healthier snack is much easier than leaving a relationship that you've come to realize is no longer right for you, but the idea is still the same. Once you move on to something better, you'll never go back to what you had before, and you'll wonder just what the heck you were doing all that time. No matter what, you'll learn a great lesson from your experiences, and hopefully be able to look back with appreciation for what was. Thank you, Pizza Pops, for keeping us alive during those formative years and always being there for us when we needed you. I know we don't see each other much anymore, and we've both moved on, but you'll always be remembered as the food that got us through that most turbulent phase of our lives, and we hope you're happy now.

Sincerely,

Every teenager who ever lived

A "Suspicious Looking Package" Was Different

Remember when a suspicious looking package was when somebody put a sock in their pants and it turned sideways? That was a much simpler time to live. That was before terror alerts and political correctness unwantedly invaded our lives, and it was better for everybody. Nowadays, the concept of a suspicious looking package is entirely different, and rather than being funny, it's worrisome. Wouldn't it be nice to go back to the times when it meant personal embarrassment, rather than mass hysteria?

You Only Knew How to Cook One Thing

For most people, the first thing they learned how to cook was one of three things: hot dogs, scrambled eggs, or Kraft dinner. You may be saying, "Hey, what about pizza pops?", but Pizza Pops aren't really cooking; they're warming something up in the microwave and hoping it won't explode, and that doesn't count. Cooking involved getting out a pot or a pan, possibly boiling some water, and allowing for the chance that you might screw the whole thing up, despite how simple it was.

When you first learned how to cook, you ate the same thing all the time because it was all you knew how to do. Any time you were left to your own devices, you survived off that one dish, whether it was macaroni and cheese, hot dogs, or whatever meal you knew how to make back then. You became a master at that one dish, and you felt like no one in the world could boil perogies or make a grilled cheese sandwich with the astonishing precision that you could. If there was a culinary award for that one basic dish, you'd be the recipient, no question.

The down side to only knowing how to cook one thing, however, was that eventually you got sick of it. It came to the point where if you had to go to the hospital the doctor would have taken a blood sample and found potato and cheese in your veins. "This guy's blood type is perogy, get some sour cream and bacon in here, stat!"

Of course, the upside of over indulging in one particular dish and getting sick of it was that it forced you to learn how to cook new things. Instead of scrambled eggs, you learned how to make fried eggs. Instead of boiling perogies, you now put them in the frying pan. Eventually, you even moved from macaroni and cheese to actual spaghetti. It was one small step in your evolution as a human being, and one giant leap in your culinary repertoire.

Yes, breaking barriers and learning how to make new meals was part of growing up, and besides learning how to walk, learning how to cook was the most baby steps thing you ever did. Unfortunately, some people never took any steps beyond that first dish, and they have suffered as a result. Those people are easy to spot as adults. They're the ones buying 30 frozen pizzas at the grocery store, or sitting in the lunchroom eating a peanut butter sandwich every single day. For goodness sakes, somebody get them some jam and help them step it up already!

You Said "The F Word" For the First Time

Before you could say the F word, you had to start with less abrasive words like hell, or damn. Those were gateway words. Crap was another. From there, you probably said the S word a few times, and it felt good. Suddenly, you found yourself in uncharted territory. You were starting to cuss, and you were moving quickly up the list of words you weren't allowed to say, getting ever closer to the mother of all bad words. And then one day, when the perfect circumstances presented themselves, you said it - the F word - and the world you knew shattered to pieces.

There were many things that may have caused you to say the F word for the first time. For example, you might have been really happy and said something like, "That is f#cking great!" Or you might have been really mad and said something like, "F*ck you!" Or you might have been terrified and just screamed "F#ck!" really loud. Whatever you said and however you said it, it was powerful, and everyone around you took notice, especially if you made the mistake of saying it in front of your parents.

That one powerful word destroyed the last vestiges of your childhood, for you and everyone who heard you say it. Your courageously foul language had shattered the parameters of what was acceptable, and even though your friends were stunned to hear you say it, they were now liberated to start using that word too, and deep down, they were thrilled about it. Suddenly, your whole inner circle had reached a new level of maturity, and you'd all taken a major step out of childhood. Once you said the F word for the first time, you could never unsay it, never go back to the way things were before.

After you'd spoken that most offensive of all words, life quickly started to change. By the time you said it, you were likely in the last stages of your adolescence, and that word marked the end of one era and your entrance into a realm you never could have prepared yourself for: the world of being a teenager, where the F word was the most commonly used term in almost any conversation.

Age and experience closed the lid on the coffin of your childhood, but saying the F word for the first time nailed it shut. Once you became a teenager and started swearing regularly, your whole world had changed. You were now free to express yourself in ways you'd never dreamed of, though your parents would do whatever they could to curb your foul language, and that included enforcing the rules of the swear jar. Unlike when you were a kid, you were actually expected to pay for your offensive language now, and that meant you had to get a job. Of course, you could have just stopped swearing, but getting a job seemed like the better option, which leads me to my next chapter.

You Got Your First Job

I worked harder at my first job than any I've had since, and chances are, you did too. Although the responsibilities and the demands on you have steadily increased from job to job, your work ethic and motivation to excel have probably decreased in tandem as you've become more and more comfortable, but that's not how it was when you got your first job.

When you got your first job, you worked like a maniac. You wanted to work harder than anyone else had ever worked at that job and be better than anyone had ever been. You didn't want to just be the employee of the month, you wanted to be the employee of all time.

Many of us found our first jobs in the fast food industry. For me, it was McDonalds. I was a model employee when I started. I never walked anywhere; I ran. I washed dishes by hand faster than the dishwasher could. I fought past swarms of wasps to take out the garbage. I slaved away over a hot stove for eight hours without a break, went home for 15 minutes, then came back for another eight because they were short staffed and asked if I could. I was the world's best employee...for about six months.

After that initial six months though, something starts to happen. It's like any relationship, really. For the first little while, you're on your best behavior. You are so grateful to have that job that you'll do anything to please your employer, much like you'll do anything to please a new partner. You'll stay late, show up early, work the night shift, put in as much overtime as they need, and do it all with a smile. That's the first six months. After that, it's all down hill.

Eventually, you start to slack off. You start to complain. You stop showing up early, start arriving late, and even find the occasional excuse not to come in at all.

You also start looking at other jobs and going, "Hmm, I wonder what it'd be like to work there?"

You do the bare minimum to avoid getting fired, and you see how long you can do that for before your boss or your partner tells you something has to change. At that point, you're faced with an important decision. Do you tell them that you've had enough and you want to start somewhere new, or do you think back to what it was like in the beginning and try everything you can to get those novel feelings and that spark back? It's never an easy decision, but it's one we've all been forced to make at certain moments in our lives.

Whether we're talking about a job or a relationship, you'll never work so hard or give so much of yourself as you did with your first. Also, whenever you know one is coming to an end, there's always a sense of sadness, a fear that you may never find something like that again. When we choose to walk away from a job or a lover, or worse, get fired or dumped, we're forced to look at ourselves and wonder what went wrong. How did something that was once so wonderful become something we just couldn't do anymore? At the time, we're left with heartache and confusion as we search our souls for answers we may never find, while simultaneously searching Craigslist and online dating sites for new jobs and new potential partners.

Then one day, years down the road, when we're at a job that's better suited for us and we're with someone who makes us happier than we ever thought we'd be, we'll think back to our first job and our first relationship and say to ourselves, "I used to work there? What was I thinking?"

You Had Dial-Up Internet

Nowadays, it's hard to believe that dial-up Internet was even a thing. Today, phoning the Internet to see if you can go online sounds crazy, but back then, it was the only thing we knew, and at the time, it was incredible.

You know what the funny thing about connecting to the Internet with a phone was? Sometimes you'd phone the Internet, and it was busy. And you accepted that. You went, "Oh, I guess someone else must be on the Internet now. I'll try again later."

Nowadays when you can't get online, you get really upset. That's because you use the Internet for almost everything: communication, banking, entertainment, education, even dating. Back in the day, you just used it as novel hobby and not being able to go online just meant you would do something else for a while. Today, not getting online means societal collapse. Things certainly have changed.

Despite how wonderful dial-up Internet was when it first came out, there were many aspects of it that you knew were terrible, but since you had no alternatives you were forced to just deal with them. For starters, remember how loud it was when you logged on? Couldn't they have made it a little quieter? What was going on between your computer and your phone to make those noises? They were the most jarring, irritating sounds you ever heard, and they announced to everyone in your house that you were going online. Did you ever try to sneak onto the Internet late at night to look at something you weren't supposed to? If so, you'll remember that it wasn't exactly a stealth mission, and unless your parents were deaf, they probably knew precisely what you were up to.

The other annoying part about dial-up Internet was that so often when you were online, having a great time, all of a sudden you heard someone from your family talking through the computer in a grainy, distant, semi-robotic voice.

"Hello? Is someone there? What's going on?"

Then, you'd yell out to whoever had picked up the phone, "I'm on the internet! Hang up the phone!"

And then it started.

"What?"
"I'm on the Internet!"
"Well I need the phone!"

"Well you're going to have to....dammit, it logged me off. Fine, go ahead! Use the phone!"

And then you would have to wait until whoever had needed the phone finished their conversation before you could go online again, and by that time, you'd probably found something better to do.

Despite a few drawbacks, there were many perks to the era when the Internet was new. Perhaps the greatest thing about the early Internet days was that you appreciated it more than you do today. Back then, if you wanted to see something, you had to really want to see it, and it took patience and dedication to finally find and download what you were looking for. Whether it was a cool new toy, a travel destination, or a picture of a naked lady, when you invested your time into seeing something, you savoured it.

Today, it's just not the same. We're over saturated with what we can see and do online. We literally have the world at our fingertips, showing up on our computers and mobile devices at lighting speed. High speed Internet has become such a normal part of life that we've grown totally accustomed to it, and as a result, we take it for granted.

That's why today, online pornography addiction is such a serious problem. In the dial-up days, it wasn't an issue, because no one had that kind of time.

It took 40 minutes to download one picture, and that was on a good day, when no one else was using the Internet at the same time as you. You usually didn't even get a whole picture, either. You were lucky to get a head, shoulders, and maybe one breast before you somehow got logged off, and by that time you had likely gone over your allotted time for the day since you had to budget yourself, as back in those days there weren't data caps, but time caps which were divided up between your whole family.

Despite how difficult it was to actually see what you wanted online, and yes, I'm talking about nudity, on the rare occasions you did get to see what you were looking for, you cherished it because of how long you'd had to wait for it, and because you knew it might be a long time before that happened again. Today, people can't wait for anything. That's why we have mobile ordering, because people can't even wait two minutes for a coffee. They want everything right away, and the slightest delay will throw them into a tailspin. My generation may be the last on Earth that will possess the virtues of patience and delayed gratification, traits that are vital to real world success. And we owe it all to dial-up.

I'm from the generation who grew up seeing one boob at a time, and I'm a better man because of it. Coming of age with dial-up Internet not only made me appreciate things more, it also forced me to become an astute decision maker who only had time for the best. It taught me that oftentimes, the best things in life require serious commitment, but there are wonderful rewards waiting for you if you can just stay focused and not give up on your goals. Whether it's being a successful writer as an adult, or seeing a naked lady online in 1994, the lessons that the early Internet taught me have had an extraordinary impact on my life, and I hope the same is true for you. Of course, we would never want to go back to the way things were because we're far too spoiled now. But don't tell the younger generations that. We still need something to scoff at them for.

You Had to Get a Date in Person

At time of writing, if you're not on Tinder, you're probably not dating. It seems that the whole world is online, and I think most of us hate it. Dating websites are like a digital catalogue of potential partners. If you don't like what you see on one page, you just flip to the next one until you find something better, and then you place an order. Well, you swipe right, but you get the idea. It's an awful way to meet people, and yet, here we are as a society.

Remember when you had to get a date in person rather than online? That's when people actually had to be smooth and charming, and think about what they said to one another. That's when people had to have game, not just a smartphone and a finger. You know who has game nowadays? Nobody, because with Internet dating, nobody needs it.

Now, I would be lying if I said I had never tried Internet dating. I've done it a couple times, and I actually kind of liked it. It streamlines the whole process for you. In some ways, it's not that much different from meeting people in real life. You can tell just by looking at someone if you'll get along and be able to carry on a conversation or not, and just like in real life, there are always surprises. At its core, Internet dating is not that different from trying to get a date in real life. However, I would argue that making a connection online is easier than walking up to a stranger and trying to get their number. You're doing the exact same thing on the Internet, but both people are protected by time and space. You've both got time to think about snappy replies and things to say that might impress a potential partner, and you've got less face to lose if the person you're interested in turns you down.

Years ago, it wasn't like that. For starters, you actually had to know the person you wanted to ask out, or at least be able to walk up and introduce yourself, unlike today, where you just have to send them a message or a wink, or swipe their profile picture in the right direction. Actually walking up and talking to someone took a lot of guts, and it's probably the reason people back in the day married their high school sweethearts so often. That's because it took so much courage to ask someone out the first time, they knew that marrying the person they were already with was easier than having to ask someone out again, and it was their way of never having to go through that awful ordeal again.

Unfortunately, I remember all too well the first time I approached a random girl and tried to chat her up, and like I'm sure it was for many of you, it was a total disaster. It was when I was in grade eight and old enough to be seriously interested in girls, and also just old enough to think that maybe I had a chance with actually getting one to like me. My friends and I were swimming at the pool, as we often did on Friday nights, when we noticed something out of the ordinary. Three stunningly beautiful girls had planted themselves on the pool deck across from where we were playing basketball, splashing around like idiots, and just having fun, not caring at all about trying to impress anyone. Well, not until we noticed those girls, at least. Once we realized they were there and within visual and auditory distance of our immature antics, we suddenly started trying to be a lot cooler than we actually were. We eased back on the hooting and hollering, stopped trying to sink baskets from the other side of the pool, and generally reigned everything in and soon found ourselves in a mid-pool huddle discussing this sudden change of events.

"Hey," I said to my friends who were clustered around me. "Do you see those girls over there?"

"Yeah, they're hot," responded my friend Craig.

"I think they go to our school," answered Gavin.

"One of us should go talk to them," replied my other friend John.

"Not me!" they all suddenly replied in unison.

That left only me, the shortest, smallest, and at the time, probably most undesirable male of the group. And I had absolutely no idea what to do.

"Go talk to them," said John.

"They are looking over here a lot," offered Gavin.

"Do it, man!" said Craig.

"What do I say?" I probed, literally having no idea how to talk to a member of the opposite sex.

"Just walk over there and say hi," said John, who really should have been the one taking charge of that operation, since he was the tallest and best looking of the group, and probably the reason the girls were looking at us in the first place. But he didn't offer up his services, and being the only one of the group who didn't have the sense to remove himself from the onus of approaching those girls, I gave in to peer pressure, despite sensing that it was going to be a suicide mission.

Once I volunteered to go, my friends fanned out and began playing basketball again, keeping a careful eye on me and the events that were about to unfold. Would I be successful and bring them back to the fold, or would I be shot down on approach like a Japanese kamikaze plane and blown to pieces before reaching its intended target? Let's just put it this way. If this really had been a military operation, the other side would have won – decisively.

It probably didn't help that after deciding to approach them, I took about 10 minutes to actually make contact. I made several aborted attempts, swimming up to them like a crocodile, half-submerged, then turning back when it decided its chosen prey was too much for it to handle.

Finally, after what was probably a series of incredibly obvious botched contact attempts, I slowly swam up to the ledge that they were sitting on and pulled myself out of the water, but left a good six feet between me and them. They continued chatting amongst themselves, pretending not to notice me, and I could see my friends watching the catastrophe unfold, with no sense of subtlety.

After sitting on the deck for about a minute, gathering my courage, I slowly slid a foot closer to them, but they still hadn't seemed to notice me. So, I slid over another foot, though I was still about four feet away, a little too far for a comfortable conversation, but as close as I felt I could get without scaring them off. And then, I did what John said to do. I just said hi, and this is exactly what happened after.

"Hi," I said to them, trying to fake some bravado.

Out of the three, only one of them turned her head and looked at me.

"Hi," she said back. She looked at me for a second, and I froze. That was all I had. I panicked. This was not going the way I thought it would. Well, actually, it was going exactly the way I thought it would, which was the problem. I needed something, anything, and I grasped for the first thing that came to my mind.

"...Do you know what time it is?" I sputtered. I couldn't believe that's all I could come up with, but it was.

And then, without saying a word, the girl who said hi pointed to a spot high up on the wall, where the biggest clock I had ever seen, at least 10 feet in diameter, was mounted, before turning her back on me and standing up to leave with her friends.

I sat on the edge of the pool in stunned disbelief, not only at the fact that I had just executed the worst pick up attempt in history, but that I had also failed to notice the world's largest clock literally staring me in the face. What I didn't fail to perceive, however, were my friends staring at me with unanimous looks of disappointment and embarrassment spread across their faces, but who were they kidding? They were the ones who volunteered me for that hopeless endeavor and hadn't offered anything in the way of backup. They wouldn't have done any better, and I knew it. Still, getting rejected in front of my friends was the icing on that bitter cake, and unfortunately, it wouldn't be the last time it would happen either.

But those were the stakes of trying to get a date in person, or even strike up a conversation with someone of the opposite sex. When you were successful, it was a blast, and when you failed, you failed miserably, often in front of people. With the Internet, that's never a worry. Now that I think about it, I see a lot more positives to Internet dating compared to when you had to get a date in real life, and I'm almost tempted to start doing it again, rather than meeting people face to face, or "organically", as some like to call it nowadays. Thanks to the Internet, I've dated two girls who were both totally out of my league, and I feel that unless we had been forced into close proximity with each other, like being stranded on a tropical island or involved in some kind of hostage taking, there's no way either of them would have ever noticed me. And really, what are the odds of something like that happening? Probably close to zero, but if being held captive leads you to your true love, it would all be worth it. And what a wedding story!

Pirating Music Meant Waiting By The Radio

We've all seen those anti-pirating commercials that say things like, "You wouldn't steal a car, so why would you steal a movie?" Whenever I see those commercials, my question is always, "But what about the people who do steal cars? This commercial has no effect on them!" All in all, it's a strange ad campaign, but I get where they're coming from. They're telling us that stealing is a crime, and we shouldn't be illegally downloading movies, or music either. Fair enough. Nowadays, it's all too easy to go online, find the thing you want, and download it for free. Well, apparently it's easy. I can't do it; I always find weird websites that don't work and install all kinds of strange files and viruses onto my computer, but in theory, pirating music is a simple, streamlined process. As you'll remember, this was not always the case.

Back in the day, if you wanted to get a song without paying for it, you only had one option, and that was to wait by the radio with a blank tape in the cassette deck and your finger on the record button, hoping that the song would eventually come on.

That was the only way to do it, unless you knew someone who had the cassette with the song you wanted on it. If that was the case, you could borrow the cassette and record that song onto a blank tape, but only if you had a double cassette player, which most people didn't. That meant that your only recourse was to wait by the radio, sometimes for hours at a time, just waiting for that one song to play, but you did it, because you had no other choice. Yes, you could have just ponied up the money to buy the album from the store, but who wanted to pay $5.99 just to get one song? That was crazy!

And so, you patiently sat by the radio, day after day, night after night, pirating the songs you wanted until you had a perfect mix tape. There was something so organic about pirating songs off the radio, and every mix tape you ever made sounded exactly the same. Each song had a DJ's voice at the beginning or end of it, or part of a commercial, and you could always hear that cool sound effect when you hit the record button, that weird "bllleeeerrrppp" sound. That raw feeling gave your tapes so much character.

The funny thing about listening to your pirated mix tapes back then was that you didn't just memorize the songs on the tape, you also memorized the commercials, the DJ commentary, and where the strange sounds were that signaled the start and end of each song. This ensured that no two mix tapes were alike, and it gave you a genuine sense of satisfaction knowing that your hard work and dedication had resulted in an absolutely authentic and original music compilation that was tuned to your specific tastes, even if it took weeks and sometimes months to make, which it often did. Rome wasn't built in a day, and neither were your mix tapes.

Of course, there were smart ways to pirate music in order to make a great mix tape. Prime pirating time was during the "top 10 at 10" or the "top 5 at 5", or whatever time radio stations were most likely to play the songs you wanted. I guess that method only worked for people who liked popular music that was radio friendly, though. If you wanted some obscure song or artist, like some weird German metal band, you had to pony up the six or eight bucks for the whole album, even though it generally wasn't worth it, since you only wanted one or two songs. It would be decades before the rise of Napster and other file sharing software, however, so you didn't have many options available and you usually just bit the bullet and bought the album.

Despite how long it took and how much patience it required, pirating music the old fashioned way was an integral part of growing up in days gone by. It's a lost art nowadays, much like baking bread and knitting. One or two generations from now, no one will even know what a cassette player is, but that's ok.

The old way of pirating music is one part of our past we can do without, because bootlegging music today is infinitely easier than it used to be if you know what you're doing, which sadly, most of us don't. Fortunately for us, there are still a few cassette decks kicking around the Salvation Army stores. Better get them while you can.

You Had Your First Kiss

Your first kiss may have been one of the most sensual experiences you ever had. Or, it may have been one of the most awkward, clumsy, or just plain grossest experiences you ever had. It varies from person to person, but one thing is for sure; you'll always remember your first.

I think that most people have two first kisses: an actual first kiss, which was terrible, and a good first kiss, which is what they really count as their first. I think most of us consider that awful kiss that came before as a training exercise, one that prepared us for the kiss we'd remember as our first. It was like an exhibition game before the start of the regular season; no one counts those, right?

I think it's safe to say that most of us felt a mixture of excitement and terror in the moments leading up to our first kiss. For some of us, we knew it was coming, and we had days and weeks to fret over it. For others, it may have happened more spontaneously, like when they were drunk at a party. That meant there was little to no planning or forethought, which also meant there was less time to worry about getting it right. For many of us though, that impending first kiss was something we simultaneously looked forward to and feared.

My first kiss, the one I refer to as my first, though technically speaking it was my second, was with a beautiful young blonde named Heather. She had everything I had ever wanted in a girlfriend, and by that, I mean she was smoking hot and had big boobs. I didn't care much about personality or intelligence back then, but hey, I was 15, the perfect age for a first kiss. Not too young, and not too old. Like Baby Bear's porridge, it was just right...though a lot more exciting.

I started dating Heather in the spring of grade 10. I had liked her all year, and although it took me awhile to work up the courage to ask her out, I finally did, and I did it in the most romantic way possible: in the middle of the spring dance, with flowers in hand, dancing to a beautiful love song. If my memory of high school dances is accurate, the song was probably "Lighting Crashes", "Tears in Heaven," or "How's It Going to Be". I waited all night to ask Heather to dance, because other guys kept getting to her before I could. I was forced to keep postponing my charm offensive and dance with other girls instead, who all asked what the flowers were for. When I told them, they each said that that was the sweetest thing they'd ever heard, and that there was no way a girl could say no to that. That really helped boost my confidence, and finally, I saw my chance.

When the next slow song came on, I literally ran across the dance floor to Heather, though I didn't have far to go, because I made sure to always stay within sight of her so as to not get beaten out by some other guy who hadn't gone to all the trouble that I had. When I was finally able to dance with her, I drew up all my courage and I gave her the flowers I had been holding all night. I then confessed that I liked her, and asked if she'd be go out with me. Assured of victory after what the other girls had told me that night, you can imagine my surprise when Heather flat out rejected me in front of the whole school. In one earth shattering moment, my heart fell out of my chest and splattered on the gym floor. As clumsy teenagers awkwardly danced all over it with their six inch heels and Sears dress shoes, I slunk away to the bleachers with my head hanging low and my tail between my legs, my broken and battered heart in tow.

I walked home that night trying to hold back the tears, but I couldn't. It was bad enough getting rejected by the girl I'd had a massive crush on all year, but the fact that it happened in front of my whole school made it even worse, and it was too much for my fragile teenage heart to take. My hot tears were a stark contrast to the cool breeze whispering through that early spring night as they fell to the pavement between gentle sobs, but fortunately no one saw me crying, except for the person in the reflective vest who was walking his dog behind me the entire way home, who I really wished hadn't been there. It was a heartbreaking night, and my first attempt at finding love had been nullified in front of my entire school. What I thought was an assured victory had turned into bitter defeat, and that night, I walked home a broken young man whose belief in love had been shattered to its core.

  Days and weeks went by, and I slowly accepted the fact that although I had liked her all year and thought she was one of the prettiest girls in school, Heather simply wasn't interested in me and I'd have to move on. While I had given up on dating her after that humiliating night, it seemed that love had other plans, and although I didn't know it at the time, my bold move had stirred something in her heart, though I wouldn't know it for about a month or so, when she suddenly changed her mind about me.

  Over the next few weeks, although I expected nothing, Heather started talking to me more and inviting me out to do things together. Later that spring, the school band went to Hawaii, and Heather and I wound up spending a lot of time together. I could tell that she was warming up to me, and when we got back home, one of her friends told me I should ask her out again. Not wanting to miss my opportunity, I asked her out at the band BBQ we had upon our return, and this time, to my immense pleasure, she said yes.

I was the happiest boy in the world! The most beautiful girl in school...well, the most beautiful girl who was somewhat in my league and would actually look at me, had said yes! I was in Heaven, and the whole world knew it. We walked home together every day after school holding hands, and just getting to touch her was ecstasy. Her hands were warm and soft, with the most delicately painted nails that accented her intoxicating femininity, while mine were sweaty and clammy because I was so nervous, though she never said anything about it.

After a week or two of walking home together and hanging out once or twice with a big group of friends, I knew I had to take things to the next level – I knew I had to kiss her. The only problem was, I had no idea how. I was 15, and I was terrified I was going to do it wrong.

In a desperate search for knowledge, I spent hours watching shows like *Saved by the Bell* and *Dawson's Creek*, as well as some *90210* reruns, in a bid to figure out just how it was done, but I still didn't know exactly how to kiss a girl properly. How much of my tongue was I supposed to put in her mouth? Just the tip? Half? Or was I supposed to shove the whole thing in there and just move it around a lot? I had no idea, but I knew I needed to find out, and fast.

Needing someone to turn to, I sought the counsel of my good friend Craig McNair, who was more experienced in this field than I was, often managing to hold a steady girlfriend for up to two weeks at a time, which was no small feat back then. Craig was a master of this sort of thing, and he gave me the best advice anyone could have given.

"Don't worry," he said. "It's natural."

It's natural. That resonated with me. Something about that advice just seemed right, and I held his words of wisdom in my mind as I prepared to do something I'd never done before: put my tongue in a girl's mouth and hope that she liked it.

Being the young romantic that I was, I planned our first kiss to happen in a perfect spot. One late spring evening, Heather and I went with a group of friends to play touch football in Mt. Doug Park, a park that bordered a forest and overlooked the ocean. During the game, I hung back a little bit and told her I had something I wanted to ask her. I took her hand and quietly snuck off the grass field to the edge of the forest, and there, leaning up against a gentle Douglas fir, while our friends played in the distance and the sun slowly set over the horizon, I kissed her for the first time, and it was magical.

Craig had been right; it was natural. Our lips touched, soft and warm, and as they opened ever so slightly, our tongues found one another. Just the tips at first, and then as we relaxed and found our rhythm, they began to caress one another, moving together in a beautiful, intimate harmony. It was the most sensual thing I had ever experienced. Our eyes were closed, our lips were locked in a beautiful embrace, and I didn't know it at the time, but together we were creating one of life's most beautiful memories: an unforgettable first kiss. I hope yours was just as good.

You Regularly Did Stupid Stuff

I'm sure that at one point, most of us have jumped off cliffs into water we didn't know the depth of, or driven a car at break neck speed around a blind corner, or gone careening down a steep hill on roller blades trying to pass a car. As an adult, you can probably say that you'd never do something like that, but as a teenager, those were just some of the many dumb and dangerous things you did on a regular basis. Back then, you did stuff like that not just because you were a thrill seeker, but also because you were stupid, and so were all your friends.

Maybe it wasn't entirely your fault that you acted so haughtily back then. You may have simply been the victim of the media's portrayal of young people doing similarly stupid things, and you figured it was part of your job as a teenager to follow suit. Think about it. No matter what horror movie you watch, the teenagers are always the first to go because they're the only ones dumb enough to be where the danger is. While the rest of the world is safe at home, they're exploring the abandoned mine, or camping out in the middle of a supposedly haunted forest. It's the same kind of idiotic stuff you did when you were young because you didn't think about consequences, and you thought you were invincible. The notion of being killed, or even just getting hurt, never entered your mind. That's why you swam in frozen lakes in the middle of winter, raced your friends down narrow back roads and passed them in the oncoming lane around corners, and dove out of moving cars like they did in the movies, just to see if you could actually do it. If you had been even remotely sensible and considered the potential consequences of your reckless behaviour, you wouldn't have done half the stuff you did back then, but then again, you wouldn't have had half as much fun either.

For example, one of the proudest moments of my life, and now one of my most "I can't believe I did that" memories, came when I was 17 or 18 years old. My friend Geoff Robson was driving me and some of our other friends home from a late night of hanging out, drinking, and doing the normal teenager things. We had stayed out particularly late that night, as we were driving home at about five in the morning. I know it's wrong now, but back then, I had a particular penchant for kicking mailboxes over. I don't know why, but I got such a thrill from doing it. Maybe it was because I never bullied other kids and had no one to take my aggression out on, but for some reason, putting mailboxes in their place made me feel like a big man.

As we were heading home that morning, doing a respectable 60 km/h down a quiet suburban street with a steep incline, I saw a mailbox on the side of the road that I felt needed a good kicking, and since no one was around, I figured it was the perfect time to do it.

"Pull over!" I said to Geoff, who was in the driver's seat next to me.

"Why?" he asked me.

"I want to kick over that mailbox!"

"No way!"

"If you don't pull over, I'm going to dive out of the car!"

"No you're..."

The next thing he knew, I had opened the passenger door and dove out of the car. Geoff thought he'd killed me because he figured I must have gone under the wheel and he'd run me over, but that's not what happened.

It still baffles me to this day, but somehow I executed a perfect dive roll out of a moving car, stood up, sprinted up to the mailbox, jump kicked it, then ran back to the car laughing my head off, while the rest of my friends stared at me in total shock and Geoff exploded at me.

"I thought I killed you!"

"No way man, I'm good. Let's go!"

And with that, we were off again, with me being totally impressed with myself for doing something that in the moment seemed so awesome, and my friends astounded at me for what I'd just done, feeling a mix of bewilderment and admiration.

I'm sure you have memories of similarly crazy things you did when you were younger, but when you look back on your life, it's those wild, ridiculous things you did that make for some of your most cherished memories. It's the times when you put it all on the line that you think back to and say, "Wow, that was really dumb, but I sure felt alive while I was doing it." Those are the moments that you look back on with fondness and remember that at one time, you were filled with an insatiable spirit of adventure.

Now, you're just a boring adult who never has any fun because you actually think things through and consider the consequences. In that regard, being short sighted in your youth wasn't so bad, because if you'd had the common sense and the critical thinking skills you do now, you never would have done anything exciting. In a way, you should be thanking your overly confident younger self for giving you so many wonderful memories to look back on, which were created by doing things so dangerous and stupid that you'll never tell your kids about them. You can only hope and pray that they won't follow in your footsteps, but deep down, you know they will. That's because doing reckless, dangerous things when you're young is part of life, and a little danger from time to time makes it worth living, though I doubt I'll ever dive out of a moving car again.

You Got Your Driver's License

Perhaps the most important day of your teenage existence, besides the day you lost your virginity, was the day you got your driver's license. It was the first real world test that life ever threw at you, and the only rite of passage we have in western society, besides becoming old enough to vote, drink and gamble.

Ancient tribes used to send their young people on spirit quests, or out into the wilderness to survive entirely on their own, thus marking their transition into adulthood. We send our young people to the DMV to first write a written test, and then do a practical with a person who hates their job and hates teenagers even more. If they pass both tests, they earn their badge of honour: a driver's license. It's the closest equivalent to a spirit quest that western society has, but unlike a spirit quest, where you die if you screw up, you can fail your driver's test multiple times and still eventually get your license, so the stakes are a lot lower.

Getting your license was an exciting and nerve wracking experience. When you first took that written test, you were nervous, but confident you'd succeed. You had studied the manual, were familiar with the road signs, and knew that if you failed, you could come back and try it again tomorrow. Passing that first test was easy for most of us, and once you had your learner's license and were legally allowed to drive, your world completely changed.

Due to careless social planning, you were now legally allowed to drive a car. Some people question whether or not 16 is too young for people to drive, and the answer is undoubtedly yes; it's way too young. That's because teenagers are the most reckless people in society, and they're stupid. I can say that with humble impunity, because I'm the first to admit that I was stupid and dangerous when I was a teenager, and so were all of my friends, even though we didn't think there was anything wrong with what we were doing at the time. All teenagers are like that – they have Superman syndrome. They think they're invincible, and they take risks no normal adult ever would. Unfortunately though, humans are flawed at any age, so it wouldn't be fair to make kids wait until their 20's and 30's to start driving. In fact, if you wanted the safest drivers around, you would let kids start driving at five or six because at that age they're all about following the rules. They would go exactly the speed limit, come to full stops at stop signs, and actually slow down at yellow lights rather than speed up to beat the red. The roads would be much safer, but for now, we've got it backwards. Anyways, back to getting your license.

Actually learning how to drive was stressful, because your parents were always with you, watching and critiquing everything you did. Now, don't get me wrong, this wasn't just nerve-wracking for you, it was traumatic for them too. That's because you thought you were already the best driver around, despite never having done it before. Your parents knew you thought that too, and that is what made the experience so hectic for them, not to mention the fact that you were driving their car. As usual, you didn't think your parents knew anything, and that included how to drive, so when they told you what to do behind the wheel, you didn't feel you had to listen. After all, they were your parents - what did they know? No doubt we all had a few close calls because of that thought process, but thankfully, here we are today, alive and well.

Now, even though driving was menacing at first, you eventually got better at it and became more confident behind the wheel. You went from thinking you knew everything, to realizing you had some learning to do, to feeling that you knew everything again. Once you had reached that point, it was time to face the final challenge of your rite of passage: your road test.

Unfortunately, road tests weren't like they were in the old days, when all you had to do was drive around a few cones and not run them over. You actually had to get out into traffic while some angry DMV employee in his or her mid 40s who seemed to hate you for no reason sat next to you with a little clip board and quietly ticked things off and wrote little comments that you couldn't see. That was a nerve-wracking experience. Every time they put a check mark or wrote something down, you panicked. You tried to think of what you'd done wrong, which only distracted you from your driving and caused you to make more mistakes, which led to more check marks and more mysterious comments from your tester. When that started happening, it was a terrible cause and effect relationship. The more you panicked, the more checks they made, and the more checks they made, the more you panicked.

It was a downward spiral that didn't take long to reach the bottom: 45 demerits, and then you failed. I was lucky. I passed by two points, but not everybody did. It was a real sense of shame to fail your driver's test, and at one point in time, your greatest fear. If you failed, everybody knew about it. You were disappointed in yourself, and even though they wouldn't admit it, you knew everyone else was disappointed in you too. The only emotion stronger than your shame was the anger you felt towards the person from the DMV, because after all, it was their fault you failed. At least, that's what you told everyone.

Fortunately, this rite of passage had an infinite amount of do overs, so even if you failed the first time, you knew you could try again. For some people, the second or third time was the charm, and eventually, pretty much everyone passed, even if they shouldn't have. Once you got your driver's license, you had finally won your freedom – the freedom to drive your parents' car or minivan around whenever they didn't need it, and life would never be the same.

Unfortunately, that freedom wasn't as great as you were hoping it would be. That's because as soon as you got your driver's license, everyone wanted you to drive them everywhere, no matter how ridiculously close the destination was. You suddenly became less like a friend and more like a free taxi service, and everybody thought you were at their beck and call to do whatever they wanted. I guess it was kind of like being a parent, and it didn't take you long to get sick of it. Suddenly, hanging out with your friends became really boring, because instead of picking a place to hang out for the night and doing something fun, you drove around from place to place and just hung out in parking lots and in parks, and it was awful.

I actually remember 16 being one of the most boring years of my life. My friends and I used to have so much fun hanging out together and playing video games, watching movies, going to the pool on Friday nights, and doing all kinds of awesome things. As soon as we could drive, we never did anything fun anymore. We just drove around and met up with our other friends who had cars, hanging out and doing nothing. When one place got boring, we'd drive somewhere else and do the same thing there, until we finally got bored enough to go home around midnight after a night of doing literally nothing except driving around and hanging out in parking lots. It was awful, and it actually made me miss the days before I had my driver's license. In fact, pretty soon, I stopped taking my parents' car out on the weekends, and I even stopped hanging out with my friends for a little while, because I couldn't stand how boring we'd become now that we could drive. Fortunately, it didn't take long for them to start to feel the same way, and soon enough, we were back doing the things we used to do: playing video games, watching movies, and going to the pool. The only difference was that now, we drove ourselves to those places. Oh, and we also yelled swear words out the window and mooned people too, something we rarely did when our parents drove.

You Could Eat A Whole Pizza

As a teenager, whenever you got together with people and decided you all wanted pizza, it wasn't a question of "How many pizzas will be enough for all these people?", it was "How many pizzas will be enough for me, because I'm not sharing with anyone else."

Nowadays, the idea of eating an entire pizza doesn't even enter your mind, but as a teenager, that was par for the course. Even as a little kid, you could eat more pizza than you can today. Whenever you'd go to a birthday party, you would have six or seven slices. It was actually a competition between kids to see who could eat the most. That's why at kids' birthday parties, there were always 20 pizza boxes on the counter. Pizza at a kid's party was the equivalent to a cow walking through a piranha-infested river. Within minutes, there was nothing left – just a skeleton of an empty cardboard box, and even that had nearly been ripped to shreds by greedy little hands tearing at its edges in an effort to eat more than anyone else.

When adults get together, the situation is entirely different. The question isn't "How many pizzas do we need for all of us," it's, "Is a large pizza too much for all of us?" You go from ordering a whole pizza for each person and worrying that it's not enough, to ordering a partial pizza for each person and worrying that it's too much.

That is perhaps the greatest difference between kids and adults: the amount of pizza they can eat. A kid will eat pizza until they can't eat any more, and the only reason they can't eat any more is because there's none left. As an adult, you can only eat as much as your body will allow, and then you're done. If you force yourself to eat more than you know you should, even just one extra slice, you're going to suffer. Once you learn that lesson the hard way though, you stay within your limit. It's the same with alcohol; when you were younger, you could drink your face off and feel fine the next day, but the older you get, the less you can handle without feeling sick. There's obviously less risk involved with eating too much pizza versus drinking too much, but both will make you feel awful and make you promise yourself you'll never lose control like that again. Of course, when you've had too much pizza, you're not worried about getting pulled over by a cop and having him go, "You were swerving a little back there...how much pepperoni have you had tonight?" When you were a kid though, you didn't worry about either of those situations, because you didn't drink and there was no such thing as too much pizza. Those were the good old days.

You Bought Condoms For The First Time

The proudest moment in a man's life is when he holds his newborn baby for the first time. The second proudest moment is when he's buying condoms for the first time in order to prevent that from happening.

Remember when you bought condoms for the first time? That was a momentous occasion, wasn't it? You had waited your whole life for that moment, and it was finally happening. You had actually found someone who was willing to sleep with you, and you could hardly believe it. You knew that once you crossed that threshold, you would leave your childhood behind forever and step fully into the adult world by the doing the most adult thing you could think of. Before that could happen though, you had to make sure you didn't create a new childhood for someone else in the process, and for that reason, you had to buy condoms.

When it came to buying condoms for the first time, there were two types of people: those who were embarrassed about it, and those who viewed it as the proudest moment of their lives. The people who were embarrassed were the ones who fearfully approached the condom aisle and grabbed the first box they saw, without taking the time to carefully consider their options. That's why they ended up with Magnums that didn't fit, or some kind of weird "tropical breeze" studded condoms that looked like some kind of alien sex toy. They also tried to disguise what they were doing by putting other things into their grocery basket along with the condoms in a vain attempt to camouflage their true intentions. When it came time to pay, they didn't just walk up to any cashier at random, either. They tried to pick the most non-judgmental looking one. They skipped the cute cashier for the first time in their lives, passed the woman in her mid 50's who may have asked for ID, and went for the defeated, haggard looking man in his mid 40s who looked like he didn't care about anything. He was their condom guy.

Then came the hardest part: actually putting the condoms on the counter and paying for them. They fearfully placed their items on the conveyor belt, hiding the condoms under a magazine or an Archie comic so that they wouldn't be seen until the last possible moment. They felt more nervous than someone smuggling drugs through an airport, and some part of them was sure that they could get in trouble for what they were doing. Once they'd paid, they hastily grabbed their bag of groceries with the condoms shoved in the bottom and slunk out of the store, desperately hoping that no one had seen them and feeling a strange sense of shame for what they had done. The whole experience had been a nightmare, and some small part of them was hoping that would be the one and only time they'd have sex, so that they'd never have to go through that humiliation again.

And then there was the other group of people, the group to which I belonged, and we couldn't have been more different than the first. We did everything the opposite of that first group. For example, instead of grabbing the first box of condoms we saw, we took our time in the condom aisle, studying every box, looking at our options, and carefully considering whether the "ribbed for her pleasure" would actually feel better, or if our partner might prefer a nice "mint sensation." After all, we had waited our whole lives for this moment; we weren't about to rush through such an important purchase. Once we'd selected a brand, we didn't try to disguise it the way the other group did either. In fact, if we were really proud of what we were doing, we didn't even have a basket to put the condoms in; we just walked around the store holding the box, hoping we'd run into someone we knew. If we did, the conversation went something like this:

"Oh hey, how are ya'? Yeah, I'm just here at the grocery store buying a couple things.

Well, just one thing actually: condoms; because I'm going to have sex."

When it came time to pay, we went to the most attractive cashier we could find, because we wanted them to know that we were sexually active and advertise our virility. That's because some small part of us was hoping that the cashier would get turned on by the fact that we were obviously desirable enough for someone to be having sex with, and may have even offered up their phone number in case things didn't work out with the person we were planning to use the condoms with. Of course, that never worked, but it didn't stop us from thinking it was a killer move and doing it every time. Once we had made our purchase, we walked out with our heads held high, knowing we'd just achieved a major life milestone, yet still having a hard time wrapping our heads around the fact that we were going to be using those condoms soon. Good thing there were a dozen in that box, because it meant we had a couple to practice with before the main event.

Whether you belonged to the first group who was filled with shame, or the second group who advertised to the world what was about to happen to them, buying condoms for the first time could make you feel a range of emotions, from utter terror to overwhelming pride. No matter how nervous you felt, however, there was always one person more uncomfortable than you, and that was the cashier. To me, that was always so weird. What were they so nervous about?

The way they acted, you'd think it was a drug deal going down. As soon as they saw the condoms, you could see them get visibly uncomfortable. They quickly scanned the box and threw it in a plastic bag for you, even making an attempt to disguise them amongst your other groceries, if you had any. Apparently, you weren't the only person who thought that buying prophylactics was a big deal, though you couldn't figure out what they were so nervous about. Of course, if your cashier was the haggard looking guy in his 40s who didn't care about anything, that wasn't an issue. Condoms got the same treatment as everything else, and that's why you loved that guy.

Regardless of whether you felt nervous or excited, ashamed or awesome, buying condoms for the first time was a memorable experience, one I'm sure we all remember. And, if you're like a lot of people out there, you also remember opening the box and checking the expiry date on the individual packages, desperately hoping you'd use at least one condom before that time came. At that point, it was a race against time. Hopefully you won.

You Drove Your Car at 100 mph

Looking back, I'm surprised I survived my teenage years. All of my friends survived theirs too, and considering the way most of us drove back then, it's a miracle we made it out alive. You probably feel the same way about that period in your own life, when you had the unrivalled cockiness of a teenager who believed they were invincible, and that they could do everything better than anyone else. That included driving a car, which is why you routinely drove everywhere at 100mph and felt it was totally safe.

Now, I myself was actually a pretty safe driver. I obeyed the speed limit, I followed the rules, and I never did anything too dangerous. My friends, on the other hand, were a different story. I have vivid memories of driving with my friend Steve in his dad's '69 Camaro, doing 100 mph down the quiet streets of our town and feeling that it was completely safe. We used to drive so fast that when we went over the slightest incline in the road, our stomachs would rise into our chests the way they do when you're on a roller coaster. We weren't on a roller coaster though; we were in his dad's pride and joy, driving like maniacs, and if we'd gotten into an accident and the crash hadn't killed us, his dad certainly would have.

I'm sure you did the same kinds of things with your friends. To you, the speed limit was just a suggestion, something other people had to abide by because they couldn't drive as well as you could. If the recommended speed limit was 60, you felt that 130 was more acceptable. If you saw a sign that said, "Danger Sharp Turn Ahead – 20mph", you took the corner at 90. "Warning, Bridge Deck Slippery When Wet" - well, the faster you got over it, the less time you had to slip. That's pretty much how you approached driving when you were a teen. In fact, there was very little difference between you and a stunt driver, except that stunt drivers got paid to drive like lunatics, and never had to explain to their parents why their car was totalled.

The funny part about how you drove back then was not how dangerous it was, it's that you felt that it was perfectly safe. That's because you trusted your friends, and since almost everyone drove like an idiot, it seemed normal. The truly shocking thing was when you drove with someone who was a safe driver and followed the rules of the road. That's when your instincts perked up and you went, "Wait a minute…something's wrong here."

Back then, you never thought about the consequences of your Speed Racer inspired driving, or what would happen if some other crazy teens were coming down the same road in the opposite direction, driving exactly like you were. That's what being a teenager was all about though: being an idiot and believing that it was fine.

Fortunately, forethought and common sense eventually kicked in and you tamed your unruly driving habits. It would have been helpful if prudence had kicked in a little sooner, say at age 16 when you first started driving, but for some reason the human brain isn't wired that way, and logic and rationality don't seem to start developing until your 20s. Despite this flaw, most of us survived our teenage years and are lucky enough to be around to think about how dumb we used to be. Today, we can look down with scorn at teenagers who are driving as dangerously as we used to, and give them a good finger wagging for their bad habits. Unfortunately, they'll probably be so busy texting that they won't even see us. For the sake of humanity, we'd better get those self-driving cars up and running soon, or we might not make it much further as a species.

"I Know Somebody Who Likes You"

"I know somebody who likes you."

When you were younger, those were the most exciting words you could hear.

"Somebody likes me? Who is it? Is it the person I like? This is amazing!"

Those were the first thoughts that ran through your head. Sadly, they only lasted about 10 seconds, and then your initial excitement was replaced by less optimistic thoughts as reality slowly dawned on you.

"Wait a minute...the person who told me they know someone who likes me isn't friends with the person I like. Darn it! Of course it's not the person I like – they don't even know I exist. Sigh…"

That entire process only took about 20 seconds, and you went from absolute elation to being right back down in the dumps, because once again, you were forced to reconcile the fact that the person you were madly in love with wasn't even aware of your existence.

To make matters worse, now you were going to have to devastate someone who had actually had the courage to open up to you. Well, they hadn't opened up to you personally – they'd gone through a third party, but still, it was a bold move and you felt bad knowing you would have to break their heart, because you knew how it felt.

I'm not sure who that situation was worse for: you, or the person who put it all on the line and sent their friend over to talk to you. I think it was difficult for both. The only person who remained unaffected was the person you actually liked, who still hadn't registered your existence on the planet. They continued on in their beautiful, perfect world, where everything was wonderful all the time and no hearts were ever broken, while you now had to nurse your own hurt feelings and bruised ego while simultaneously trying your best to mask your disappointment and let that other person down as gently as you could.

And so, trying your best to come up with an excuse as to why you weren't interested, you knowingly perpetuated the cycle of unrequited love by telling their friend that you just wanted to be friends, or you weren't ready to date, or that your dad would kill you and anyone you brought home, or whatever other excuse you came up with. And, like we so often do, rather than giving someone a chance who *did* know you existed and *did* like you, you chose to remain miserable and alone, secretly pining after someone you didn't have the courage to admit your feelings to, or even ask their friend to tell them for you. And maybe, just maybe, everyone in that unreciprocated love triangle missed out on something good.

Life's funny that way, but that's how it goes so much of the time. We always want people who don't want us, and we don't want the people who want us. It's the eternal struggle, and in the circle of love, everyone seems to be facing the wrong direction. Sometimes though, if you're lucky, the person you like actually likes you back. In those moments, you don't need someone to tell you, "I know someone who likes you," because you just know. Those moments are rare and precious, because they are the moments when we fall in love.

And they are the most beautiful part of being alive.

You Fell In Love For The First Time

There may be nothing more beautiful than falling in love for the first time. That is one of life's most cherished memories, because it only happens once. It is something that words can't describe, because love is a force, and it cannot be broken down, dissected, or explained. It can only be felt, and perhaps never as deeply as when you feel it for the first time. Because I can't adequately describe what it feels like to fall in love for the first time, I'll simply share my own story. All of our stories are different, but I'm sure that parts of mine will resonate with you, if not in the details, than in the feelings and the memories that are evoked, and help you remember that most magical time in your life when you fell in love for the first time.

Remember when I said the person you liked never liked you back? Well, for once in my life, the stars aligned perfectly, I got it right, and it was the most magical feeling I'd ever experienced.

I met Erin when I was 17, the summer I started working at McDonalds. She was the most beautiful girl I'd ever laid eyes on. She had long, silky brown hair, touched with blonde, falling half way down her back and usually tied into a ponytail or a neat bun, which helped to accentuate the face of an angel and the body of a goddess. She was a living, breathing embodiment of the world's most beautiful young woman who looked like she'd walked straight off the pages of a men's magazine and into my life. She was totally out of my league, and I knew it. She also had a boyfriend, and I knew that too. I didn't think there was a chance in hell she'd ever like me, but it didn't stop me from falling in love with her.

The fact that I knew she was out of my league actually boded well for me, because I didn't get nervous around her, knowing full well there was no way she'd ever be interested in me. I didn't try to impress her, put on an act, or come off cooler than I was, which helped me to do the most important thing you can when trying to get someone to like you: it helped me to relax and be myself.

When I was at work, I looked for any excuse to talk to her. The fact that I was having problems with a girl at school who I was trying to date, who I thought was more in my league, though it turned out she wasn't, proved to be a perfect way to start opening up to Erin and getting to know her. I don't know how the conversation started or who initiated it, but suddenly I found myself talking to Erin about this girl at school who I was unsuccessfully trying to date – let's just call her Jen.

One of Jen's friends had pulled the classic, "I know someone who likes you," moves with me, and for the first time in my life, it was actually someone I was interested in, so I was excited to hear the news. As a result, I started talking to Jen more, who was one of the prettiest girls in school, but not stuck up or aloof like many of the other attractive girls were. We started hanging out after school and on the weekends, talking on the phone, going to movies, and doing all the stuff people do when they like each other. The problem was, it wasn't going anywhere. She wouldn't hold my hand, let me put my arm around her, or kiss me, and it was weird. It all seemed very one-sided, and although Jen told me she liked me and wanted to spend time alone together, there was an incongruity between what she was saying and what she was doing.

After about two months of things going nowhere with Jen, I knew I needed to abort my mission of dating her in any serious way, the way I wanted to be dating someone when I was 17 and an idealistic romantic. After spending so much time trying to make things work with someone who had seemingly no interest in me and had been leading me on the entire time, I was filled with frustration. As a result, one night at work I started venting about it to Erin, the girl I was secretly in love with but thought I could never be with.

It was later in the evening, around seven o'clock, after the dinner rush was over. I think Erin asked me what I was doing that weekend, and without realizing what I was doing, I started spilling my frustrations about Jen. I told Erin about this girl who I liked, who supposedly liked me, who I hung out with alone, watched movies with and tried to put my arm around, but who never returned an ounce of affection or did anything to show that she liked me. Somewhere in the midst of my ranting, without being conscious that I was doing it, I started doing impressions of the kinds of things Jen would say to me. I didn't realize it, but I had started doing my "girl voice," which Erin found hilarious. She couldn't stop laughing, but I wasn't trying to be funny. I was exasperated, steaming like a kettle, but Erin loved every second of it. What I didn't know at the time was that that was the night, and the conversation, that opened the door to us falling in love. When I look back, that was one of the best nights of my life, because it was the beginning of me falling in love for the first time, and it was happening with the girl of my dreams.

Something shifted after that night. Even though Erin still had a boyfriend, and even though she was still out of my league, I could sense that there was something wonderful growing between us, even if I didn't know exactly what it was yet. Suddenly, she was finding excuses to talk to me. Often, I'd catch her staring at me from across the restaurant with her beautiful blue green eyes, and when I looked at her, she didn't look away. She just stared right into my eyes with this silent beauty that I found more attractive than anything.

As time went on, our relationship continued to blossom. We wound up talking more about my difficulties with Jen, and Erin gave me some advice about the situation, which was basically to stop wasting my time with her. She told me that a girl would be stupid not to be interested in me, and even as clueless as I was back then, I knew that she was dropping some serious hints and beginning to open up to me. It was amazing. I was beginning to see signs that the girl I'd been in love with since the second I saw her was starting to have feelings for me, and unlike Jen, she wasn't afraid to show them.

Every second I spent with Erin was Heaven, no matter what we were doing. I loved going to work when she was there, and I was miserable when she left. There was nothing more disappointing than starting work just as she was getting off, because it meant I missed her all night, and there was nothing better than knowing I was doing a closing shift with her, because it meant we got to talk and be together all night. At that point in my life, no one had ever enjoyed working at

McDonalds as much as I did, and it was all because of her.

Pretty soon, Erin told me I needed to get ICQ (remember ICQ?). I had no idea what it was, but the next day, I had it installed on my computer. For those of you who don't know or don't remember, ICQ was one of the world's first instant messaging systems. It was like texting on your computer, before texting was a thing. Once I had ICQ, we started talking all the time, instead of just when we were at work. Fairly quickly, roles began to reverse, as Erin started opening up to me about problems she was having with her boyfriend. It was at this point in my life that my heart started beating twice as fast on a full-time basis, because I was starting to get a sense of where things were heading, and it was literally my most beautiful dream manifesting before my eyes.

Shortly after, Erin opened up to me about the fact that she wasn't happy with her boyfriend, and that she didn't want to be in the relationship anymore. Then, she told me something that made my heart light up like the Fourth of July, even though I was Canadian.

"I don't think I want to be in this relationship anymore…plus there's someone else I'm interested in."

My thoughts and my emotions felt like they were on the Scrambler at the amusement park.

"Is it me? It has to be me. Of course it's me. No...it can't be me. These kinds of things don't happen to me. There's no way it's me...is it me?"

My mind did endless acrobatics trying to figure out whether or not I was the "someone else" she was interested in. Given my social standing and dating history, it seemed almost impossible to believe that Erin was talking about me, but deep down, I knew that she was.

I don't remember how I responded when she told me that. I probably said something stupid, but nonetheless, she had gone out on a limb, and I wasn't about to leave her there, even if I still wasn't totally convinced she was talking about me. Soon after that conversation, she gave me her phone number and we started talking on the phone. At that point in time, I'd never felt so excited about anything in my life. Every time we talked or saw each other, my heart beat faster, my hands trembled, and when we touched, there was electric chemistry coursing between our bodies. It was so palatable that we could actually feel it.

Things progressed quickly from there. One of the first times we talked on the phone, we wound up talking for eight hours, from 11pm to 7am the next morning, and the time flew by without us even noticing. The next night, we talked for ten, and it was the most magical night of my life. That night, we both said, "I love you," and meant it. I'd never said that to anyone before, but like everything else about our relationship, it caught me completely off guard, and it was totally unplanned – but it was real.

When we said, "I love you" for the first time, it opened up a flood of emotions, and they poured forth like water bursting from a damn. Once that dam was breeched, there was no stopping us, and that night, we gave in to every thought, feeling, and emotion that we had for each other. In the morning, our love had been laid bare, and we knew that we had to be together, no matter what.

That was Sunday and Monday nights. After that, we made plans to hang out the following Friday, and I'd never enjoyed a week so much in my life. I'd never had to endure a longer one, either. Although it was only days away, it felt like years. We met as often as we could before Friday came, but we had to be very secretive about it. That's because a lot of her ex-boyfriend's friends worked with us, and she didn't want them to find out what was going on between us, especially since she had broken up with him that week. I didn't want them to find out either, because they were a tough crew, and I didn't want to get beaten up, although it would've been worth it.

On Wednesday, I met her in the parking lot when she got off shift. I sat in my car, so as to keep out of view of prying eyes, and she stood there pretending to talk to me, but really we were holding hands, feeling the electricity coursing through our bodies and staring into each other's eyes, both in awe at what was happening between us. On Thursday, she drove me home after work and came inside to hang out for awhile, even though Friday was still the main event. We sat on my bed, feeling the magnetic pull of our bodies, and we couldn't keep our hands or our lips off of each other. When we kissed for the first time, it was like two meteors colliding into each other, the strength and the gravity of their impact unable to be measured. To this day, I have never felt a kiss like that. It was our first, and there was more emotion and passion in that kiss than any I have experienced since. I've had some amazing kisses in my life since then, but that one is still special because of its depth of feeling. It may have had something to do with how long we had to wait for it, as we'd been building our love, our attraction, and our connection over the last six months, and when we finally got to express it, it was the most beautiful form of madness.

That's the only way I can describe it: beautiful madness, because that's what it was. We longed for each other even while we were embraced in the most passionate kiss of our lives, and no matter how much we got of one another, we wanted more. We caressed each other uncontrollably, our lips locked and sealed in an unforgettable moment of ecstasy as our tongues swirled and danced around one another, fuelling the fires of unrivalled lust that raged within us. She straddled me and held me down on my bed, and the next thing I knew I was on top of her, our pelvises grinding into one another so hard I thought I would break through my jeans as we feasted off each other's uncontrollable, sexual energy.

And then my parents came home and we had to stop.

After experiencing the most impassioned moment of my life and ushering her out the back door before my parents came inside, I knew that Friday would be even more incredible than what we'd just experienced, and it was all I could think about.

After what had seemed an eternity of waiting, Friday night finally came. There are only little bits of that night that I now remember, but I can still see myself clear as day, sitting in my dad's truck in the dark parking lot of Panagopoulos Pizza, in the middle of January, waiting for the girl of my dreams to come to me. I had the pizza waiting, and before I knew it, Erin was standing at the passenger window, looking more beautiful than any human ever had. I melted into my seat knowing that she looked that good just for me.

That night, I was the luckiest guy in the universe, and I knew it.

I don't remember much else from that night, other than lying on top of her and staring into the eyes of Heaven and Earth's most beautiful angel. I could literally feel the energy of my heart pouring into her as her heart energy poured into me, both of those energies connecting to create a divine space that was the manifestation of true love. It was a divinely blessed connection, as if the angels themselves were surrounding us and flooding us with all the love that has ever existed in creation.

None of that night felt real to me. It was all a beautiful dream, as if the very air between us was shimmering with a golden aura of divine love as our hearts, souls, and bodies connected for the first time in the way we'd been longing for. To this day, I can still remember how it felt, and like our first kiss, I have never felt anything quite like that again.

For as long as we were together, that feeling of divine love never went away. Every second I spent with her was bliss, and I knew that I wanted those feelings to last forever. I honestly believed that at 17, I'd found the one I was meant to be with forever, and that we would be together for the rest of our lives. Sadly though, as is so often the case, that love would not stand the test of time, even if it felt like it should have.

Far too soon for me, Erin decided that she didn't want to be together anymore, and it was the most devastating experience of my life. I'd fallen in love for the first time, and experienced a kind of ecstasy and unparalleled happiness I didn't know existed, but as a result, I'd also experience my first heartbreak, and the shattering disillusionment that comes with it.

Love is beautiful, but the other side of it is so damn hard. A broken heart is one of the most crippling things we can endure, yet it is worth it, because if we are that broken at the end of something, we know that while we had it, it was more beautiful than we could have ever imagined. That's the paradox of love; it's the most wonderful and painful thing in the world, and even though we may feel it many times throughout our lives, we may never feel it as deeply and as passionately as we did when we felt it for the first time.

We all have our firsts, and even though that love may have physically disappeared, it's still there in our hearts and our souls, a beautiful memory in time, recorded in our consciousness for eternity. It's a wonderful gift to be able to look back on and smile as we remember what used to be, when we fell in love for the first time. Thank you, Erin, for being my first.

You Had Your First Heartbreak

Heartbreak hurts every time, but never so much as the first time. I think the reason that getting your heart broken the first time is the most painful is because you don't have any life experience, and no matter how young or good looking you are, you're absolutely convinced that you'll be alone for the rest of your life, which only compounds your sadness. When you're older and you've experienced the ending of an intimate relationship before, it can still be devastating, but deep down there's a quiet knowing that even though you're broken hearted now, things will eventually get better and one day you'll be alright again.

There's a little voice inside of you going, "I know it hurts, but you're going to be ok. We've been through this before, and we'll get through it again. And one day, when this is all over, we'll find love again. So don't worry – everything is going to be ok."

When you're suffering from your first heartbreak though, you don't have that reassuring voice from within. You still have a voice, but it's not saying, "Everything's going to be ok," it's saying, "WHAT THE HELL DID YOU DO!? You had the perfect person and you screwed it up! You idiot! We're going to be alone forever!"

Besides lacking life experience, your first heartbreak is also the worst because it's connected to the first time you fell in love, and both experiences were totally new to you. You got to feel the deep, spiritual beauty of falling in love with another person, but as a result, you also had to feel the Armageddon of a broken heart. When that happened, it felt like you were dying inside, because really, a part of you was.

I was 17 years old when I had my heart broken for the first time, and what made it so shattering was how quickly it happened after falling in love. I was a mere child of this world, yet I was convinced that I had found the girl I wanted to spend the rest of my life with, and I was certain the feeling was mutual. I mean, she told me it was, so you can imagine my surprise and ensuing devastation when the girl who told me that she wanted to spend forever with me suddenly stopped talking to me and completely cut me out of her life a mere three weeks later. I guess our interpretations of forever were different.

I went from Heaven to Hell in the blink of an eye, and suddenly I found myself exiled from Eden, a true Adam in a hostile, shattered world. The girl I loved was gone, and although I would have done anything to win her back, and believe me, I tried, she wanted nothing to do with me. The worst part was, she didn't even tell me why it was over; she just shut me out of her life and refused to speak to me, and that made it even more painful because I couldn't understand why, and therefore, couldn't find closure. I didn't want closure, though; I just wanted to be with her.

I eventually discovered that the reason she cut me off so suddenly and absolutely was because she'd gotten back together with her ex-boyfriend. Remember him, the guy she had broken up with in order to be with me? Life experience would have told me that I should have seen that coming, but at 17, I was short on that most important quality.

It wasn't just finding out that she was back with her old boyfriend that hurt, it was the way I found out. One Saturday afternoon in late February, a week or two after my desperate Valentine's Day offensive that went completely unacknowledged, I was working the grill at McDonalds, my lifeless heart dangling around my feet, hanging on by a piece of connective tissue and barely keeping me alive. As the timer went off to remove the patties, I loaded them into a tray and turned around to put them in the heat cabinet, when suddenly, somebody punched me in the throat, the gut, and the balls all at the same time. I dropped the meat tray and it shattered on the floor, along with the last little pieces of my fractured heart.

There, standing five feet away from me on the other side of the counter, was Erin. Standing next to her, holding her hand, was her ex, and now seemingly current, boyfriend. In the middle of that insane lunch rush, time suddenly stopped as I stood there staring at her while McWorkers whipped around me, unable to process the evidence in front of me. In the background, some barely audible voice was calling my name, but I couldn't hear it.

I'll never forget the look on her face, or the way she spoke to me in that moment. She didn't say anything in words, but she looked into my eyes, and for the first time since she'd stopped talking to me the month before, she said something. She said, "I'm sorry." It wasn't in words, and it wasn't in writing. It was in the deep, unspoken, spiritual communication that we're all capable of understanding. It was the first time in my life I had experienced that, and it broke my heart all over again.

What happened next was like in one of those war movies when a bomb goes off beside a soldier, but the blast doesn't kill him. It just makes everything go quiet and move in slow motion, and there's a loud ringing in his ears as he watches the chaos unfold around him and tries to make sense of it all, when someone suddenly grabs him and starts screaming at him to bring him back to reality.

"Adam! Clean up those meat patties! Get another round on the grill!"

That was my manager, who cared more about profits and production than human emotions, but his tactic worked. Suddenly, time began moving again as I snapped back into reality and took stock of the world around me. A broom was thrust into my hands, and I stood there sweeping up the meat patties and the pieces of my broken heart, my back to Erin so that she couldn't see the tears forming behind my eyes. I then dumped the patties and the shards of my shattered heart into the trash, knowing that no one would ever have use for them again.

That was a sad day in my life. It was absolute confirmation that I had lost the only girl I ever loved, and I knew that I was the only person in the world who had ever felt a loss so apocalyptic. After hoping for so long that she would snap out of her silence and come around, I now knew that it was hopeless. She was never coming back. It was a deep inner knowing that I didn't want to acknowledge, but sadly knew it was true. I didn't begin to move on right away though, because I couldn't. My heart had been surgically removed from my chest, and there was simply a void where a vital organ had once been. It would be several months before I would start to feel anything but sadness again.

    Like a bitter winter, however, a broken heart doesn't last forever, and like it always does, time slowly started to heal me and planted a new seed where my old heart used to be. I don't mean that someone new came into my life, but I did start to find joy again. I still missed Erin terribly, and I knew that she had sacrificed something beautiful, at least from my perspective. There was nothing I could do about it though, and once I accepted that and decided I didn't want to stay stuck in sadness, I was finally able to start putting her behind me.

    I began to occupy my time with other things. I started hanging out with my friends more, and playing street hockey again. I put a band together. Most importantly of all, I discovered the band that would become an incredible influence on the rest of my life: Blink 182. Somewhere in the midst of all that, when I was living the kind of life I loved and becoming a better version of who I used to be, my heart continued to mend itself while all kinds of wonderful new people came into my life. Eventually, I even met someone new who I fell in love with. She too was incredibly beautiful, had the body of a goddess, and interestingly enough, was also named Erin.

Even though I managed to move on, I often still thought about the first girl I fell in love with, and part of me never really got over her, at least not until I was much older. I think we're all like that. We'll always remember our first, but as hard as it was getting over them, I often think that the second person you fall in love with can be even more beautiful, because in a way, their love is even stronger. That's because they're the one who is going to heal your tattered heart, and the one who is going to teach you about love all over again. Most importantly, they're the one whose soul is so beautiful that you're willing to risk it all for again, and that, my friend, is a beautiful thing.

You Lost Your Virginity

"No, I don't," you're saying. "I was drunk."

That's ok, so was I, but I still remember it. You know what my strongest memory of losing my virginity is? It's that it didn't feel half as good as I had always thought it would. Now, maybe that's because I was drunk, or that neither of us had any idea what we were doing, but losing my virginity was mostly a disappointment, and I know I'm not alone in this. I didn't lose it to the person I wished I had, and I did it more out of guilt than love, which I'm sure is another common occurrence.

When I was a virgin, I thought that sex would be the greatest thing in the world. I believed it would feel infinitely better than anything I could imagine, and losing my virginity would be the crowning achievement of my life. Sadly, it wasn't so.

Now, that's not because I wasn't attracted to the girl I lost it to, or that it was over as soon as it had begun, but for some reason, it was entirely anti-climactic, and my main memory of the event was how disappointed I was. Regrettably, I'm sure the feeling was mutual.

I thought losing my virginity would be like sex is in the movies, but it wasn't. We weren't moaning and screaming, thrusting ourselves at each other with reckless abandon, or digging our nails into each other's backs as we both simultaneously climaxed in unparalleled ecstasy. Instead, we were two teenagers who'd been drinking, very quietly and carefully having sex for the first time in my bedroom while the rest of my family was asleep upstairs, and at the time, it was the greatest let down of my life.

Chances are, your first time wasn't so different from mine. Or maybe it was. Maybe your first time having sex was the wild, carnal, ecstasy inducing experience that mine wasn't, and you can't relate to this at all. Or maybe you lost it to someone you truly loved and cared about, the person you truly wanted to give yourself to, and you can't understand where I'm coming from. Well, if that's the case, I'm happy for you, whether it was carnally erotic, or the most beautiful thing you'd experienced with another human being. Sadly, that wasn't the case for me, but there was one part about losing my virginity that was better than anything I'd ever expected or imagined, something I'd remember for the rest of my life, and that was what came afterwards.

Shortly after my girlfriend left my house, a little after midnight, my best friend came over. He had been at a party up the road and had decided to come by my window unannounced to see if I wanted to go. I quietly opened the back door and let him in, then led him to my room, where the candles were still burning, the bed was in tatters, and the room still smelled like sex. He threw me a wickedly knowing grin.

"You did it?"

"Yeah," I said, proud of my new manhood and the fact that I'd just fulfilled every teenage boy's life goal. "Mission accomplished."

We high-fived, celebrated, and then quietly crept out the back door into the darkness of that snow covered early winter night, only minutes after midnight, heading for a party that Sean had promised would be wild.

As long as I live, I'll always remember what followed. Once we got to the house where the party was being held, we let ourselves in the front door. The party was in the basement, and as we descended the stairs, we could hear the bass thumping and the music getting louder. At the bottom of the stairs, Sean opened the door to the basement suite and boldly stepped into the room, which was packed wall to wall with raucous partiers in their late teens and early 20's who were dancing, drinking, and just plain partying, and I followed in behind him.

As soon as he'd taken two steps into the room, Sean did something I never expected. He put his hands above his head and waved his arms like a man on a deserted island signaling a passing ship for rescue, while simultaneously shouting to the DJ, "Stop the music!!!"

Instantly, the music stopped, and a stunned crowd turned as one to look at Sean, wondering what could possibly be so important as to disrupt their riotous party.

"Hey, everybody!" Sean pointed to me. "This guy just lost his VIRGINITY!!!"

As one, the crowd erupted. "YEAH!!!!"

The next thing I knew, dozens of strangers were high-fiving me and putting drinks in my hands, patting me on the back and shaking my hand.

"Right on, man!"

"Way to go, bro!"

"Dude, awesome! I remember my first time!"

The music turned back on, and people started dancing again, just as they had before, only this time, with something more to celebrate. I was the hero of the party, and I didn't know a single person there.

I don't remember much else from that night, other than the fact that I drank too much and was enamored with positive attention and praise from my peers for the rest of the night. The best part about losing my virginity had nothing to do with the actual event, and it's one of the greatest memories I have. I love that moment in time, and I hope you love yours just as much. Oh, and if the girl I lost my virginity to is reading this, don't worry; everything that came after was amazing. Well, for me at least.

You Thought You Were Invincible

When I was 18, I had a motorcycle, and I was never afraid of getting hurt. I believed that if a car hit me, it would be like in the *Superman* movies, where I'd make a huge dent in the car, crippling it beyond repair, and would walk away completely unscathed. Now in my 30s, I won't even go for a walk at night without a flashlight, lest some distracted driver fail to see me crossing the road. I'm even thinking about getting a reflective vest to really make myself visible, but that's probably a few years away.

I'm sure that when you were young, you thought you were invincible too. I know I'm not the only young guy who believed that if he got hit by a car, the car would be the one on life support rather than him. That's why you did the crazy, wild, reckless things you did back then. It's why you dove out of moving cars, jumped off roofs, and hurled yourself off cliffs into the unexplored waters below. It's why you climbed mountains without ropes or harnesses, and rode bikes or rollerbladed downhill so fast that you passed cars. You never thought about being safe because you never thought about getting hurt. You believed you were invincible, and it was an awesome way to live.

Looking back, it's amazing that you survived your teenage years. From skiing and snowboarding down mountains in the off-limits back country to driving your car at 100mph down twisting back roads, you habitually did incredibly dangerous things that you would never do now. That's because as an adult, you've lost your sense of invincibility. You no longer think of yourself as an unstoppable super hero, but rather as a fragile, frail, walking sack of water without a whole lot of extra protection, and for that reason, you are very careful with everything you do.

The transformation from an invincible mindset to one of fragility took a long time to manifest, however. It wasn't an instant shift, but a slow and gradual process that happened almost without you realizing it, though there was usually some kind of inciting incident that triggered that change. For many people, the transition may have begun when they got into a car accident for the first time, or got injured doing something stupid, like failing to clear a rocky outcropping while cliff jumping at the lake in order to impress a girl. For my younger brother and I, it was the time we watched a parkour video on YouTube of people scaling buildings and jumping off roofs, and thought, "We can do that!"

Five minutes later, we had climbed to the top of the two-storey baseball house in Majestic Park and stood overlooking its perilously high edge, which looked a lot higher from up there than it had from below. Still thinking we were invincible and believing we could execute such a feat just like the people in the parkour videos, we both took running starts and hurled ourselves off the edge, doing our best to somersault as we landed.

As I hit the ground and tried to roll like the guys in the video had done, my knees felt like they exploded, and I don't know how I didn't break my neck, since I hit the ground with what felt like terminal velocity and immediately threw myself into a sloppy somersault that was not nearly as graceful as what I had believed I was capable of.

I came out of my somersault and rolled onto my side, not knowing if I'd broken my legs or not. I had never experienced such pain in my entire life. It literally felt like my knees had exploded, and I was terrified that I'd rendered myself a cripple. I lay on the ground writhing in pain, and managed to look over to my brother, who was experiencing a similar situation. We locked eyes and shook our heads, barely able to fathom what had just happened.

After a few moments of utter agony, I managed to sit up and feel my legs. Nothing felt broken, and I found that I was able to move them, though I felt like a truck had hit me. Garett was doing the same thing, and to our relief, we were both able to stand up and walk home, though much slower and with a lot less gusto than before. That was the first time I had ever really gotten hurt doing something stupid, and the first time I realized that no, I was not Superman, and if I wanted to live to see my old age, I had better start being a lot more careful.

No matter what your inciting incident was, the first time you really hurt yourself doing something dangerous was a wakeup call, and it was through those painful lessons that you gradually became aware of your own fragile mortality. That's why as an adult, you don't do those kinds of things anymore. It's the same reason you sometimes feel so lame and boring nowadays, but as you learned so painfully in your youth, it's better to be someone who is lame, boring, and alive, than someone who died doing something that seemed cool at the time, but in retrospect, was actually really stupid.

For those of you who have kids, memories of the reckless things you did in your youth are a real concern for you now. That's because you remember all the dangerous stuff you did, and you're terrified that your kids are going to do the same kinds of things. Rest assured, they will do stupid things, but hopefully not as stupid as what you did when you were their age. I imagine this puts parents in an awkward situation.

They don't want their kids to repeat the mistakes they themselves made, so they're torn between telling them not to do certain things in an effort to make them mindful of the dangers involved, but also aware that by doing so, they may be giving them ideas they'd never have thought of on their own.

That's why when I was heading out for the night with my friends one time, my dad said to me, "When you and your friends are out driving tonight, I don't want anyone surfing on the hood, ok?"

That's literally word for word what he said to me, and it blew my mind. Never in my life would I have thought of doing something that stupid, but once he put the idea in my head, it got me to thinking, "Hey...that might be fun."

If you have kids, you can caution them all you want, but as you know from your own death defying youth, the only thing that can change someone is experience. Life is the greatest teacher there is, and all you can do is hope that your kids learn from their mistakes and smarten up before it's too late. That will ensure that they can live long, full, happy lives and grow up to be just like you, an overly cautious adult who is lame, boring, and afraid to do anything even remotely dangerous. Oh well, at least you had your fun when you were young. Now if you'll excuse me, I'm off to buy that reflective vest I was talking about.

Life Seemed Easier

Life seemed easier as a kid. You know why? Because it was. You had very few responsibilities, and even if you didn't meet them, there were no real consequences. My only obligations as a kid were to set the dinner table and get dressed for school in the morning. I wasn't very good at either, but it didn't matter. If I screwed up, someone would step in to set the table for me, and it's not like my parents were about to send me to school without pants on, so no matter what, someone had me covered if I couldn't man up to the task. It's not the same when you're an adult. If you screw up now, there can be hell to pay. You can lose your house, your career, your loved ones – you can lose your entire life. You couldn't lose any of those things when you were a kid, because they weren't yours to lose. There was no pressure on us back then, and it was wonderful.

In contrast, life as an adult is filled with all kinds of pressures, from work, to relationships, to money, to you name it. We've got a million and one things to worry about, and we've got to simultaneously take care of them all. If we don't, no one else is going to step in and do it for us, and there are real repercussions for failure. When we were kids, we were carefree. Even as we got older and became adolescents and teenagers, we still had it easy. We could wake up, eat breakfast that had often been made for us, go to school, do very little work, come home, have a snack, watch TV, play sports or video games, hang out with friends, come in for a dinner that had been made for us, clear a couple plates, then play more video games or watch TV until bed time and repeat it all again the next day. It was as easy as life could get, and we didn't appreciate a thing about it. What we'd give to be able to live that kind of life again now, but we can't. It's gone forever, and exists only in our memories.

Still, sometimes it's nice to look back on those times and think about how wonderful life was. We didn't have careers or money, or mortgages and bills, or even intimate relationships to occupy our minds, and because of that, we were so much happier. We didn't feel the stresses of real life, because we weren't even aware that those stresses existed. Our lives consisted of doing things we loved, whilst having almost no responsibilities. The only time you'll get a second chance at that kind of lifestyle is if you make it to retirement, and that's only if you've worked hard your whole adult life and are lucky enough to have a pension. Without that, you'll never experience that kind of carefree nirvana again. Of course, by retirement age, you'll have your health to worry about, so the pure simplicity of childhood is something we can truly only experience once in a lifetime.

At least we can look back with fond memories and remember how wonderful life used to be when things were so much simpler. Even if we can never go back to the way things were, it's still nice to think about how good we had it at one point in time. In a way, it's kind of like looking back on a relationship with someone you once loved who is no longer with you. Even if you can't have something, or someone, the way you used to, the memories are still beautiful, and that in itself is a great gift.

Here's to the beauty of what once was, and in our hearts, will always be.

From the Author

This is my first published work, and I hope you had as much fun reading it as I did writing it. I wanted to create something that would capture your imagination, and help you think back to a simpler time when life was a little easier. My sincerest wish is that you found joy while reading this book, that it made you laugh, and even shed a tear or two. Thank you to my friends, family, and soul mates who played a part in its creation, and also to my readers, who helped make what was once just a dream into a reality.

Adam L'Heureux

Manufactured by Amazon.ca
Bolton, ON